WITHDRAWN

Hopeful Journeys

University of Pennsylvania Press
EARLY AMERICAN STUDIES
RICHARD S. DUNN,
Director, Philadelphia Center for Early American Studies, Series Editor

Also in the series:
Rosalind Remer. *Printers and Men of Capital:*
Philadelphia Book Publishers in the New Republic. 1996

Hopeful Journeys

German Immigration, Settlement,
and Political Culture in Colonial America,
1717–1775

AARON SPENCER FOGLEMAN

University of Pennsylvania Press

Philadelphia

Hopeful Journeys has been selected by the Pennsylvania German Society as its 1996 annual publication, Volume XXX.

Table I.1 is reprinted from *The Journal of Interdisciplinary History* 22 (1992), 698, with the permission of the editors of *The Journal of Interdisciplinary History* and the MIT Press, Cambridge, Mass. © 1992 by The Massachusetts Institute of Technology and the editors of *The Journal of Interdisciplinary History*.

Library of Congress Cataloging-in-Publication Data
Fogleman, Aaron Spencer.
Hopeful journeys : German immigration, settlement, and political culture in colonial America, 1717–1775 / Aaron Spencer Fogleman.
    p. cm. — (Early American studies)
Originally presented as the author's thesis (Ph.D.) — University of Michigan, 1991.
  Includes bibliographical references and index.
    ISBN 0-8122-3309-3 (cloth : alk. paper). — ISBN 0-8122-1548-6 (paper : alk. paper)
    1. German Americans—History—18th century.   2. Immigrants—United States—History—18th century.   3. United States—Emigration and immigration—History—18th century.   4. Germany—Emigration and immigration—History—18th century. I. Title.
II. Series.
E184.G3F724   1996
305.83'1073'09033—dc20   95-43562
                                                                           CIP

Contents

List of Tables and Graphs

GRAPHS

List of Maps

Acknowledgments

I HARDLY KNOW HOW TO BEGIN TO THANK all the people and institutions who supported me during this project. The list of acknowledgments is long and the appreciation I have for all in it is deep.

First I would like to thank Richard Dunn, not only for inviting me to submit this work in his new series and supporting me through the process, but also for his support during part of the research phase a few years ago. A grant from the Philadelphia Center for Early American Studies allowed me to spend a year in the Philadelphia area archives and libraries. Many of the ideas for this book originated in Professor Dunn's Friday afternoon seminars and in the evening discussions in Michael Zuckerman's living room, as I listened to others present their work and presented some of my own. Also, Susan Klepp's comments on the final manuscript were very helpful.

I must also once again thank the co-chairs of my dissertation committee at the University of Michigan, John Shy and Kenneth Lockridge. The assistance, support, and encouragement they provided in Ann Arbor has continued on this project and other projects, even though geography now separates us. I would also like to thank Maris Vinovskis, who made many helpful suggestions along the way, and Albert Hermalin, of the Population Studies Center in Ann Arbor, who did his best to keep my demography on the straight and narrow path. All deviations are my own fault.

I also owe thanks to many historians and archivists at several other institutions who supported my work. In addition to the grant from the Philadelphia Center for Early American Studies, large grants from the Horace H. Rackham School of Graduate Studies at the University of Michigan and the German Historical Institute in Washington, D.C., were extremely helpful. The staff members of the Library Company of Philadelphia and the Historical Society of Pennsylvania, especially James Green and Linda Stanley, guided me through their collections and supported me with a summer fellowship.

Others who helped me include the staff members of the Moravian Archives in Bethlehem, Pennsylvania, and in Winston-Salem, North Carolina, all of whom provided invaluable assistance with their incredibly rich collections. Vernon Nelson answered countless questions about the Moravians of the eighteenth century (and today) and helped make my stay in Bethlehem one of the most enjoyable I have ever spent anywhere. Many thanks also to the staff members at the Pennsylvania State Archives in Harrisburg (especially Donna Munger and Jonathan Stayer), at the Museum of Early Southern Decorative Arts in Winston-Salem (especially Martha Rowe), and at the William L. Clements Library in Ann Arbor.

The Fulbright Commission supported my study in Freiburg from 1984 to 1986. In Freiburg, Hans Fenske and Klaus Deppermann helped me greatly and educated me on migration and radical pietism respectively. Later, Wolfram Angerbauer of the *Landratsamt* in Heilbronn introduced me to the literature and archives of the Kraichgau. The staff members of the city archives in Sinsheim and the town hall of Schwaigern were also very helpful.

The University of South Alabama provided important assistance during the final phases of this project. Grants from the Research Committee and the College of Arts and Sciences helped pay for travel and other expenses. Also at the University, Eugene Wilson produced this volume's cartography, and Michael Thomason helped with the photographs. The assistance of the university library staff, especially Deborah Cobb, was invaluable.

Other grants that provided financial support for this project include a Michael Kraus travel grant from the American Historical Association, a travel grant from the National Endowment for the Humanities, and a grant from the Michigan Chapter of the Colonial Dames of America.

There are many other individuals who helped me over the years. These include H. James Henderson and George Jewsbury, who got me started a long time ago; many fellow graduate students at Ann Arbor, including Keith Arbour (who suggested the title for this work), Dave Hsiung, and Jon Atkins; and two "Philadelphia people" no longer in Philadelphia, Rosalind Remer and Susan Branson. From Ann Arbor to Philadelphia to Germany, I think of you often, especially during the winter.

AARON S. FOGLEMAN
Mobile, Alabama
February 1995

Introduction: An Immigrant Society

IMMIGRATION TO AMERICA CALLS TO MIND images of millions of Europeans crowding into eastern port cities, struggling to get ahead, to escape the slum and carve out a better life, either in the city itself or on the frontier. While it is self-evident that the immigrants sought opportunity, and that many also sought some kind of freedom, the degree to which they left behind the Old World or brought some of it with them is debated. When did they become Americans? What kind of Americans did they become? Or did America become them?

Most Americans have encountered these images or questions in one way or another, but attention has inevitably centered on the years 1815 to 1914, when some 38 million immigrants from Europe and Asia arrived. Much of what we think of as "America" came to be in this period, and immigrants were vital to the country's shaping. After World War I immigration continued at a significantly slower pace until the renewed wave of Spanish-speaking and Asian immigration during our time. But of course the story begins before 1815.

Before the millions of Europeans and Asians arrived in the nineteenth century, another large influx occurred in the decades before the American Revolution, and its magnitude and consequences, as well as the personal struggles involved, were no less significant: in the first three-quarters of the eighteenth century the immigration of hundreds of thousands of non–English-speaking Europeans and Africans transformed American society. In 1700, nearly a century after Jamestown, only about 250,000 white and black inhabitants populated the colonies, while the Native American population along the coastal plain and in the Piedmont region had declined dramatically from perhaps 700,000 inhabitants before European settlement. The vast majority of the white inhabitants were either born in England or descended from English immigrants. Only about 11 percent of the non–

TABLE I.1 Estimated Decennial Immigration by Ethnic Group into the Thirteen Colonies, 1700–1775.

DECADE	AFRICANS	GERMANS*	NORTHERN IRISH	SOUTHERN IRISH	SCOTS	ENGLISH	WELSH	OTHER	TOTAL
1700–1709	9,000	⟨100⟩	⟨600⟩	⟨800⟩	⟨200⟩	⟨400⟩	⟨300⟩	⟨100⟩	⟨11,500⟩
1710–1719	10,800	⟨3,700⟩	⟨1,200⟩	⟨1,700⟩	⟨500⟩	⟨1,300⟩	⟨900⟩	⟨200⟩	⟨20,300⟩
1720–1729	9,900	⟨2,300⟩	⟨2,100⟩	⟨3,000⟩	⟨800⟩	⟨2,200⟩	⟨1,500⟩	⟨200⟩	⟨22,000⟩
1730–1739	40,500	13,000	4,400	7,400	2,000	⟨4,900⟩	⟨3,200⟩	⟨800⟩	⟨76,200⟩
1740–1749	58,500	16,600	9,200	9,100	3,100	⟨7,500⟩	⟨4,900⟩	⟨1,100⟩	⟨110,000⟩
1750–1759	49,600	29,100	14,200	8,100	3,700	⟨8,800⟩	⟨5,800⟩	⟨1,200⟩	⟨120,500⟩
1760–1769	82,300	14,500	21,200	8,500	10,000	⟨11,900⟩	⟨7,800⟩	⟨1,600⟩	157,800
1770–1775	17,800	5,200	13,200	3,900	15,000	7,100	⟨4,600⟩	⟨700⟩	67,500
Total	278,400	84,500	66,100	42,500	35,300	⟨44,100⟩	⟨29,000⟩	⟨5,900⟩	⟨585,800⟩

* "Germans" refers to German-speaking peoples, many of whom came from areas outside the modern borders of Germany, especially Switzerland and Alsace.

Note: Figures in Table I.1 were rounded to the nearest one hundred immigrants. The estimates in the table are divided into three categories: most accurate (no demarcation), less accurate ( ), and least accurate ⟨ ⟩.

Source: Aaron S. Fogleman, "Migrations to the Thirteen British North American Colonies, 1700–1775: New Estimates," *Journal of Interdisciplinary History*, 22 (1992), 691–709, contains a detailed discussion of the sources used in compiling Table I.1

Native American population were black. Yet by 1776, the combined white and black population of the thirteen colonies had increased tenfold to 2.5 million—a spectacular development that still fascinates demographers today, just as it did at the time. By 1776, large numbers of Germans, Scots, Irish, and other "strangers" populated the colonies, in addition to hundreds of thousands of Africans and African-Americans. The ethnic English population had become a minority.[1]

The society that fought the Revolution was an "immigrant society" in many respects. Population and immigration estimates for the eighteenth century are difficult to make because of the lack of good statistics, but the information that we do have (summarized in Table I.1) suggests that a significant amount of the colonial population was born in either Europe or Africa, especially after 1740. Indeed, if the figures in the table are reasonably accurate, the proportion of immigrants to the base population during the generation before the Revolution was higher than it would ever become in the nineteenth or twentieth centuries. In other words, encountering people born overseas was as common in mid–eighteenth century America as it would become in the later periods that have received much more attention from historians of immigration.[2]

But it was not merely the presence of large numbers of "foreign born" that transformed much of colonial America into an immigrant society. Indeed, the eighteenth-century immigrants *and their progeny* permanently altered the ethnic and demographic patterns of the colonies in directly visible ways. By the time independence was declared and a war fought to preserve it, nearly half (south of New England, more than half) of this rapidly growing, diverse population was either born in the Old World (Europe or Africa) or descended from eighteenth-century immigrants. Most of the immigrants and their descendants lived in highly visible ethnic enclaves in largely segregated, rural landscapes. As a result of the new kind of immigration after 1700, it was possible by the 1750s and 1760s to walk from Philadelphia to the Carolina backcountry and hear a variety of languages and dialects spoken.[3]

What this means is that the roots of the American population on the eve of the Revolution extended as much into eighteenth-century Europe and Africa as into seventeenth-century America. The immigrants and their descendants constituted a vital part of the population—probably the majority south of New England (especially south of New York and New Jersey). America was a society with a rapidly growing population due to the excess of births over deaths, but this growth was also due to immigration—which was important in and of itself, and because it contributed to even further growth by natural means.

The enormous immigration that occurred after 1700—especially after about 1730—had a dual impact on the fast-growing, triracial population of America: it brought both opportunity and hardship, freedom and servitude. For many European immigrants it brought both opportunity, but for Africans (nearly half of all immigrants) it meant slavery. And for Native Americans, every acre of opportunity achieved for the new arrivals signified their loss.

Large-scale immigration had a double effect on Europeans as well. On the one hand the European immigrants, who came from small, overcrowded farm villages, found what seemed to them breathtaking landscapes of opportunity in America; the villagers at home could not comprehend such landscapes even after reading descriptive and articulate letters from family and fellow villagers who had made the journey. Yet such descriptions of opportunity brought even more immigrants, and when their numbers reached record levels at mid-century, conditions in America worsened, in part because of their arrival. Henry Melchior Muhlenberg, Christopher Saur, and Gottlieb Mittelberger are only three of the better-known commentators of the 1750s who condemned the abuses of the immigrant shipping trade, the redemptioner and indentured servant system, and the shrinking opportunities for new arrivals seeking land in the backcountry of Pennsylvania.[4]

In this climate of increasing opportunities from the European vantage point, and shrinking opportunities and crisis from the American vantage point, how did the immigrants make it in their New World? Which individuals and groups did make it? Which did not, and why?

*   *   *

In the midst of this multi-ethnic immigrant society were the Germans. Although the estimated number of German-speaking immigrants from 1700 to 1775 amounts to only a fraction of the millions who came to the United States in the nineteenth and twentieth centuries, they were arguably the largest European immigrant group in the eighteenth century.[5] The immigration with which this study is concerned was actually the third in a series of distinct phases of German migrations to British North America, each with its own causes and character. These phases occurred from 1683 to 1709, from 1709 to 1714, and from about 1717 to 1775.[6]

Religious persecution in central Europe and the pursuit of utopian experiments were the predominant reasons for the first phase of German immigration in the period 1683–1709. Many small, well-organized radical pietist groups, fleeing desperate conditions in central Europe, migrated together to their new asylum in Pennsylvania. In addition to the state of nearly-continuous warfare in southwest Germany and Switzerland, a renewed wave of religious intolerance and persecution against pietistic religious sects broke out in the late seventeenth century. At the same time, William Penn and his agents traveled through these areas, making contacts with Mennonites and others, converting some to Quakerism, and interesting others in the Holy Experiment. The groups led by Franz Daniel Pastorius, Johannes Kelpius, and Daniel Falkner were typical of this first phase. Though their numbers were small—perhaps about three hundred immigrants by 1709—they left a legacy that endures to this day.

Religious immigration motivated by persecution and/or utopian ideals continued throughout the colonial period, but beginning in 1709, a much larger and different kind of immigration overwhelmed and dominated German America.[7] From 1709 to about 1714, thousands of Germans and Swiss, motivated by an agricultural disaster in 1709 and an English settlement experiment, fled to New York and North Carolina in a single mass emigration. The English government had been trying for years to recruit German settlers for the colonies to manufacture shipbuilding products on the Hudson River in New York. They published many promotional pamphlets and books, but few potential emigrants had responded. In 1709 a new incentive was added to one of these tracts: Now Queen Anne promised to pay for their journey to America and to support them upon arrival. To further ensure that the offer would attract the attention of the many thousands of potential emigrants in southwest Germany, the queen's picture was placed on the cover and the title page was printed in golden color. The tract became known as the "Golden Book," and it was circulated widely in the Rhine Valley just as one of the worst agricultural disasters of the century hit all of Europe.[8]

But the English soon became victims of their own plan: Unprecedented numbers of emigrants rushed down the Rhine to the port city of Rotterdam to take advantage of the queen's offer. About 30,000 attempted to emigrate, but their numbers so overwhelmed the English authorities that only half made it across the Channel, and many of these were later sent home. Eventually, about 2,400 sailed in ten ships to New York, while 650 settled in New Bern, North Carolina.[9] As with the first phase, there was a sense of desperation to this emigration that was not present in later years. Most of the emigrants came from the Palatinate or the immediately surrounding area. This region had suffered the most from the wars and de-population of the late seventeenth and early eighteenth centuries. While many other areas in southwest Germany began recovering after 1650, con-ditions had improved only minimally in the Palatinate. Overpopulation did not help cause the emigration of 1709, as is sometimes suggested, because the population there was still well below pre-1620 levels. Rapid population growth did not occur until after the conclusion of the War of the Spanish Succession in 1714. The English shipbuilding plan failed because of poor planning, lack of funds, and the rise of a new Tory government in London (which disapproved of it), but the Germans stayed in America. This signi-fied the first time they had come to the New World in large numbers. By 1714, most lived not in Pennsylvania, but in New York.

The subjects of this study arrived during the third phase (roughly from 1717 to 1775) and were part of a much larger and different kind of immi-gration. Only a small (but significant) minority belonged to some group of radical pietists fleeing extreme religious persecution, and relatively few were part of a large group of migrants desperately fleeing a war or agri-cultural disaster (although the latter was sometimes the final impetus). In-stead, the majority of those who came during the third phase represented a small part of a decades-long out-migration of hundreds of thousands of German-speakers. Long-term conditions of overpopulation and land scar-city in Europe (discussed at length in Chapter 1),[10] combined with the active recruitment of Germans to settle in the colonies, where labor was in short supply and land in abundance, induced more than 80,000 German-speaking immigrants to try their luck in the New World. They sought land and opportunity, both of which seemed to be declining in Europe but abundant in America. For them, emigration was a calculated risk, one of many choices they could have made to try to improve their steadily de-teriorating situation at home.

By about 1760 there were significant, noticeable German-speaking populations in most of the British North American colonies (see Map I.1). Twelve ships carrying German immigrants arrived in Halifax, Nova Scotia, from 1749 to 1752. Five ships landed in Massachusetts from 1750 to 1753, and their passengers founded small settlements, including one in Maine. New York was no longer the primary destination after 1714, but it became an important secondary entrepôt and remained so throughout the century. Many immigrants remained in the city, but many others settled along the upper Hudson and the Mohawk rivers. Some Germans from the 1709–

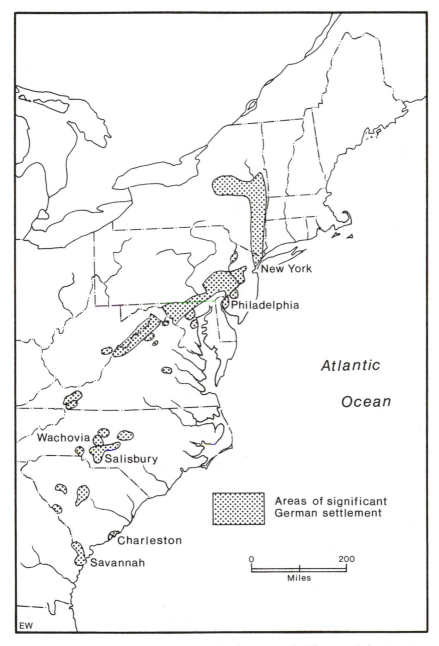

Map I.1. Principal Locations of German Settlement in the Thirteen Colonies, circa 1760.

1714 immigration eventually moved into New Jersey, settling in Essex and especially in Bergen County, but most who lived in New Jersey by 1760 had entered through Philadelphia. They settled primarily on the Delaware in Hunterdon and Sussex Counties, upriver from Philadelphia. Some also settled across the river from Philadelphia in Burlington County and in the southwestern corner of the colony in Salem County.[11]

A large majority of all German immigrants, especially those who came during the third phase, entered through Philadelphia and settled in a large area that Carl Bridenbaugh called "Greater Pennsylvania." This area included Philadelphia and other parts of southeastern Pennsylvania, parts of New Jersey, and the southern backcountry as far south as the North Carolina Piedmont (see Map I.1). Most of the Germans, Scots-Irish, Scots, English, and others migrated from Pennsylvania to the southern backcountry along the Great Wagon Road, which ran through the Shenandoah Valley of Virginia and into the Carolina Piedmont, or on at least one other important immigrant trail east of the Blue Ridge Mountains in Virginia. At least for a while, this diverse lot of immigrants and their descendants maintained economic ties with Philadelphia in the same way suburbanites maintain ties with the city center in a modern metropolis.[12]

The heaviest concentration of Germans within Greater Pennsylvania in 1760 lay in southeastern Pennsylvania and in western Maryland. By that time more than fifty thousand Germans had arrived, and they made up the largest ethnic group in these areas. Although there were significant immigrations through Baltimore and Annapolis, and Alexandria, Virginia, throughout the eighteenth century, most of these arrivals settled along the coast. By 1790 (if not earlier), 86 percent of all Maryland Germans lived in the backcountry counties of Frederick, Washington, and Allegheny. They made up 50 percent of the white population and 44 percent of the total population in those counties.[13]

Many of the Pennsylvania Germans had moved into the Shenandoah Valley of Virginia by 1760. Numerically, these settlers overshadowed the Piedmont Germans, who had come through the Chesapeake and settled Germanna (1714), Germantown (1719), Hebron (1725), Little Fork (1734), and Frankford (1738). Moreover, they were the largest ethnic group in the lower end of the Valley. Above them was the large "Irish" tract, and at the upper end of the Valley, Germans settled at New River (1743) and Mahanaim (1745).[14]

The deepest penetration of significant numbers of Pennsylvania Germans into the southern backcountry took place in the North Carolina

1. Jonathan Hager, who arrived in Philadelphia in 1736, built this stone house in 1739. The house is still standing in Hagerstown, Frederick (now Washington) County, Maryland. (Photograph courtesy of the Jonathan Hager House and Museum.)

Piedmont. Following well-established immigrant trails through western Maryland and Virginia, they pushed into North Carolina in the 1740s and continued to do so in large numbers throughout the century. Although Germans never outnumbered English settlers in the region as a whole, there were significant ethnic enclaves along the Great Wagon Road around Salisbury, in Rowan County, and in and around the German Moravian tract in Surry County. They also settled on the tributaries of the Cape Fear River in western Orange and eastern Guilford counties, and to the southwest in Lincoln County. In fact, Germans made up the majority of the population in northeastern Mecklenburg County (modern Cabarrus County).[15]

Most Germans living in South Carolina in 1760 had immigrated through Charleston, not Philadelphia. A small but distinguishable "Dutch

2. One of the few surviving colonial structures built by Germans in North Carolina, this stone house, built by Michael Braun in 1766, stands near Salisbury, in Rowan County. (Photograph by James P. Barringer, Jr., of the *Salisbury Post*.)

Town" was located in the northwest quadrant of the port city. In 1732 Germans also settled near the coast in Purrysburg, not far from Savannah. Shortly thereafter they began moving into the backcountry and settled Orangeburg (1735), Saxe-Gotha (1737), and an area between two tributaries of the Congaree River known as "Dutch Fork." In 1764 several hundred Germans settled Londonderry Township on Hard Labor Creek, near the Savannah and over fifty miles upriver from Augusta, Georgia.[16]

By 1760, many of the German settlements in Georgia were already in decline. Salzburgers and a handful of Moravians were among the first to colonize Georgia, and Swiss and Swabian immigrants soon followed. They settled in and around Savannah; just upriver in Ebenezer and Bethany; and farther south, on the coast, in Frederica. Within a generation, many left the colony for South Carolina, Pennsylvania, and elsewhere. By 1790 no Georgia county was as much as 5 percent ethnic German.[17]

*   *   *

In this study, I attempt to link the questions, issues, and sources of central European social-demographic history to the migration, settlement, mobility, and politics of eighteenth-century British North America during the critical decades preceding the Revolution. Moreover, I try to link the experience of the Germans, the only substantial non-British European immigrant group in the eighteenth century, to the larger issues of the day during this period of crisis in late colonial America. My argument is that a collective strategy best suited the immigrants from the time they left their communal peasant villages in Europe until they consolidated their new positions politically in colonial American society. The origins of this strategy lay in the peculiar conditions that developed in southwest Germany and Switzerland in the late seventeenth and early eighteenth centuries, as well as in the new conditions of pre-revolutionary America. From the crowded villages and prolific radical pietist religious movements of their homelands to the ethnically and religiously diverse, crisis-ridden colonies of British North America, many immigrants found that by sticking together they could survive the journey and perhaps even flourish in their new world.

There was in some ways a significant amount of continuity, rather than disconnection, among the lives of German-speaking immigrants in colonial America. They made a calculated risk when they left the conditions of scarcity and growing state or aristocratic interference in their lives, which they had often resisted. They went to North America because they had heard stories of abundant land that could be had on easy terms. Many said the voyage could be dangerous, perhaps even catastrophic, but if they survived and stayed out of debt during the passage, they stood a good chance of becoming one of the success stories told in letters to those who stayed behind.

This is a story about those who took a chance and found that by maintaining some of their old ways and creating new ones they could succeed. Part 1 examines the world they left behind and includes an overview of the causes of German-speaking emigration to the colonies, developments at the village level, and patterns of migration. The eighteenth-century im-

migrants left an old world of peasant village communities undergoing tremendous change. Many of the attitudes associated with that change would
emerge among the immigrant population in the colonies. Part 2 examines
settlement patterns of the immigrants in the colonies, their successes and
failures, and their involvement in colonial politics. Nearly 80 percent of
the German-speakers went to Pennsylvania, at least initially, and they used
many of their old ways and connections in their struggle to get ahead.
Most tried to acquire land within largely German areas. Some succeeded
and some failed. But they quickly adapted to the new, growing, triracial
environment. When they became involved in colonial politics and, eventually, in the imperial crisis, they did so on their own terms.

As the immigrants adapted to their new environment, they not only
used Old World village and family connections in their struggles to succeed, but also developed a new, larger ethnic identity with German speakers from other villages and regions. This ethnic identity remained strong in
later generations and throughout the upheavals of the Revolutionary Era.
By 1790 almost all of the immigrants and their descendants still spoke German, married other Germans, went to German churches, and lived near or
next to German neighbors. Thus in the process of their struggle for success,
they helped create a new, diverse, competitive America and—without becoming less German—became "Americanized" by their adaptation to their
new land.

PART ONE

THE WORLD THEY
LEFT BEHIND

The immigrants did not leave a void, nor did their Old World customs, beliefs, and connections entirely disappear when they crossed the North Atlantic. Instead, their past ways helped shape their behavior in the North American continent. They successfully left behind a changing world—a world recovering from the devastation of the previous century—by reviving some old practices and beginning some new ones. Understanding the overall framework of change within which the migrations occurred will help us better understand who the immigrants were and what they were doing in their new world.

3. The residence of Carl Friedrich and the city of Karlsruhe, the capital of Baden-Durlach, from a 1739 engraving by Johann Matthäus Steidlin and Co. (Courtesy of the Generallandesarchiv Karlsruhe.)

I

A Changing World and the
Lure from Abroad

By the mid-eighteenth century, Carl Friedrich, the margrave of Baden-Durlach, could contemplate with some satisfaction the situation of his realm, which consisted primarily of three disconnected clusters of territories scattered along the right bank of the upper Rhine in southwest Germany. From his magnificent new baroque palace in Karlsruhe, the enlightened margrave ruled a territory that was recovering from the destruction that war and pestilence had wrought for decades during the previous century. Public buildings, also in the new baroque style, appeared everywhere in the compact reconstructed villages of the realm. After more than forty years of relative peace, the once devastated population had recovered and rebuilt the land. In fact, throughout Carl Friedrich's long reign (1746–1811) there would be no war in Baden-Durlach.

Thus the margrave had grounds for optimism as he attempted to build an ideal state. This ambitious, enlightened ruler implemented reforms in the judicial system, industry, agriculture, science, education, and social welfare. Eventually, he would abolish the use of torture (1767) and free the serfs (1783). He believed that if his subjects prospered, they would be able to contribute even more to the treasury, which would enable him to build more baroque structures, make his army stronger, and further extend his bureaucracy, thus allowing him to collect even more revenues. If his state became strong enough, it might be able to resist any future aggressions from its neighbors.

But many problems in Baden-Durlach prevented Carl Friedrich from attaining his goal of a secure, prosperous, and enlightened state. Some of his advisors told him that the territory was becoming overpopulated, and that this was leading to economic problems for many subjects, possibly even for the entire realm. Indeed, the official censuses of the realm, while not as accurate as they would become in the next century, listed about 82,000 inhabitants in 1746 and 109,000 by 1785.[1] Moreover, the growing realization that his government could not manage his far-flung state exactly as he wished troubled the margrave. Centuries-old traditions, as well as village parochialism and self-interest, led many peasants to ignore some of the decrees and resist some of the moves made in Karlsruhe. Sometimes, they were successful: They resisted Karlsruhe's attempts to draft spinners to work in the newly opened cloth mills. Some resisted the government's attempts to carve up the common fields for private use; others disobeyed edicts banning deforestation; and many ignored attempts to regulate inheritance practices.

One difficult, growing, and—according to some of his mercantilist advisors—potentially devastating problem recurred in Baden-Durlach during this time: emigration. Emigration, they believed, drained away the most important resource for the wealth of a state—its people. The problem had existed for centuries, and this latest phase had begun a half century earlier, but it had not reached significant levels until this point. In fact, by the end of Carl Friedrich's reign, more than 11,000 families had emigrated from Baden and Breisgau (along the right bank of the upper Rhine), and a large portion of them, perhaps one-half, had left Baden-Durlach. Thus the population by 1785 would have been considerably higher than 109,000 had there been no emigration—a fact that alarmed and frustrated the state-building mercantilists.[2]

Carl Friedrich shared the problem of emigration with most other rulers in southwest Germany and Switzerland. In the eighteenth century hundreds of thousands of subjects emigrated from these regions to distant lands. They left growing, solidifying, but still scattered territorial states like Baden-Durlach as well as smaller ecclesiastical states and tiny principalities ruled by knights or other, lesser nobles. They journeyed to lands, east and west, that were so distant, and which presented such great difficulties for establishing one's self and family, that there was little or no possibility of return if things did not work out. Most of these peasant farmers and craftsmen followed the paths traveled for centuries to traditional destinations in eastern Europe. A small minority, however, journeyed even farther, to new lands, to the "island of Pinßel Fania" (Pennsylvania).

What was happening in southwest Germany and Switzerland, the origin of almost all emigration from German-speaking lands? (See Map 1.1.) How did state-building, recovery from war, and population growth transform the landscapes of these regions? Why did this lead to the emigration

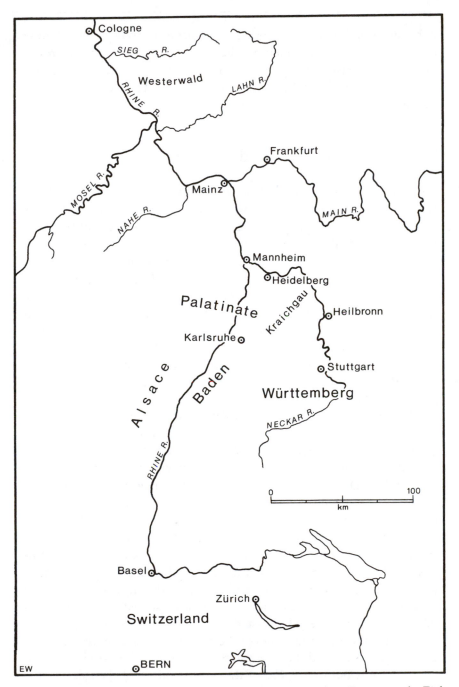

Map 1.1. Principal Areas of Emigration from German-Speaking Europe in the Eighteenth Century.

of hundreds of thousands of subjects, and what made some of them choose to go to British North America? The answers to these questions reveal many of the crucial elements that helped shape the attitudes of immigrants when they looked for places to settle and confronted the authorities in the colonies.

Recovery and Reconstruction

From the late seventeenth to the mid-eighteenth century, the inhabitants of southwest Germany and, to some extent, Switzerland underwent a period of recovery and reconstruction that transformed and redefined the social, political, economic, religious, and demographic fabric of their societies—societies that warfare in the seventeenth century had nearly destroyed. Throughout the eighteenth century the larger states grew even larger and exerted increasing influence on villagers' everyday lives. The shift from the traditional three-field system with village common lands toward more modern, intensive agriculture was accelerated. Ethnic and religious diversity increased tremendously in the region, even as the respective established churches—Lutheran, Reformed, and Catholic—attempted to "purify" their subjects. The pace of change varied from region to region, but the net effect in all regions was enormous.

It is difficult to exaggerate the effects of seventeenth-century warfare on southwest Germany. War essentially ripped much of society from its roots as large percentages of the population succumbed to the plague or combat, and many more fled the region. Society in general became much more mobile. Destructive warfare continued throughout the century (and did not truly abate until 1714), especially in the Palatinate, which probably lost more of its population than any other region.[3]

The seventeenth-century wars, especially the Thirty Years' War, provided the impetus for the enormous changes that took place in the southwest during the eighteenth century by nearly destroying the demographic, political, social, and economic fabric of the area. As regional and local political, social, and economic activities resumed, both rulers and ruled returned to some old ways and also began many new ones.

During the wars, the armies of the great European empires and kingdoms largely destroyed the local political structures of most territories in the southwest, but by the end of the century, many of the rulers in the region began putting together the pieces of their shattered regimes. They proceeded at different rates—some, such as the Palatine Electorate could hardly begin before 1700 because of continued destruction during the wars of the late seventeenth century—but slowly the local rulers began gaining more control over their subjects' lives.

The reconstruction of the state in southwest Germany during the eighteenth century represented the resumption of a centuries-long trend of state-building and centralization taking place in the early modern period. Throughout Europe, state governments established and deepened their hegemony over regional and local government, even village life, by extending their bureaucracies (hence tax apparatus), legal systems, and military strength throughout their lands, all at the expense of the cities, guilds, estates, and weaker neighbors. The disasters of the seventeenth century temporarily reversed this trend in the smaller states of southwest Germany, but by the eighteenth century the pattern resumed.[4]

In the southwest, the process of state-building was closely connected to population policy (*Bevölkerungspolitik*) and, ultimately, emigration. Most rulers of the larger states (for example, Württemberg, Baden-Durlach, and the Palatine Electorate) believed that a rational population policy was central to building or rebuilding a strong, prosperous state. As early as the 1660s some rulers were beginning to implement the theories of Johann Joachim Becher, a mercantilist political scientist who emphasized the importance of promoting in-migration and restricting out-migration in building a strong state.[5]

Throughout the eighteenth century the mercantilists gained influence in the courts of the territorial rulers in the southwest. Johann August Schlettwein, one of the most respected and influential political economists of his day, served in the court of Carl Friedrich at Karlsruhe from 1763 to 1773. Schlettwein believed that the more subjects a state had, the stronger it would become. Faced with the argument that overpopulation and the accompanying extreme parcellation of landholdings was causing severe problems for many subjects, Schlettwein studied the census tables and concluded that his territory was actually *underpopulated*. Overpopulation was possible, but only when every square inch of land was under maximum cultivation, when all possible raw materials for industry were being used, and when more than sufficient labor was available to maintain all necessary industrial efforts for the state.[6]

Following the advice of Schlettwein and other mercantilists, many territorial rulers in the southwest maintained policies that promoted in-migration and restricted or forbad out-migration outright. But neither the margrave of Baden-Durlach nor any other territorial ruler was capable of controlling his subjects like chess figures.[7]

Although total control of their populations was impossible, rulers of both large and small territories were able to erect extensive bureaucratic structures to tax subjects who did wish to leave the realm, something that would have been impossible in the seventeenth century. In the seventeenth century, with local and territorial government dissolved, large numbers of subjects fled in terror when plague-carrying armies advanced into the region: these emigrants did not report to the authorities and pay the usual taxes. In the relatively peaceful eighteenth century, however, tens of thousands of emigrant families in the southwest paid a large fee for leaving the realm and another for removing their property.[8]

In preparing to leave the realm the emigrants encountered not only the expanding state apparatus, but also one of the most important remnants of seigniorial privilege—serfdom. Serfs, the majority of the population, were part of a complicated web of traditional rights and privileges that left them legally "owned" (*leibeigen*) by their rulers. The cornerstone of eighteenth-century seigniorial privilege in the southwest was the ruler's right to control the movement of his subjects. If serfs desired to emigrate, they first had to apply and pay a large fee for manumission. The territorial ruler, through his extensive bureaucracy, granted manumission and then collected the fee.[9]

What this means is that both the growing state apparatus and the remaining seigniorial institutions affected the emigrants as much as or more than any other subjects. While the majority lived in villages and were *leibeigen*, their status manifested itself most significantly when they wished to emigrate.[10] And when they did emigrate, they paid enormous fees for manumission, removal of property, and the act of emigration itself, all of which helped the rulers finance the reconstruction and extension of their respective states.[11]

An alternative to paying the manumission and emigration fees was to emigrate illegally, and, given the enormous rates charged, it is little wonder that many did. This *Schwarzauswanderung* was most significant in the weaker territorial states, such as the Palatine Electorate, and in the very small territories, such as those in the Kraichgau (see Chapter 2). But the tens of thousands of government records left behind by those did pay attest to the success of many of these territories in taxing the subjects they could not keep at home.[12]

The world of the villagers was changing not only due to the increased role of the state in their lives but also due to an acceleration in the shift toward a more capitalist economy. Throughout the early modern period a transformation in agricultural practices occurred in western Europe, from subsistence farming using the common fields system to intensive, capitalist farming using new methods. The rate of change varied from region to region, and subsistence farming still flourished in many areas of the southwest in the mid-eighteenth century, but the common fields had all but disappeared by 1800.

An intense assault on the land occurred in the eighteenth century, as both peasants and elites implemented new farming methods. In their search for more land, peasants began plowing and planting fields that before had lain fallow. University professors began teaching agronomy, which led to improvements in cattle and sheep breeding. The highly speculative viticulture, as well as fruit trees, potatoes, and other high-yield crops came into greater use, as did clover and dung, to restore minerals to the soil. Further, many areas of southwest Germany (especially the Black Forest) were nearly deforested, as peasants cleared new ground for planting and to provide timber for Europe's expanding navies.[13]

Some peasants profited from the transition to a more capitalistic agriculture, and others lost ground. Many peasants who acquired larger plots of land, or city dwellers who acquired land in the countryside and rented to rural peasants, did well. On the other hand, those whose only means of livelihood lay in scratching out a living by farming on shrinking, far-flung plots suffered increasingly as the century progressed.[14]

Southwest Germany was also becoming more religiously and ethnically diverse in the eighteenth century. Since the sixteenth century none of the three dominant religions of central Europe (Roman Catholic, Reformed, or Lutheran) was able to dominate the region, and all were strongly represented in the numerous independent states and territories there. Within the larger churches there were movements, such as Pietism among the Lutherans and Reformed, that were a source of diversity and conflict.

In addition to the three traditional religions of central Europe, a large and growing number of small, radical pietist groups were strewn across the landscape of the southwest. Their numbers were small, but they would become important to the settlement of Pennsylvania and other areas. Some, such as the Mennonites, Swiss Brethren, Moravians, and Waldensians, dated from the Reformation or earlier, and began moving into the southwest German river valleys in the seventeenth and eighteenth centuries.

Others were new groups that took root in the area as their leaders saw visions of the Apocalypse in the catastrophes wrought upon their region. Disillusioned with what the traditional religions had to offer, they turned to chiliastic, sometimes mystical countermovements despised by both religious and secular authorities. These new groups included Quakers (recruited in the middle Rhine region by William Penn and others), the Saalhof pietists in Frankfurt am Main (led in the 1670s by Eleonore von Merlau and Johann Jakob Schütz), and a small group of mystic pre-millennialists led by Johannes Kelpius. At the turn of the century in Wetteravia, a scattered group of hermits led by Alexander Mack began forming a group that would become known as the New Baptists, or Dunkers (eventually the Church of the Brethren). There were many other small religious groups that formed around various charismatic leaders in this climate of disorder, fear, and disillusionment. The net effect of these movements was to create extreme religious diversity in the collection of societies clustered along the middle Rhine in southwest Germany.[15]

But it was more than just the growth of small, radical pietist groups and the presence of all three of the major churches in this region that created the cultural diversity in the southwest. When rulers such as Carl Friedrich of Baden-Durlach encouraged large-scale immigration into their depopulated territories, tens of thousands of French Huguenots, Swiss, and Flemish settled in the region to take up lands abandoned during the devastation of the seventeenth century.[16]

Thus by the early eighteenth century, southwest Germany had become a collage of ethnically diverse states representing all three of the officially sanctioned religions (often located in the same territory) along with a host of small, radical pietist groups, not to mention a significant Jewish population. Although many religious and political leaders did not like it, the need to gain new subjects after the losses resulting from seventeenth-century warfare, as well as their relative inability to enforce conformity, led to a significant measure of toleration for some of these groups—at least for awhile. In short, religious and ethnic diversity, immigration, and tolerance combined to form a collection of societies in parts of the middle Rhine region very similar to the diverse make-up of Pennsylvania.

Ultimately the nature of the recovery and reconstruction led many to leave the realm. Letters home, colonial newspapers, and other sources from immigrants in the American colonies often condemned the growing state bureaucracies and tax burdens, as well as serfdom and a hardening religious order. Further, many who were not doing well in the growing capitalist economy sought their fortunes elsewhere. Still, many of these developments, while influencing the attitudes and behavior of the former subjects in the colonies, only indirectly "caused" emigration from southwest Germany and Switzerland. More direct causes will be investigated next.

Demographic Pressure, Scarcity, and Emigration

One of the most important developments in southwest Germany and Switzerland in the eighteenth century that contributed not only to much of the change described above but also to the emigration of hundreds of thousands of subjects from the region was uninterrupted, long-term demographic growth. As the population reached record levels by the middle third of the century, much of traditional life at the village level became untenable for peasants, serf and free, and they were forced to make a range of choices in order to adapt. One of those choices was to seek their fortunes elsewhere.

In some ways demographic developments in the eighteenth century reflected a continuation of centuries-old patterns of growth and pressure, followed by significant social change. The population of Europe increased roughly 70 percent from 1720 to 1800 — essentially a population explosion. Such "explosions" had occurred periodically in European demographic history, but when this one began, the population was already at a record level.[17]

From the eleventh to the seventeenth century a pattern developed in which socioeconomic change was connected to demographic cycles in many parts of Europe, including southwest Germany and Switzerland. A shift toward more extensive agricultural methods and partible inheritance occurred during periods of severe population loss, and the practice of more intensive farming and impartible inheritance increased during long-term periods of population growth. Movements into towns and cities from the surrounding countryside and the development of manufactures also occurred during peak population periods.[18]

Also connected to the natural cycles of growth and decline in the population during these centuries were long-range out- and in-migrations. Significant levels of out-migration (primarily to eastern Europe) occurred when population levels reached peaks in the twelfth and thirteenth centuries, and again in the late sixteenth and early seventeenth centuries. Conversely, in-migration occurred in the late seventeenth and early eighteenth centuries, when the population level was down. This rhythmic ebb and flow would continue until a permanent decline in mortality and fertility, as well as large-scale industrialization and urbanization, redefined the framework for the movements of peoples in modern society.

The pattern established in the previous five centuries, in which demographic decline was followed by recovery and then socioeconomic change, including in- and out-migration, repeated itself in the seventeenth and eighteenth centuries. While population growth merely stagnated in many areas of Europe in the mid-seventeenth century, it declined drastically in the territories along the Rhine during the Thirty Years' War (1618–1648), and many of these territories continued to suffer enormous losses in the wars of the late seventeenth century. Some regions and subregions suffered more than others, but the southwest lost as much as 40 percent of its population by 1648. Not all of these losses were due to deaths—many people fled their homes and returned years later—but the number of deaths was indeed high enough to alleviate the population pressure that had been building since the sixteenth century.[19]

In the late seventeenth century, the population of southwest Germany began to grow dramatically. Natural population growth increased because of the decline in mortality and an increase in fertility: The severity of warfare and disease declined, and inhabitants began marrying earlier and having more children. Adding to the already increasing population was the large-scale in-migration into the southwest after 1648.

During this period of rapid growth and recovery, inhabitants of the southwest practiced extensive agriculture and partible inheritance. Following the devastation of the earlier wars, labor demand and land availability in the southwest was high, which allowed the custom of partible inheritance to flourish after it had been abandoned in many other parts of central Europe. Couples thus had an incentive to marry earlier and have more children—there would be plenty of land for all when they came of age.

Eventually, the high rate of natural increase, combined with immigration, led to overpopulation, as by the mid-eighteenth century the population reached the record levels of 1570–1620 and then continued to grow.[20] The increase was greatest in the river valleys and foothills of the southwest, where partible inheritance was still practiced. Favorable climate and soil quality in the upper Rhine Valley allowed the practice of more intensive agriculture, and peasants became dependent on new methods of farming. But they clung to their traditional inheritance custom, and, inevitably for many, landholdings became too small to support a family, even when they used the newer methods.[21]

When proponents of rational agrarian reform convinced the authorities in states like Baden-Durlach that unrestricted population growth and parcelling of landholdings (*Güterzersplitterung*) might harm the well being of the realm, and when the authorities began to take action, many peasants reacted with resentment and noncompliance. In 1724 the government in Karlsruhe forbad immigration, thus reversing the seventeenth-century policy designed to repopulate the territory after the Thirty Years' War. Furthermore, the government outlawed marriage for people under the age of twenty-five and the division of land into "too small parts." But the peasants, resentful of this attempt at intervention into local customs, continued to practice partible inheritance. By mid-century the problem had become much more acute, and in 1760 the court issued a general proclamation forbidding the division of fields, pastures, and vineyards under $\frac{1}{4}$ *Jauchert* — about *one-fifth of an acre* — and $\frac{1}{8}$ *Jauchert* for gardens; still, the practice continued.[22]

Faced with the prospect of making a living off a parcel of land a mere fraction of the size worked by their grandparents, in a land where the apparatus of government increasingly interfered with the affairs and customs of the village, many peasants chose to seek their fortunes elsewhere, as they had done in previous centuries under similar pressures. Graph 1.1 shows that an upswing in emigration from three important areas of the southwest occurred in the middle third of the century, as the population reached pre-1620 levels and then continued to grow.

Wolfgang von Hippel arrived at similar results using the same kinds of sources for Upper Swabia, the Upper Neckar, the Hohenzollern territories along the borders of southern Württemberg, the southeastern areas of the Black Forest, and the area along the northern shores of Lake Constance. Sudden, sharp peaks of emigration, caused by climatic and agricultural disasters, occurred throughout the century, but with the exception of the brief emigration after the catastrophic winter of 1708–1709, climatic-agrarian disasters coincided with emigration only in the latter two-thirds of the century. As in the areas represented in Graph 1.1, the largest wave of emigration in the areas studied by von Hippel occurred in 1770–1771, after some of the worst crop failures of the century followed a disastrous winter in Europe. Emigration was minimal in the first third of the century, but thereafter, as population pressure became more acute, it gradually increased between the peak years.[23]

Overpopulation and heavy emigration usually occurred in areas practicing partible inheritance. In southern Baden, for example, the overwhelming majority of parishes with heavy emigration, measured in terms

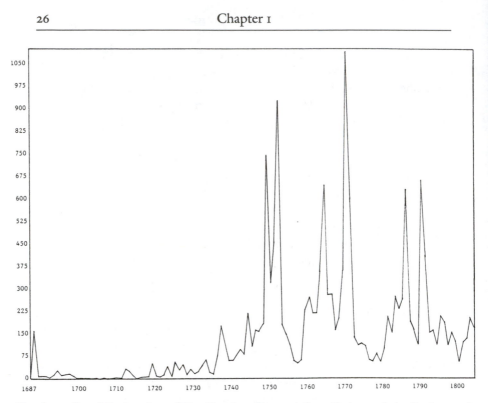

Graph 1.1. Legal Emigration of Families (not Persons) from Baden and the Breisgau, the Lower Neckar, the Bishopric of Speyer, and the Territories of the Imperial City of Ulm, 1687–1804. *Sources*: Compiled from three collections of published lists by Werner Hacker: *Auswanderungen aus Baden und dem Breisgau; Auswanderungen aus dem früheren Hochstift Speyer nach Südosteuropa und Übersee im XVIII. Jahrhundert*, Schriften zur Wanderungs-geschichte der Pfälzer, vol. 28 (Kaiserslautern: Heimatstelle Pfalz, 1969); "Auswanderer aus dem Territorium der Reichsstadt Ulm, vor allem im ausgehenden 17. und im 18. Jahrhundert," *Ulm und Oberschwaben: Zeitschrift für Geschichte und Kunst*, 42/43 (1978), 161–257; *Kurpfälzische Auswanderer vom Unteren Neckar, Rechtrheinsiche Gebiete der Kurpfalz* (Stuttgart and Aalen: Konrad Theiss Verlag, 1983).

of total population, practiced partible inheritance or a mixture of partible and impartible inheritance (see Table 1.1). With only a few exceptions, these parishes lay in the Rhine valley and foothills, where population growth and the transition to commercial agriculture were most pronounced.[24]

Most of the parishes practicing impartible inheritance in southern Baden lay in the mountainous Black Forest, where the rugged terrain hindered intensive agriculture and family farms were much larger. This area experienced relatively little of the destruction and depopulation so promi-

TABLE 1.1 Inheritance Customs by Level of Emigration from Southern Baden Parishes during the Eighteenth Century.

	NUMBER OF PARISHES									
	LEVEL 1		LEVEL 2		LEVEL 3		LEVEL 4		TOTAL	
Inheritance Custom	n	%	n	%	n	%	n	%	n	%
Partible	78	58	41	31	11	8	4	3	134	100
Mixed	35	67	16	31	1	2	0	0	52	100
Impartible	76	90	8	9	1	1	0	0	85	100
Total	189	70	65	24	13	5	4	1	271	100

Note: Emigration levels refer to number of legal emigrant families from 1688 to 1803 per parish population in 1809. Level 1 = 0.0–2.9; Level 2 = 3.0–5.9; Level 3 = 6.0–9.9; Level 4 = > 10.0.

Sources: Hacker, Auswanderungen aus Baden und dem Breisgau (emigrations); and Helmut Röhm, Die Vererbung des landwirtschaftlichen Grundeigentums in Baden-Württemberg (Remagen: Selbstverlag der Bundesanstalt für Landeskunde, 1957), "Map 1" (n.p.) and Straub, Das badische Oberland (inheritance customs).

nent in the Rhine valley and foothills during the seventeenth-century wars, and population growth in the eighteenth century was much lower. Consequently, few subjects emigrated from this region.

The special circumstances in two monastic territories in the Black Forest (St. Blasien and St. Peter), both of which experienced heavy emigration, illustrate the correlation between population growth, inheritance practices, and emigration. The subjects in the parishes of St. Blasien (located in southern Baden) never made the transition from partible to impartible inheritance, as did most of their neighbors in the Black Forest. Consequently, they experienced extreme land splintering in the eighteenth century, and emigration was heavy.[25]

In nearby St. Peter, ultimogeniture was the traditional inheritance form, but changes beginning in the late seventeenth century and continuing in the eighteenth century led to overcrowding and emigration nevertheless. During this period large numbers of peasants from the valley and foothills who were accustomed to practicing partible inheritance began moving onto the monastery's possessions. The Benedictine monks rented the newcomers' fields that had been abandoned during the difficult war years. (Unlike most regions of the Black Forest, St. Peter suffered tremendously during the seventeenth-century wars.) These tenants remained for generations, contributing to population growth and eventually making permanent claims to monastic lands. In short, significant emigration from these parishes in the Black Forest (within southern Baden) resulted from many of the same factors that motivated emigration from the Rhine valley and foothills—overpopulation and extreme division of landholdings.[26]

Whether in the more fertile valleys of the Rhine and its tributaries, or in the scattered, exceptional cases elsewhere, the problems of overpopulation and land splintering that had plagued southwest Germany periodically since the eleventh century recurred once again in the mid-eighteenth century, and once again there was significant emigration from the region. Whenever population pressure increased beyond what traditional practices in agriculture could support—as it did in the early fourteenth, sixteenth, and eighteenth centuries—people began to emigrate, especially to eastern Europe. The numbers emigrating grew in each phase, reaching new levels in the eighteenth century when emigrants ventured to Russia and America. Without demographic control or collapse (as there had been in France after 1800), millions of Germans eventually emigrated in the nineteenth century.[27]

Destinations

Large-scale emigration began in the middle third of the eighteenth century because it was at this time that population pressure began to reach a critical stage for many segments of the population even as other segments prospered. Emigration occurred where it did, rather than in other areas of Europe where there was also population pressure on the land, because of strong "recruitment" (*Werbung*) in southwest Germany and Switzerland, which attracted potential settlers to newly acquired lands in eastern Europe and America. By the eighteenth century, these regions had a centuries-long reputation as a place where one could recruit large numbers of potential settlers. Without recruitment of some kind, there would have been no emigration.

Three of the most important kinds of recruitment came from governments, private organizations, and individuals. In the early modern period, large-scale emigration did not occur unless countries with strong state policies directly or indirectly promoting the settlement of their new territories recruited immigrants. For the inhabitants of southwest Germany and Switzerland, Britain, the Habsburg Empire, Prussia, and Russia filled this

role. Britain established settlement colonies in the New World that flourished as increasing numbers of Europeans were encouraged to emigrate
in the seventeenth and eighteenth centuries. As the Habsburgs expanded
into southeastern Europe and Galicia, they actively recruited Germans to
settle in their new lands to help develop the economies there and provide a
buffer against their enemies. Similarly, Prussia developed its lightly populated eastern regions and newly conquered Polish territories by bringing in
large numbers of southwestern Germans and French Huguenots. Russia,
a latecomer to this style of social engineering, began promoting German
immigration under Catherine the Great in 1763 and continued to do so
well into the nineteenth century.[28]

Many countries, such as France and the Netherlands, did not develop
state policies in which large settlement colonies played a role. Both countries had colonies in the New World and in south and southeast Asia but—
with the exceptions of the Dutch settlement of South Africa, which remained small until the eighteenth century, and the relatively small French
settlements in Canada, Louisiana, and Guiana—there was little attempt by
these governments to stimulate large-scale migrations.[29]

Large-scale migration did not occur unless the state directly or indirectly supported it, but private organizations and individuals played an
important role in transporting people to their destinations in both eastern Europe and North America. Land settlement schemes run by speculators attracted settlers, and their agents (called newlanders, or *Neuländer* in
North America) handled transportation. Sometimes the authorities sanctioned such schemes, but often they did not. Also, when religious groups
migrated to eastern Europe or America, regardless of whether they purchased land from speculators, they often had to organize everything for
themselves.[30]

In addition to state governments and private organizations, incentive
and encouragement to emigrate also came from individuals such as friends,
families, relatives, and neighbors who had already successfully settled in
distant lands. Letters home (sometimes with exaggerated claims of success) provided a wealth of information for potential emigrants. In a few
cases, return migrants brought news and information as well. As the number of German settlers grew in the colonies, so did the volume of letters
and personal contacts, which brought even more immigrants to the newly
settled areas.

Several governments recruited heavily in the overcrowded southwest,
sometimes making extremely attractive offers, and received hundreds of

thousands of responses. In 1723 Hungary offered fifteen years of freedom from taxation and other public dues to craftsmen who would agree to permanently settle there. In the same year, Habsburg officials offered free transportation, housing, land, tax relief for three to five years, religious privileges, and free status (*Leibfreiheit*) — as opposed to serfdom — with no feudal dues (*Frohnen*) or subjectship to local lords for those who would settle in the Banat (a region in modern Rumania and Serbia). In 1763, the Russian government offered free transportation, travel money, assistance with housing and livestock purchases, five to thirty years of freedom from taxation and other assessments, inducements for developing manufactures, religious freedom, freedom to leave Russia if they later changed their minds, and the freedom to build closed colonies with their own constitutions and no interference from authorities. In 1763 the French government had some success recruiting settlers for their colony in South America (Guiana) by offering to provide transportation costs to the colony via Rochefort, a bounty based on the number in the family arriving there, two years of full upkeep in the colony, a third year of partial upkeep, a house with furnishings and some land, tools, clothes, freedom from public assessments, unrestricted exercise of religion, permission to return to France after five years if they so desired, and other benefits. In 1769 Prussia offered travel costs, land with full ownership and bequeathal rights, ten years' freedom from assessments on uncultivated land, free status, and freedom of movement (*Abzugsfreiheit*).[31]

The eastern lands offered the overcrowded, wanderlust-stricken peasants of the southwest and Switzerland enough land, resources, religious freedom, and protection from enemies (such as the Turks) to begin building flourishing German communities throughout the region. Moreover, the government would assist groups of forty or fifty families in establishing their own semiautonomous villages, physically set apart from native peoples in the area.[32]

The British government supported the circulation in southwest Germany of many pamphlets and books encouraging emigration in the late seventeenth and early eighteenth centuries. But what could the British government or colonial governments and individuals offer Germans in the thirteen colonies, and why would some choose to go there, instead of eastern Europe, as Germans had traditionally done? In fact, British officials offered few of the attractions that other governments offered to settlers in eastern Europe, and when they tried, they could not deliver. London supported the circulation of many pamphlets and books in southwest Germany in the late seventeenth and early eighteenth centuries, but after the disastrous settlement experiment in New York of 1709–1710 (see Introduction), the British never again sponsored schemes in North America that offered bounties of land, housing, tools, and special tax incentives for large numbers of immigrants. Ultimately, the government even took steps to prevent individual colonial governments from subsidizing immigrant settlements.[33]

Another disadvantage for those who chose North America over eastern Europe was the Native American threat. While the Turkish threat was receding throughout the eighteenth century in the Habsburg lands, and the government offered guarantees of protection and freedom from impressment for German immigrants, in North America the danger to European settlers from natives in frontier regions was nearly constant. Moreover, the government in Pennsylvania, where most immigrants went, was pacifist for most of the colonial period and did relatively little to protect its frontier. British recruiters attempted to counter this disadvantage by including descriptions of Native Americans in their recruitment literature which portrayed them as docile, exotic neighbors, thereby stimulating a fascination among many Germans that still exists today.[34]

The lack of special privileges, the difficult and expensive journey, and the Native American threat may, in part, explain why so few emigrants—perhaps less than 15 percent of the total number—chose to go to British North America. Only about 14 percent (3,193 of 22,284 families) of the legal emigrations from the four regions represented in Table 1.2 were to America. These are the four regions with published records of legal emigrants from which substantial numbers did, in fact, go to British North America. When one adds the tens of thousands of families from other regions (from which few went to America), the total number of emigrants journeying west instead of east becomes extremely small indeed. One historian has estimated, perhaps conservatively, that total emigration from Germany approached 900,000 during the eighteenth century; less than 15 percent went to the thirteen colonies or the United States.[35]

But the question remains: Who were the 85,000 who did go to the thirteen colonies, and, given all of the disadvantages, why did they choose to go west instead of east? Some American historians have suggested that the European immigration was a kind of self-selective process in which many "liberal," opportunistic individualists within the general population took the great risk of crossing the Atlantic and thereby infused these attributes into the developing American character.[36] This supposition is dif-

TABLE 1.2   Emigration to America as a Percentage of Total Emigration from
Four Select Regions of Southwest Germany in the Eighteenth Century.

REGION	EMIGRANT HEADS OF FAMILY	EMIGRANTS TO AMERICA	
		N	%
Ulm and its territories	813	128	16
Northern Baden-Durlach	2,406	629	26
Lower Neckar (in the Palatinate)	2,231	544	24
Western Palatinate and the Saarland	16,834	1,892	11
Total	22,284	3,193	14%

Sources: Compiled from Hacker, Baden und dem Breisgau; "aus dem Territorium der Reichsstadt Ulm; Kurpfälzische Auswanderer; Auswanderungen aus Rheinpfalz und Saarland im 18.
Jahrhundert (Stuttgart: Konrad Theiss Verlag, 1987).

ficult to substantiate. (Indeed, many who have suggested it have not tried
to substantiate it.) Substantiation would require a thorough study comparing emigrants to nonemigrants within European society as well as a
comparison of emigrants migrating west to North America as opposed to
emigrants who migrated east to Russia, Prussia, and the Habsburg lands.
Even if completed, such a study could only document tangible differences,
such as wealth, occupation, and religion.[37]

The promise of religious tolerance or freedom, often stressed by
American historians, has perhaps been overemphasized. In some ways, the
British policy on religion was more restrictive than that of eastern Europe.
Officially, the British did not accept Catholics (a large proportion of the
southwest German population), although many Irish and German Catholics did settle in the colonies. On the other hand, members of all three
major religions in the southwest received guarantees of tolerance in various
eastern lands. Catholics could settle in almost all the Habsburg territories,
while Lutheran and Reformed members could settle in Transylvania and
in Prussian-controlled regions. Russia tolerated all three religions among
German immigrants. Even in Hungary (officially Catholic), many Calvinist nobles successfully recruited large numbers of Protestants from the
southwest and Switzerland. Further, in spite of British North America's
reputation in the eighteenth century as a haven for the small radical pietist
groups, a significant part of these groups, went east including Hutterites,
Moravians, Mennonites, and others, rather than west.[38]

Two characteristics of the thirteen colonies may have drawn some emigrants westward, in spite of the disadvantages. First, enormous amounts of land seemed to be available for the taking in the colonies. Although land was also available in the east, the amounts were generally smaller and often distributed among entire villages or settlements rather than to individuals. In the colonies, word had it that an individual could acquire "plantations" of two or three hundred acres, maybe more. Second, while special privileges were no longer granted to immigrants in America, the relative freedom of the general population from the state military and fiscal apparatus appeared perhaps even more attractive than the benefits granted to the emigrants in the east. These advantages were communicated to potential emigrants not just in the propaganda of land schemers, but in the large and growing number of letters home from fellow villagers and in testimony from return visitors who had succeeded in America.[39]

The immigrant letters and return visitors told tales to those who stayed behind of a land where three or four families might own as much land as belonged to the entire village at home. Not only was land abundant and affordable, but taxes were low and the "freedoms" available to the general population were generous. Durs Thommen, for example, emigrated to Pennsylvania in 1736 with his family and many others from Niederdorf, near Basel. After arriving they wrote home that the trip was very difficult and expensive, and that the agents and crews had not always told the truth about these conditions. But Thommen also wrote that,

I took a place with 350 *Juchert* (about 435 acres), two houses and barns, and have, believe it or not, 6 horses, 2 colts, 15 cattle, and about 35 sacks of oats, 46 sacks of wheat, 25 sacks of rye, and 23 sacks of corn. For all this land I have to pay no more than 7 shilling, or about 7 times 5 Swiss batzen, for tithes, quitrents, and other dues. In this country there are abundant liberties in just about all matters.[40]

Letters such as these had a powerful effect on the people in the home village. Years after his migration Johann Georg Jungmann of Hockenheim (in the Palatinate) told a familiar story of how his family decided to emigrate when his father received a letter from Pennsylvania in 1731 which described how many Germans were arriving in that colony and doing well. The next spring the family sold everything they had, made their way to Neckarhausen, and from there downriver to Rotterdam, where they boarded a ship bound for Philadelphia.[41]

Gottlieb Mittelberger's famous journey to Pennsylvania in 1750 sums up the dilemma for those considering traveling west instead of east. This Lutheran schoolteacher and organist from Enzweihingen in Württemberg published his well-known description of the journey to *discourage* emigration. He wrote that he required seven weeks just to reach Rotterdam from Heilbronn on the Neckar, and he had to pass through thirty-six customs houses on the way. He hypothesized that a five- or six-week stay in Rotterdam was normal. The trip from Rotterdam to Cowes, England (on the Isle of Wight), lasted eight days, but could take up to four weeks if the winds were contrary. In Cowes, passengers once more paid customs duties, as they entered the British Empire and navigation network. Mittelberger's voyage from Rotterdam to Philadelphia on the *Osgood* took fifteen miserable weeks. His experience was not necessarily typical, but he had to endure "smells, fumes, horrors, vomiting, various kinds of sea sickness, fever, dysentery, headaches, heat, constipation, boils, scurvy, cancer, mouth-rot," as well as bad food, an exploitative captain with a thieving crew, thirst, storms, and the deaths of many fellow passengers, especially children.

Had Mittelberger ended his tale with his awful description of the voyage, he might have succeeded in frightening many from the decision to emigrate westward. But instead he went on to describe Pennsylvania as a place with abundant land, wildlife, and liberties—just what many in southwest Germany and Switzerland felt they were sorely lacking—making the difficult voyage to attain what Mittelberger described seem worth the risk.[42]

So the America immigrants took the hard route and hoped that the payoff would come with acquisition of one of the huge tracts of land they had heard about. Given the overcrowded conditions in their villages, the scarcity of land, and the demands of growing state bureaucracies that had led many of them to emigrate in the first place, it is not surprising that German-speaking immigrants in the colonies would become hypersensitive to political matters involving land issues. They had forgone special privileges in eastern Europe in the hope of attaining better conditions in America, but they could not allow their position as immigrants to cause them to receive *fewer* privileges than those possessed by the native inhabitants. These considerations shaped their stance toward their new rulers—the royal and proprietary administrations and the colonial legislatures in America, especially in Pennsylvania.

* * *

The hundreds of thousands of Lutheran, Reformed, and Catholic church members who settled lands from the Volga to the Americas in the mid- and late-eighteenth century left behind a much different world from that of the small numbers of Mennonites, Quakers, and other radical pietists who had settled in Pennsylvania in the late seventeenth century. In 1700 southwest Germany was still an underpopulated region where large-scale in-migration occurred. Most inhabitants were serfs who lived in villages, worked the surrounding lands under the traditional three-field system, and maintained strong local control of their affairs. By the late eighteenth century, many of the serfs had been freed and the state apparatus influenced their lives to a much greater extent. No longer plundered and burned periodically by the rampaging, plague-carrying armies of the great powers of Europe, as they had been throughout the seventeenth century, the territorial and local authorities built the baroque churches, town halls, and other official buildings so prominent in the village landscapes of the German southwest today. Agriculture had become more commercialized, but the landscapes were crowded, and many farmed a few scattered patches of land and/or plied a craft in villages plagued by land splintering, scarcity, and poverty.

During this century of change many subjects left the region, as they had done in previous centuries when times were hard. Most went to eastern Europe, as their ancestors had for centuries, but some chose instead to go to a new destination—British North America—where word had it there was so much land and freedom from encumbrances on its use that one might never again face poverty.

Carl Friedrich, the margrave of Baden-Durlach, tried to manage these changes from his new palace in Karlsruhe in an "enlightened" way that would strengthen his state, but how did the peasants living in the thousands of nuclear villages of southwest Germany and Switzerland react to these developments? More specifically, how did the subjects of a region where most who emigrated went to the thirteen colonies react to the changes occurring in eighteenth-century society, and how might this change have shaped their future attitudes in their new homeland? To answer these questions we will look closely at village life and patterns of migration from one such region in the southwest, the northern Kraichgau.

2

Peasant Communities
and Peasant Migrations

LATE ONE NIGHT IN MAY OF 1743, a group of unmarried young men from Schwaigern met in a barn outside of town for a revel. Schwaigern, located in an area of rolling hills near the Rhine (just southeast of Heidelberg) known as the Kraichgau (see Map 2.1), was a market town that served as the seat of the ruling von Neipperg family. The young men had gathered to celebrate the imminent departure of four of their number: Georg Luttmann, Christian Steinbrenner, Johann Michael Wagner, and Johann Jacob Eichhorn. They began the secret celebration before midnight with food and drink in Johannes Kober's barn. A blind musician named Christoph Schuster (*der "blinde Stoffel"*), provided music while they sang and danced until dawn.

The town authorities noticed the racket, however, and descended upon the merrymakers. Soon the musician found himself serving a twenty-four-hour sentence in the witch's tower (*die Hexeturm*) for not seeking official permission to conduct his concert. (Only a generation before, an accused witch had been kept in the same tower—hence its name.[1]) A crowd gathered around the four *Auswanderer* (emigrants) and began clamoring for their arrest and detention in the tower. Instead, the four eluded their pursuers, ran through the town whooping and hollering, and then vanished through the town gate, never to be seen in Schwaigern again. They made their way to nearby Heilbronn (on the Neckar River) and began their journey to Pennsylvania that very day.[2]

Although it was only about thirty miles from Karlsruhe, the residence of Carl Friedrich, Schwaigern and the entire Kraichgau region lay outside the territorial boundaries of Baden-Durlach, and a different kind of state system prevailed. There was no margrave, duke, or other territorial ruler of the region (enlightened or otherwise), but rather a plethora of small, semi-autonomous realms ruled by lesser nobles. Further, there was no large state policy restricting emigration and no debate among court advisors and political economists over restriction or a general "population policy." Emigration policy—and all policy—was localized, varied, and difficult to enforce.

Yet in spite of the differences in political organization between Baden-Durlach and the nearby Kraichgau, there were important similarities between the two regions and the inhabitants of each. Both lay in the heartland of southwest Germany, where emigration was heaviest. Both areas were recovering from the devastating wars of the seventeenth century, and, by the middle eighteenth century, ethnic and religious diversity as well as overpopulation and extreme land splintering characterized their landscapes. Further, both were rural, agrarian societies, and most inhabitants were serfs living in villages and towns. In fact, many of the similarities between Baden-Durlach and the Kraichgau characterized much of southwest Germany and Switzerland in the eighteenth century.

Not everyone who emigrated from southwest Germany and Switzerland in the mid-eighteenth century left with such blatant disrespect for the authorities as had the four young men from Schwaigern, but their story reveals much about what had become typical of the emigration to North America. In the period that followed the destruction that occurred in the seventeenth century and the rebuilding and repopulation of the early eighteenth century, most Germans of the third phase of immigration into colonial British America (1717–1775) did not leave in large religious groups fleeing persecution or seeking perfection, as had Germans in the first phase. Nor did these immigrants participate in huge, organized settlement projects in the colonies, as had those in the second phase. Instead they left in small groups with other members from their villages and towns, and the destination for most was Greater Pennsylvania.

Though usually forbidden by the authorities, emigration from the southwest and Switzerland had become an uncontrollable fact of life by the middle third of the eighteenth century. The territorial rulers, the lesser nobles, and the village authorities (including the church) exercised more control over their subjects during this period than they had during the seventeenth century, but they still could not stop hundreds of thousands from leaving the realm.

Much of the population in the southwest, including many who would

4. View of Schwaigern, circa 1680, from an engraving by Andreas Kieser. (Reproduced by permission of the Haupstaatsarchiv Stuttgart. All rights reserved.)

emigrate to North America, were peasants living in villages or towns like Schwaigern and in regions like the Kraichgau. The Kraichgauers lived in nuclear, subsistence agrarian villages and towns where local authority (town and church officials) was becoming stronger, not weaker. Here lesser nobles struggled against the villagers themselves and the growing territorial states in order to establish and maintain their hegemony over these clusters of tiny political entities. And it was from the northern parishes of this region that about 2,000 inhabitants emigrated to Greater Pennsylvania, more than 300 from Schwaigern alone.

During this period of recovery and establishment or reestablishment of order, authorities at all levels in the small territories, towns, and villages tried to control the movements of their growing populations, just as the rulers of the larger neighboring states did. But in some areas of the Kraichgau, the pressures of population increase and emigration to Greater Pennsylvania had become so great by the 1730s and 1740s that it was impossible to stop. In Schwaigern, authorities attempted to compensate by making efforts to insure that those who did leave played and paid by the rules: Serfs had to be manumitted, and all inhabitants had to receive permission to emigrate and then pay the appropriate dues to compensate the community and the noble to whom they owed allegiance.

The crowd in Schwaigern became hostile toward the young emigrants because they were leaving without permission and without paying. Most emigrants from Schwaigern paid their dues during this period of strict enforcement. In 1743, not just the four young revelers, but also twenty-eight others emigrated to Greater Pennsylvania, and all but five left legally. At least three of the five who did not leave legally (the *Schwarzauswanderer*) were among the group of known revelers—Johann Michael Wagner, Georg Luttmann, and Johann Jacob Eichhorn. To add insult to injury, the illegal emigrants left by celebrating their actions noisily, by breaking local ordinances, and then by running through the streets and disturbing the peace on their way out the town gate.

A close look at the communities of the northern Kraichgau reveals more fully the nature of communal relations and helps us understand who the Kraichgauers in Greater Pennsylvania were, how they emigrated, and what aspects of their Old World peasant culture and background they brought with them to the New World.

The Case of the Northern Kraichgau

The Kraichgau is a region between the Rhine and Neckar River valleys, just south of Heidelberg, due west of Heilbronn, and northeast of Karlsruhe (see Map 2.1). Stream-carved valleys cut through the region, and limestone cliffs covered with loamy soil and red marl, and keuper hills projecting upward, provide an uneven but rich topography. Politically, or historically, the "Kraichgau" refers to a scattered collection of tiny, semi-independent territories strewn haphazardly across this landscape. These territories united in the early modern period in a loose, voluntary confederation of knights known as the *Kraichgauer Ritterschaftskanton*. The territories lay at the confluence of three of the largest states in the southwest during the eighteenth century: the Margravate of Baden-Durlach, the Palatine Electorate (*Kurpfalz*), and the strongest state in the southwest, the Duchy of Württemberg. In 1599, membership in the confederation consisted of seventy-five knights, some rich and some poor, who owned seventy-two separate territories, the average size of which was less than fourteen square miles. The "northern" Kraichgau consisted of fifty-three

Map 2.1. Northern Kraichgau Parishes Investigated in This Study.

1. Adelshofen	19. Eschelbronn	36. Neidenstein
2. Adersbach	20. Fürfeld*	37. Obergimpern
3. Asbach	21. Gauangelloch	38. Reichertshausen
4. Bad Rappenau	22. Grombach	39. Reihen
5. Bammental	23. Hasselbach	40. Rohrbach
6. Bargen	24. Helmstadt	41. Schatthausen
7. Bonfeld*	25. Hilsbach	42. Schluchtern
8. Berwangen	26. Hoffenheim	43. Schwaigern*
9. Daisbach	27. Ittlingen	44. Sinsheim
10. Daudenzell	28. Kirchardt	45. Stebbach
11. Diedesheim	29. Massenbach*	46. Steinsfurt
12. Dühren	30. Mauer	47. Tairnbach
13. Ehrstädt	31. Meckesheim	48. Treschklingen*
14. Eichtersheim	32. Michelfeld	49. Untergimpern
15. Elsenz	33. Mönchzell	50. Waldangelloch
16. Epfenbach	34. Neckarbischofsheim	51. Weiler
17. Eppingen	35. Neckargemund	52. Wiesloch
18. Eschelbach		53. Zuzenhausen

* No information on legal emigration available.

parishes (*Gemeinden*).³ In the eighteenth century, most of the parishes contained subsistence-farming peasant communities, such as Ittlingen and Hoffenheim, but a few, such as Schwaigern and Sinsheim, were small market towns. In 1809, the first year for which there is a reasonably accurate census covering the entire area, and after well over a century of steady population growth, the total population of the fifty-three parishes was 41,700, or about seventy-eight persons per square kilometer.⁴

The ethnic, religious, and political mosaic that made up the Kraichgau resembled the larger portrait of southwest Germany, as well as that of Greater Pennsylvania. Thousands of Swiss immigrants and some French Huguenots helped repopulate the area after the heavy demographic losses of the seventeenth century.⁵ The Lutheran church dominated the region, but many Kraichgauers belonged to the Reformed or Catholic churches, and Mennonites and some Jews were present in some of the communities. No one territorial state controlled most of the parishes: Fourteen were possessions of the Palatine Electorate during the first three-quarters of the eighteenth century, and thirteen were part of the *Kraichgauer Ritterschafts-kanton*. The remaining twenty-six parishes belonged to a variety of lesser nobles, none of whom possessed more than three. Six of the parishes maintained the rights of a city (*Stadtrecht*), which included the right to hold a market and the absence of serfdom for most of the inhabitants. The remaining forty-seven parishes were villages.

One source for the extreme heterogeneity of the American colonies was the diversity among the German-speaking immigrants, in addition to that created by the arrival of different language groups from Europe and Africa. In fact, there was significant diversity within the immigrant population from the Kraichgau alone. Seventy-four percent of Kraichgauer immigrants in Greater Pennsylvania were Lutheran, 21 percent were Reformed, 2 percent were Mennonite, and 1 percent were Catholic (the religious affiliation of 2 percent is unknown). Many Swiss names were included among the nearly 2,000 Kraichgauers who went to Greater Pennsylvania, and all came from separate political entities rather than from one territorial state.

Although this diverse, tangled collection of peasant communities was in many ways typical of southwest Germany in the early modern period, the Kraichgau differed from some of the surrounding areas in one important respect: Here, no strong, homogenous state was developing, as in Catholic Austria or Lutheran Brandenburg-Prussia. Nor was there a regional power controlling the area, as in the Lutheran state of Württemberg or Catholic Bavaria. In fact, not even the weaker territorial states, such as the Palatine Electorate or Baden-Durlach, dominated the Kraichgau. Instead, tiny, loosely united principalities, such as the von Neipperg, von Gemmingen, and von Bettendorf territories, were the norm.

Consequently, the developing "state" played a different role in the lives of the Kraichgauers than it did in many areas of the southwest, such as in Württemberg, or even the Palatine Electorate and Baden-Durlach. During the rebuilding period of the late seventeenth and early eighteenth centuries, it was the second estate, not the state itself, that made increasing demands upon the inhabitants. As the knights and other, lesser nobles of the Kraichgau tried to reassert the status and authority they had lost during the decades of destruction in the seventeenth century, they often clashed with the villagers who were struggling to rebuild their communities. During these clashes, the villagers often sought out the "state," that is, the larger territorial rulers, for protection against their local rulers.

Aristocratic Resurgence and Peasant Resistance

The inhabitants of the northern Kraichgau owed allegiance to dozens of separate aristocratic rulers. The rulers of those parishes not included in the Palatine Electorate found themselves in a hostile environment during the early modern period. Not only were they located among three larger powers (the Electorate, the Margravate of Baden-Durlach, and the Duchy of Württemberg), they also lay between two superpowers of continental Europe—France and Austria. From this precarious position, the knights of the Kraichgau struggled to maintain their independent sovereignty over their tiny holdings. For as long as possible, they skillfully played off the surrounding princes against the emperor in Vienna. The greatest enemy of the knights before the Thirty Years' War was the Palatine Electorate, where the official religion alternated between Catholicism and the Reformed faith. The knights had quickly become Lutheran during the Reformation and so tended to have closer relations with Lutheran Württemberg. But the defeat of the princes in the Schmalkaldic Wars and encroachments from the Swabian Circles inclined them toward the emperor in Vienna. The knights needed the protection of the Catholic Habsburgs from the Protestant princes in order to maintain their independence, while Vienna needed any loyal ally it could find in its struggle against the princes.[6]

Before 1620, the Kraichgau parishes were overpopulated, but during

5. The von Neippergs of Schwaigern were one of many lesser noble families who ruled the numerous small estates and territories in the Kraichgau. Eberhard Friedrich (1655–1725) ruled during the rebuilding years after the seventeenth-century wars. He oversaw the construction of the new palace (*Schloß*), 1702–1704, and many other buildings. (Courtesy of the Bürgermeisteramt, Stadt Schwaigern.)

the Thirty Years' War and the wars of the late seventeenth century, the armies of the great European powers nearly obliterated village after village in the Kraichgau, while the knights struggled merely to hang on to their territories. By 1648 Adelshofen had lost twenty-eight families (about half the village population), and was then repeatedly plundered and set ablaze in the 1670s and 1680s. Most of Ittlingen lay in rubble and ashes as a result of the Thirty Years' War. The population of Kleingartach dropped from about 120 to 33 between 1620 and 1648. Massenbachhausen lost its entire population during the Thirty Years' War, and was resettled after-

6. Wilhelm Rheinhard von Neipperg (1684–1774), son of Eberhard Friedrich, ruled when most of the emigrants left Schwaigern. He strengthened the realm's ties to Vienna through his conversion to Catholicism and military service, for which he received the title *Reichsgraf*. (Courtesy of the Bürgermeisteramt, Stadt Schwaigern.)

ward by outsiders. In 1674 the French took Sinsheim, and fifteen years later they burned it to the ground. In 1689 they also destroyed Wiesloch, and four years later they occupied and partially destroyed Fürfeld. In 1621 Tilly's troops plundered Hoffenheim and tortured many of its inhabitants. In 1634 this unfortunate village suffered further plunderings by

7. Graf Leopold von Neipperg (1728–1792), son of Wilhelm Rheinhard, and his family. He served as a career diplomat for the Vienna court. (Courtesy of the Bürgermeisteramt, Stadt Schwaigern.)

Swedish and imperial troops. By 1639 only nineteen residents remained. In 1647 there were fewer houses standing than there had been in 1518. When Hoffenheimers refused to support the war against the Turks in 1663, many of them were executed. In 1699, Hoffenheim, along with Wiesloch, Sinsheim, Zuzenhausen, Meckesheim, and Mauer, were completely destroyed by fire.[7]

As the nobility emerged from this long series of disasters, they continued to struggle to maintain their independent existence and identity, not only vis-à-vis the surrounding powers, but now against their own subjects as well. The villagers struggled to recover and reestablish their societies as they once were, or as they thought they had been. During the process they were forced to defend themselves against the encroachments of the knights and other nobility who were their rulers.[8]

The impetus for the new encroachments by the nobility on the villagers was both financial and political. The nobles needed new revenues to rebuild their own destroyed residences, and they also sought to direct the rebuilding of village structures. Having lost their power to direct the community during the war years, the nobility hoped to clearly establish their authority in the new baroque villages by directing the construction of the new churches, town halls, and other community structures.

But the new residences and village structures were extremely expensive, and the huge demographic losses suffered during the war years had eroded the tax base of the territories. In a series of independent offensives against their villagers, the knights of the Kraichgau attempted to raise the necessary funds by increasing feudal dues or by vigorously enforcing the payment of traditional dues in the hopes of clearly reestablishing their authority in their realms. The rebuilt villages would reflect a new social order in which the church and community would be strong, and the noble, in his new baroque residence, would be clearly at the top.

The clash between the nobility and the villagers in the Kraichgau reached its height in the late 1710s and early 1720s, just before large-scale emigration to Greater Pennsylvania began. While it is doubtful that the offensive by the aristocrats "caused" many to emigrate, it is clear that many of the Kraichgauers in the North American colonies were peasants who had come from a place where inhabitants of strong, tightly knit nuclear villages had struggled with the local nobles, who were trying to increase their presence, status, and wealth in society. A few examples from some parishes that experienced heavy emigration during the eighteenth century demonstrate this point.

The small backwater village of Hoffenheim, which would experience a heavy emigration to Greater Pennsylvania in the 1730s, forties, and fifties, had suffered tremendously from warfare in the previous decades and had resisted exploitation by its lords in the early eighteenth century. Two families, the von Österreichs and the von Waldenburgs, owned Hoffenheim jointly, and in 1705 they reissued an agreement from 1618 that established their rights and privileges. The von Österreichs had leased their half of

Hoffenheim to an extremely poor noble family, the Äscher von Bünningens. Both ruling families were Catholic, and this, along with attempts to change the old agreements regarding privileges and dues, caused problems with the Lutheran population of the village. The von Bünningens brought in the first Catholic priest in 1693 and encouraged several Catholic families to settle in the parish in the following years, so that by 1715 there were forty communicants and sixteen schoolchildren in the Catholic community. In that year, the ruling families (*Herrschaft*) appointed a dubious and incompetent pastor to head the Lutheran flock, in order to further weaken them—or so the villagers thought.[9]

In 1717 the peasants in Hoffenheim began to resist what seemed to them to be a subversive and abusive *Herrschaft*. In August, in one of many examples of inhabitants of the peasant communities in the Kraichgau appealing to one of the larger territorial states for assistance in their struggle against the local nobility, the peasants drew up a list of complaints and sent them to an imperial commission. The list sums up the frustrations of a village of subsistence-farming peasants trying to hold on to the remnants of their old ways: They blamed the new encroachments of the nobility for some of their problems and more traditional sources for others. The peasants complained that there were not enough visitations from their new pastor, that their dues were becoming excessive, that the logistics of paying them were unreasonable, and that the village commons were not being properly cared for.[10] The imperial commissioners very likely rejected the Hoffenheimers' complaints. When the commissioners showed up in October to witness the villagers' swearing of loyalty to the von Österreich family, the actual half-owners who had been leasing their share to the von Bünningens, the Hoffenheimers threatened them and refused to comply.[11]

Conditions did not improve, and in 1726, the Hoffenheimers drew up another petition that summed up the long history of the village's problems, many of which, including overpopulation, were closely related to the conditions surrounding emigration. Once again they attempted to circumvent their local rulers, this time presenting the petition to imperial authorities in Freiburg in the Breisgau. They complained of lazy, abusive, and gluttonous officials and lawyers employed by the ruling families who did not even live in the village yet received large salaries to legitimize the importance of their position. They also complained about the condition of serfdom (*Leibeigenschaft*) in general.

Hoffenheim was one of the poorest villages in the region. The petitioners recounted the long, devastating years of warfare and crop failures that had impoverished the village. Hoffenheim was becoming crowded, the forests were disappearing, and sustenance was becoming more and more scarce ("die Nahrung geschwechet"). With these uncontrollable conditions bearing upon the peasants, the actions of the nobility and their apparatus were proving intolerable. Things had become so bad that the villagers were becoming suspicious of each other, even of the honest, decent, long-established villagers and their children.[12]

Freiburg rejected the appeals of the Hoffenheimers to rid the village of their self-serving officials, claiming that the villagers had nothing to complain about and should carry on as usual.[13] Two years later, one Hoffenheimer emigrated to Pennsylvania, and in the three following years at least thirty-two others followed.

Many nobles of the Kraichgau applied new pressures on their villagers at about the same time, as they sought to reestablish their own presence and rebuild their territories during the postwar period. In 1717, inhabitants of Weiler submitted a petition to officials of the Palatine Electorate to intervene on their behalf against their local ruler, Georg Friedrich von Venningen, who had just moved to the village and, in open violation of the agreement with the Electorate of 1572, had burdened the villagers with new and heavy work requirements (*Frondiensten*) to build his residence. Von Venningen replied to the officials in Heidelberg that the charges were unwarranted because he was also having them make other improvements for the village in general. The villagers of Weiler appealed for the state's help against the more direct threat—the local aristocracy.[14]

Adelshofen began to rebuild after 1700, and many of its inhabitants suffered during the process. The villagers built a new residence for the von Neipperg family, and a new church, town hall, and school for the parish. To pay for all this, the authorities instituted a series of new ordinances and duties, as well as mandatory work requirements. Many villagers opposed the new duties, and many also emigrated in later years.[15]

One of the most flagrant offensives launched by the nobility in the Kraichgau against the villagers occurred in Ittlingen. The history of village-noble relations in this small, subsistence farming community reflects a larger pattern developing in the region in which peasants rebuilding their communities in the early eighteenth century were well aware of their interests and rights and resisted any encroachments by the nobility on those rights. The peasants were not powerless rural settlers who played no role in the political developments of the region; rather, they often took direct action when they perceived a threat to their interests—a pattern that would resurface among the Germans living in the North American colonies.

In 1699 the von Öttinger family (under agreement with one of the two ruling families of Ittlingen, the von Gemmingens) attempted to increase duties in violation of an agreement dating back to 1579, but the inhabitants succeeded in blocking this move by complaining to the *Reichsritterschafts-direktion* (an imperial court for another confederation of knights) in nearby Heilbronn. This was the first of many appeals the Ittlingers would make to state authorities for protection against the local nobility. In the late 1710s the impoverished, heavily indebted von Kochendorf family began increasing feudal dues (*Frohnen*) to pay for a new residence. They also began enclosing the common fields for their own private use. They banned meetings of the village assembly and began selling off village interests to outsiders: a salt monopoly was sold to a Jewish merchant and the 200-year-old common bakery to a private individual. Further, they began inflicting excessive punishments for slight infractions of local ordinances. Perhaps the villagers' most visible warning sign of future trouble came when the *Herrschaft* took over the cellar of the town hall (which was village property) and converted it into a jail.[16]

The Ittlingers did not take these new encroachments lightly. When the von Kochendorfs had a fence built around the village meadow, the villagers tore it down, a scenario that was repeated twice. Furthermore, the villagers expelled the Jewish merchant who had purchased the salt monopoly. The villagers were unsuccessful in blocking the establishment of the jail, however. Seeing no end to the violation of their rights by the nobility, the villagers submitted a twelve-point complaint to the *Reichsritterschaftsdirektion* in Heilbronn for relief.[17]

By now the von Gemmingens and von Kochendorfs considered the villagers of Ittlingen in rebellion. Still determined to exact revenues for maintaining their presence in the parish and pulling themselves out of poverty, they took extreme measures against the village in 1720. First, they raised the fees for grazing rights (established by an agreement in 1584) for the villagers' hogs on the common. When the Ittlingers refused to pay and complained to Heilbronn again, the von Gemmingens and von Kochendorfs brought in twenty armed men to take the village hogs. Sunday-morning church attendance was mandatory in Ittlingen (as it was in most villages in the Kraichgau), and while the whole village worshipped, the *Herrschaft*'s men made their way into the forests and led the entire village herd of hogs (160 head) to Gemmingen, about five miles away.

That afternoon the Ittlingers were up in arms about the theft of their hogs. The village citizens (*Bürger*) met at the town hall to discuss what to do. Two tavernkeepers and a blacksmith were the group's leaders. Some young men followed the trail of the hogs to Gemmingen and then reported back to the villagers in Ittlingen. Many wanted to descend on Gemmingen, the home of the von Gemmingen family, and retrieve the herd by force. Others urged moderation. During the town meeting someone produced a Bible and read from the twenty-eighth chapter of Deuteronomy, which includes a long list of curses and judgments. Afterward, the tavernkeepers asked everyone to come forward, place their hand on the Bible, and swear they would not give up the struggle against the *Herrschaft* until they had won. If they did not do this, God would punish them in the manner prescribed in Deuteronomy. All but one villager at the meeting threw in their lot with the group. Cool-headedness prevailed, however, and the villagers opted to use restraint. Instead of an assault on Gemmingen, they chose to register a complaint in Heilbronn, which ruled in their favor.

The *Herrschaft*, however, ignored the imperial court's ruling against them and began selling the hogs at bargain prices. They then threatened to take the villagers' cattle and lock up the tavernkeepers who were ringleaders in the revolt. Soon thereafter the *Herrschaft*'s twenty armed men reappeared and tried to steal the village sheep. They were caught by the villagers, however, and after shots were fired, the *Herrschaft*'s men retreated, leaving the villagers with their sheep. Fearing possible imperial intervention against their cause, the von Gemmingens and von Kochendorfs lost their nerve and sought a truce. After long negotiations that divided the villagers into those who wanted to deal harshly with the nobles and those who remained loyal, the imperial authorities mediated a compromise in which the ruling families made partial repayment for the lost hogs.

The compromise settlement over the issue of the hogs did little to ameliorate relations between the villagers and their *Herrschaft*, however, as both sides geared up for more conflict a few weeks later. In 1721, the von Gemmingens hand-picked a new Lutheran pastor, who began preaching obedience to the authorities.[18] But the pastor went too far in his zeal to support his benefactors. For six months he lambasted the villagers from the pulpit for their disobedience. One Sunday the pastor harshly condemned the villagers who had participated in the meeting in which the Bible was used to help instigate disloyalty to the *Herrschaft*, and he called for their punishment. Two days later the villagers met in the town hall to discuss what to do about the new preacher. By this time rumor had it that he was preaching these sermons at the request of the *Herrschaft*. Also, many believed that the preacher had participated in a cover-up involving a nobleman who had shot a villager (one who had signed the petition sent to Heilbronn).

The Ittlingers had gained a favorable reputation among neighboring villages for standing up to their abusive *Herrschaft*, but now people were beginning to laugh at them for taking so much verbal and other abuse and doing nothing about it. The meeting sent a delegation of six men to the preacher's house, where they demanded that he revise his style of preaching or they would go to church elsewhere and not support him financially. The preacher's response did nothing to gain favor with this group of highly politicized, angry, and mistrustful peasants: He replied that he had a theological degree from the university at Heidelberg, and that it was not necessary for him to defend his style of preaching to them. At this point the von Gemmingens and von Kochendorfs once again backed down. They informed their preacher that he would receive no funds from them for construction of a new parsonage and church. This gesture allowed tempers to cool. The preacher toned down his sermons and managed to keep his post for more than twenty years.[19]

Thus the Old World background of the Kraichgauers in Greater Pennsylvania was not one where democracy flourished, but the villagers were by no means apolitical. They reacted vigorously to any perceived threat to the community. While the seventeenth century was a time when the marauding armies of Europe's strongest states left them devastated and powerless, the absence of the most severe warfare in this region during the eighteenth century allowed significant leeway for these peasant communities to fight for their interests. In this border region between the larger powers of southwest Germany, the villagers allied themselves with the imperial state apparatus to resist the encroachments of the abusive local aristocracy. The interests of the community—not loyalty to any party, rank, or faction in society—shaped their political activities. Especially in times of crisis, they appealed to whomever necessary to get what they wanted. This pattern would reemerge, but in a somewhat different form, in democratic Pennsylvania, where traditional nuclear communities were few and far between, and the highest authorities to whom Germans could practically appeal would be the colonial legislature and proprietary governor.

Village Boundaries and Overcrowding

One result of all this conflict between the villagers and the aristocracy in the Kraichgau during the eighteenth century was the development or redevelopment of strong, cohesive, peasant villages and towns. After the destruction and depopulation of the seventeenth century, the survivors and their

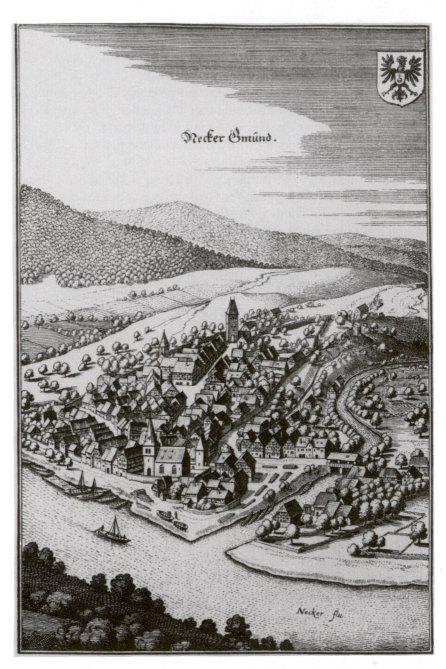

Necker Gmünd.

Necker flu.

8. A mid-seventeenth-century view of Neckargemünd, a market town on the northern fringe of the Kraichgau, just upriver from Heidelberg (see Map 2.1). At least twenty-three persons emigrated from here to Pennsylvania in the eighteenth century. From a copper engraving by Matthäus Merian, in Martin Zeiller, *Topographia Palatinatus Rheni et Vicinarum Regionum* (Frankfurt: M. Merian, 1645).

Wißeloch.

9. Matthäus Merian's engraving of Wiesloch, a market town in the northern Kraichgau, from where at least fourteen inhabitants emigrated to Pennsylvania. (From Zeiller, *Topographia Palatinatus.*)

Sinßheim.

10. Merian's view of Sinsheim, also a market town in the northern Kraichgau. At least seventy-two persons emigrated from here to Pennsylvania. (From Zeiller, *Topographia Palatinatus*.)

11. Eppingen, a market town and one of the largest of the northern Kraichgau parishes investigated in this study. At least sixty-six persons emigrated from Eppingen to Pennsylvania. (From Zeiller, *Topographia Palatinatus*.)

children, together with Swiss and other immigrants, began to reestablish
nuclear, localist-oriented, subsistence peasant communities. The general,
though disconnected, movement of the aristocracy to increase revenues
quickened the process of community formation. The actions of the aristocracy in villages like Hoffenheim, Ittlingen, Adelshofen, and many other
subsistence farming villages in the Kraichgau helped draw the peasants into
close communities to meet the new threat. It was from these kinds of villages, which soon became overcrowded and burdened with extreme parcellation of landholdings, that the immigrants to Greater Pennsylvania came.

The communities of the northern Kraichgau consisted of forty-seven
villages and six towns.[20] Most inhabitants of the villages were serfs who
practiced subsistence agriculture or a craft for the local population. Ittlingen, for example, produced virtually no surplus in agricultural products.
In 1720, the entire village's herd of hogs numbered only 160. Furthermore,
when the *Herrschaft* stole the herd (to raise desperately needed cash to pay
off debts and help fund some of their new projects, among other reasons)
they were only able to sell about half of the hogs in nearby Gemmingen,
even at cut-rate prices. There simply was no market for such a quantity of
hogs. The village economies were geared toward low-level production and
local consumption. With no large market available to get rid of the stolen
hogs for a sizeable profit, the von Gemmingens and von Kochendorfs
finally had to have some of them butchered and sold in small quantities at
low prices. In this area of the Kraichgau it simply was not possible to turn
quick profits when dealing with large quantities of goods.[21]

Most inhabitants of the six towns were free and maintained official
permission to hold markets. They were craftsmen serving the local populace or farmers who lived in town and walked, rode, or drove a cart or
wagon to fields scattered throughout the parish. They produced small sur-
pluses that they traded at the local market. The markets themselves usually
served only those in the surrounding area.

The villages and towns in the Kraichgau, and indeed in most of southwest Germany, were almost without exception nuclear in shape (*Haufen-
dörfer*) or some slight variation thereof. They were not long, extended
one-street towns (*Straßendörfer*). At the center of the town of Schwaigern,
for example, were the marketplace and the town hall (see Map 2.2). The
large von Neipperg residence and the Lutheran church surrounded them,
along with the remnants of a wall, the witch's tower, and a tightly packed
residential area. A road enclosed the entire town and separated the inhabi-

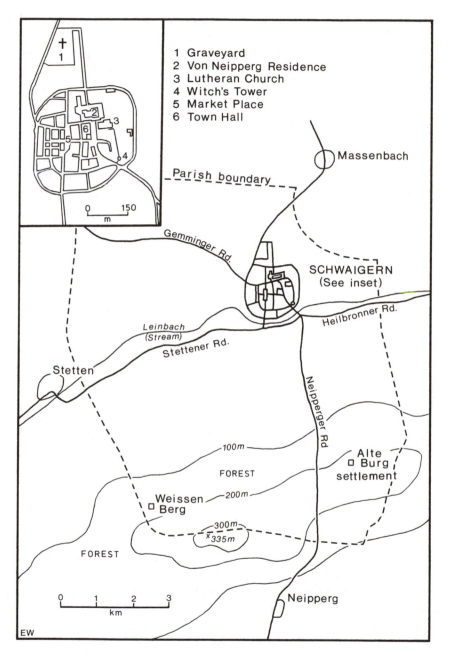

1 Graveyard
2 Von Neipperg Residence
3 Lutheran Church
4 Witch's Tower
5 Market Place
6 Town Hall

Massenbach

Parish boundary

Gemminger Rd.

SCHWAIGERN
(See inset)

Heilbronner Rd.

Leinbach
(Stream)

Stettener Rd.

Stetten

Neipperger Rd.

Alte
Burg
settlement

100m

FOREST

200m

Weissen
Berg

300m
×335m

FOREST

0   1   2   3
km

Neipperg

EW

Map 2.2. The Parish of Schwaigern in the Northern Kraichgau: Old Boundaries.

tants from the fields they worked. With few exceptions, the inhabitants of the parish lived within the confines of the road.[22]

Not only were the Kraichgau communities tightly built and the quarters close within the village, but the settlements themselves were also built extremely close to one another. In fact, they were so close that one could normally stand on the periphery of one village and see the next village just down the road or across a few open fields. From a slight elevation several villages were and are easily visible. The distance between the adjacent communities of Schwaigern and Massenbach, for example, is only about two miles, and that between Schwaigern and Schluchtern is slightly more. From Ittlingen one could walk or ride only two miles and reach the next village, Reihen, or two and one-half miles in another direction and arrive at Kirchhardt. The distance from Hoffenheim to either Sinsheim or Zuzenhausen is one and one-half miles. Even the distances between the market towns are relatively short: fourteen miles from Schwaigern to Sinsheim, and seven from Schwaigern to Eppingen. From Sinsheim, which lies roughly in the middle of the region, to Neckargemünd at the northern fringe (on the Neckar River) the distance is only about eleven and one-half miles.

The settlements' close proximity to one another means that the land available to the inhabitants for cultivation was very limited. The median size of the parishes (that is, the village or town and the land surrounding it) in the cohort was 2,062 acres. Several hundred people lived in each settlement, with their numbers growing steadily throughout the eighteenth century. By 1809 the median population of each settlement had grown to 703—about three and one-half acres per person. But land was not equally distributed within the villages, so many were trying to survive on less than this.[23]

By the second decade of the eighteenth century, as farmers in the northern Kraichgau extended the fields under cultivation to the limits of their parish boundaries, disputes arose between parishes as to where the borders actually lay. A border dispute between Bonfeld and the adjacent parish of Kirchhausen began in 1717 and continued off and on until 1761. In 1728 Hoffenheimers took up arms against soldiers of the Palatine Electorate in a border dispute, but no shots were fired. Hoffenheimers had further boundary disputes with the adjacent parish of Daisbach in 1744, 1749, and 1781. The village of Ittlingen renewed all the stone markings of its parish borders in 1751, but this did not prevent an armed border dispute from erupting with Hilsbach in 1768. During the wars of the seventeenth century, as village after village was destroyed, records were often lost and people were concerned primarily with survival. In the immediate postwar period, the parishes were so underpopulated and land so abundant that the exact lines where one parish ended and another began seemed unimportant. The large number of sometimes violent border disputes in the mid-eighteenth century indicates that land was becoming more valuable as it became scarcer. Exact knowledge of how much land the parish possessed and where it lay became extremely important.[24]

Thus, while the general background of demographic recovery, new aristocratic encroachments, and the rebuilding of village structures and community cohesiveness was important to this group of fifty-three villages and towns in the northern Kraichgau, the crucial local factors that led so many families to emigrate were the same as for the rest of southwest Germany: increasing scarcity of land, overpopulation, and extreme land splintering resulting from the practice of partible inheritance. By the 1720s and especially in the 1730s and 1740s, many elements of the population, sometimes entire villages, either found they could not fully recover from the disasters of the seventeenth century or if they had recovered, now fell into desperate economic circumstances. For many Kraichgauers in villages like Hoffenheim, the aspirations of the nobility eventually subsided, but the economic situation grew more bleak.

Some of the villagers, such as Hans Horch, were still relatively well off. Horch was one of the richest farmers in the parish from 1700 to 1750. He owned seventy-one separate pieces of land, together about twenty-six acres in size. More typical, however, was the case of the Neu family. When Christof Neu's wife died in 1744, he worked his tiny, scattered parcels of land for a year, then decided to retire and give his six children their inheritance. Each of the children received about 2.4 acres of fields, meadowland, gardens, and vineyards scattered throughout the parish. One of the sons, Georg Michael, received the family home by lot, worth about 250 guilders. In return, the children had to support both Neu and his sister in their retirement, providing them with a small yearly allowance in cash, plus grain, fruit, vegetables, and a quantity of hemp. Single family members would support married couples as needed. Neu and his sister would remain in the family home. This arrangement continued for several years until better prospects presented themselves from abroad.[25]

There was an enormous contrast between the Kraichgauers' troubled and crowded circumstances in these subsistence, nuclear villages and what they had heard and read about dispersed settlements and huge land tracts available in the commercial, capitalist world of Greater Pennsylvania, but many still could not imagine it until they saw for themselves the seemingly incredible distances between towns and individual farmhouses in the New World. In Pennsylvania, a group of six or seven families often owned as much land as did an entire village populated by hundreds of people in the Kraichgau. When Johann Michael Wagner, one of the four young revelers from Schwaigern, arrived in Pennsylvania, he was overwhelmed by the size of the farms and the distances between farmhouses. When he wrote home a year or two after his arrival in the colony, he compared the new distances with those in Schwaigern, remarking that, "In this country it is as if one house were in the Alten Burg [see Map 2.2], one in the Hinden Berg (not shown), and another in the Weissen Berg, so are the conditions in this country, so stand the houses in the forests."[26]

Letters from Greater Pennsylvania describing a land of abundance and of freedom from restrictions poured into the villages of the Kraichgau in the middle third of the eighteenth century. The lure of large tracts of land in a more prosperous community proved too much for two of Christof Neu's sons in Hoffenheim. In 1751, Hans Georg Neu and his brother, Johannes, emigrated to Pennsylvania with nineteen other Hoffenheimers. Indeed, more than one hundred persons emigrated to Greater Pennsylvania from that small village alone.[27]

Family and Village Migrations

What happened to the Neu family of Hoffenheim also happened to hundreds of other Kraichgauers. Living in difficult, crowded conditions in their small parishes, where relations with the authorities were often tense, they read the promotional literature on Pennsylvania and the letters of previous emigrants from the village, and chose to seek a better fortune there. Those who began the relatively large migrations of the late 1720s and early 1730s followed in the wake of a few hardy souls who had gone years before them under different conditions. These families and individuals of the second phase of emigration to colonial America (see Introduction) had reported that Pennsylvania, as opposed to New York, North Carolina, or some other colony, was the best place to settle. Emigrants from the northern Kraichgau parishes of Daudenzell, Eschelbronn, Ittlingen, Eppingen, Bonfeld, Massenbach, Rohrbach, Wiesloch, and perhaps others had participated in the disastrous migration and settlement project in New York from

1709 to 1714. They, too, were fleeing the climatic-agricultural catastrophe that had struck Europe during the winter of 1708–1709. The first emigrants from Schwaigern were probably related to the witch who was imprisoned in the tower and burned in 1713; their flight may have been related to this incident. These early migrations were forerunners of the long, drawn-out movement of Kraichgauers to Greater Pennsylvania, which reached its height in the years from 1727 to 1754.[28]

In addition to the general demographic-economic conditions, official recruitment, and publications by governments (see Chapter 1), many local factors influenced the course of emigration to Pennsylvania. The return of previous emigrants, the letters they sent from the colonies and the friends or hired messengers they sent to the home villages, and the strong, cohesive village communities and networks were also important factors. As the trickle of emigrants from the Kraichgau to Greater Pennsylvania became a flood in the second quarter of the eighteenth century, these local factors influenced the way the villagers migrated and how they initially settled in the colonies.

Whether the initial emigration to North America was to New York or Pennsylvania, it established new routes for villagers in the Kraichgau who had been emigrating to eastern Europe for centuries. Often, emigrants from one village continued to migrate to specific townships in Pennsylvania where fellow villagers had settled.[29] In the six sample parishes shown in Table 2.1, a small number of emigrants preceded the large wave of 1727–1732 in all but Hoffenheim and Weiler. And with the exception of Weiler and possibly Eppingen, the emigration, once begun, continued at significant levels for decades. Weiler experienced two large group migrations in 1727 and 1732, which represented 84 percent of total emigration to North America from that small village. But the pattern for all other villages reflects the general trend of all German-speaking emigrations to North America during the eighteenth century: A relatively small number preceded the vast majority, which emigrated during the third phase (1717–1775).

The northern Kraichgauers tended to emigrate with other family members and villagers on the same ship or in the same year. When the four young revelers from Schwaigern outraged their fellow townspeople in 1743 by celebrating their departure in such an unacceptable fashion, they represented merely the rowdy portion of a large group migration from the town: Thirty-three Schwaigerners left for Pennsylvania that year (see Table 2.1). All of Schwaigern was aware that this was happening, as all but

TABLE 2.1   Emigration to North America by Year from Six Sample Parishes in the Northern Kraichgau, 1709–1775.

YEAR	SCHWAI-GERN	ITTLIN-GEN	HOFFEN-HEIM	WEILER	MASSEN-BACH	EPPIN-GEN	TOTAL
1709					3		3
1710					6	4	10
1713	1						1
1716	5						5
1717	2	1					3
1721	1						1
1722						6	6
1727	5	4		34		19	62
1728		12					12
1729	6						6
1730	9		1	3		1	14
1731	26						26
1732	50	14	8	33	20	17	142
1733		15	24				39
1734	2						2
1736	7				9		16
1737	18	8	1				27
1738	31	6	2	1	2		42
1739	2		1				3
1740	5	1					6
1741	5						5
1742		18			9		27
1743	33		4				37
1744						6	6
1747	1	15				1	17
1748		1					1
1749	67	30	10		13	1	121
1750	7	3	15	1	9		35
1751	1		21			3	25
1752	1		7		3	1	12
1753	1		2	1		1	5
1761			1				1
1762	6	3					9
1763			1				1
1764	6		2				8
1765				3			3
1769	1						1
1772						2	2
1773	1						1
Unknown	5	26	2	4	1	6	44
Total	305	157	102	80	75	68	787

Sources: Burgert, *Eighteenth Century Emigrants*, Hacker, *Unteren Neckar*, and Henry Z. Jones, *The Palatine Families of New York*, 2 vols. (Universal City, California: Henry Z. Jones, 1985).

five (three of the revelers and two others) had requested official permission and paid the appropriate fees. Even though the four revelers left as young, single men, they began their journey as a group, and by the time they boarded a British ship in Rotterdam, they had caught up with other Schwaigerners and made the ocean crossing with them.[30]

In fact, the villagers rarely traveled alone or as single families when they emigrated. Eighty-five percent of emigrants from the six sample parishes traveled with family members (see Table 2.2, column b). Ninety-six percent traveled with other persons from the same parish on the same ship—either from the same or a different family (see column c)—and 97 percent traveled in the same year as other persons from the same parish (see column d). Only 4 percent traveled alone (see column a), and a smaller number were the sole emigrants from one of the sample parishes in any given year. Even this low percentage includes those traveling with family members having different surnames or from neighboring villages and godparents and children.

Extended-family networks were common in these village societies, and so it is not surprising that such networks influenced the way people migrated. According to tabulations of common surnames in Schwaigern throughout its period of emigration (1713–1775), more than half of the emigrants from this parish were members of families with at least seven members who emigrated (see Table 2.3, columns d and e), and more than two-thirds were members of families with at least five members who emigrated. That is, over half the Schwaigerners who went to Greater Pennsylvania lived in that colony with at least six other persons from Schwaigern with the same surname. Only 5 percent were individuals with unique surnames among the entire cohort of emigrants from that parish, and even some of these were related by marriage to other emigrants. These extended-family migrations provided the framework within which the connections needed for successful settlement in the colonies were established. In a voluminous transatlantic correspondence with parents, children, siblings, cousins, in-laws, and god relatives, settled immigrants provided important information on travel conditions and the new land itself, and they assisted their family members upon arrival.

Emigration in groups with other members of the village was critical for the Kraichgauers and many others bound for Greater Pennsylvania. Few were wealthy when they left, and those who were frequently lost all they owned during the expensive and often harrowing process of leaving their territory and traveling for months down the Rhine to Rotterdam,

TABLE 2.2   Tendencies of Emigrants from the Six Sample Parishes in the
Northern Kraichgau to Travel to Pennsylvania with Residents of the Same Parish,
1717–1775.

	MANNER OF TRAVEL WITH OTHERS FROM SAME PARISH							
	(a)		*(b)* Same surname and ship		*(c)* Same ship		*(d)* Same year	
	Alone							
Parish	n	%	n	%	n	%	n	%
Eppingen	5	10	41	69	47	90	53	91
Hoffenheim	7	7	81	79	95	93	97	95
Schwaigern	7	2	263	87	275	98	295	97
Massenbach	2	3	52	81	62	97	65	100
Weiler	4	5	70	89	72	95	73	96
Ittlingen	5	3	142	92	147	97	152	99
Total	30	4%	649	85%	698	96%	735	97%

Note: The total number of emigrants from each parish is Eppingen, 64; Hoffenheim, 102;
Schwaigern, 305; Massenbach, 66; Weiler, 80; and Ittlingen, 157. Missing data vary for each
calculation and for each parish, but the range is low (from 2 to 6 percent for all parishes taken
together).

Sources: From Burgert, *Eighteenth-Century Emigrants*; Hacker, *Unteren Neckar*; and Wagenplast Notes.

across the English Channel to Cowes, on the Isle of Wight, and then across
the Atlantic.

*   *   *

As the Kraichgauers and other immigrants sailed up the Delaware
toward Philadelphia, they grew excited with anticipation. The difficult voyage, of which earlier immigrants had warned them, was over. They were
about to make their first contact with a new government and new authorities. They would have to deal with the difficult tasks of settling up with
the captain and other creditors, recovering from illnesses, and taking the
first steps to establish themselves. How would they react to the new, dispersed, capitalist environment in which there were few communal, subsistence, peasant villages such as those they had left in the Kraichgau? What
would happen to the old bonds of extended family, religion, and commu-

TABLE 2.3 Emigration from Schwaigern to Pennsylvania by Number in Family, 1713–1775.

					CUMULATIVE		
(a) Number in family	*(b)* Number of families	*(c)* Total persons			*(d)* Number of families	*(e)* Total persons	
		n	%			n	%
20	1	20	7		1	20	7
13	2	26	8		2	46	15
12	1	12	4		4	58	19
11	1	11	4		5	69	23
10	1	10	3		6	79	26
9	3	27	9		9	106	35
8	3	24	8		12	130	43
7	4	28	9		16	158	52
6	4	24	8		20	182	60
5	6	30	10		26	212	70
4	7	28	9		33	240	79
3	11	33	11		44	273	90
2	8	16	5		52	289	95
1	16	16	5		68	305	100%
Total	68	305	100%				

Note: "Number in family" refers to those having a common surname. With few exceptions this is an indication of kinship at the village level. Not all emigrants were part of the same nuclear family, nor did they necessarily emigrate together.

Sources: From Burgert, *Eighteenth-Century Emigrants*, and Wagenplast Notes.

nity that had held their lives together during the period of recovery after the seventeenth-century wars, during the conflict with the local nobility, and through the stresses of leaving the village and sailing to Philadelphia? These old communal ties, as well as their attitudes toward abusive authorities who would usurp their rights, would not evaporate in the new circumstances of Greater Pennsylvania. Instead, they would continue to shape the lives of these peasant immigrants, but in different ways. Indeed, these rural, pre-industrial migrations provide an unusual opportunity for studying peasant communities and attitudes in flux.

PART TWO

———

NEULAND

When the immigrants arrived in their new world, they found that continuing the collective strategy of their villages best suited their interests. "Old World" factors such as family, village, and religion, as well as the new factor, ethnicity, were crucial components of this strategy. This "modernity of tradition" facilitated their entrance into the multi-ethnic, capitalist economy of Greater Pennsylvania. The collective strategy also surfaced in the political arena, as the immigrants and their descendants sought to solidify and protect their gains under their new rulers.

3

Community, Settlement, and Mobility in Greater Pennsylvania

As THE HUNDREDS OF SHIPS CARRYING German-speaking immigrants approached Philadelphia, the largest city in North America and one of the largest cities in the British Empire, their passengers tried to put behind them the circumstances of their long, difficult voyage. Many experienced death, exploitation, hunger, and thirst, and almost all experienced storms, sickness, and weeks or months of boredom. The four young revellers from Schwaigern had a very difficult trip lasting twenty-three weeks. Johann Michael Wagner wrote home that the crew packed the passengers on his ship like herrings and that 128 died during the voyage. Among the dead were one of his companions, Christian Steinbrenner, and four others from Schwaigern. His ship, the *St. Andrew*, finally reached Philadelphia on October 7, 1743.[1] As difficult and tragic as the journey had been for Wagner and many others, for a moment, as they peered over the railing of the ship and caught their first glimpse of Philadelphia, this didn't seem to matter. When Christopher Saur, a pharmacist from Wittgenstein who later became a well-known Separatist printer in Germantown, arrived in October 1724, twenty-two cannon shots were fired as they cast anchor, and soon thereafter a crowd formed and began distributing food and inquiring about debts the passengers owed.[2] Most did not receive the kind of treatment Saur did, however. Gottlieb Mittelberger, a Lutheran schoolteacher who emigrated in 1750 from Enzweihingen in Württemberg carrying an organ for the congregation at Providence, wrote,

The glimpse of land revives the passengers, especially those who are half dead of illness. Their spirits, however weak they had become, leap up, triumph, and rejoice within them. Such people are now willing to bear all ills patiently, if only they can disembark soon and step on land. But, alas, alas![3]

12. "An East Prospect of the City of Philadelphia; taken by George Heap from the Jersey Shore, under the direction of Nicholas Scull Surveyor General of the Province of Pennsylvania." Engraved and published by Thomas Jeffreys, London, 1756. Perhaps more than 75 percent of all German-speaking immigrants in the thirteen colonies landed here. (Courtesy of the Library Company of Philadelphia.)

Mittelberger went on to write a bitter account of the treatment German immigrants received upon arrival in Philadelphia. It was published in Stuttgart in 1756 with the intention of cooling the emigration fever sweeping through Württemberg at the time. By mid-century, when the main immigrant stream was arriving, a network of Philadelphia and Rotterdam merchants had developed a profitable business in bringing over German immigrants, and conditions for the passengers worsened. Hence Mittelberger's cry of "alas."[4]

How did the "strangers" flooding into Philadelphia during the third phase of immigration survive this difficult, sometimes tragic experience? How did Old World cultural factors, as well as new factors in North America, help them adjust and get settled? As the immigrants arrived in the colonies, they quickly realized that a collective strategy could help them make the transition. In the changing, capitalist world of Greater Pennsylvania, where most of the German-speaking immigrants ultimately settled, retaining elements of the Old World village community and adopting the New World phenomenon of ethnic cohesiveness were often the keys to success at a time when many never recovered from the financial, physical, and other setbacks of the journey. This chapter examines four important components of the immigrants' collective settlement strategy: community, ethnicity, religion, and mobility.[5]

Community

The immigrants had come seeking land and freedoms, but when they arrived they encountered many difficulties. Few letters had warned them of inflation, the increasing scarcity and costs of prime agricultural land, the threat of war in the backcountry, and other problems awaiting newly arrived immigrants. Many older immigrants commented in the Pennsylvania German press and in official correspondence to European authorities on the increasing difficulty of getting established in the colonies and on how continued immigration further compounded the problem. Yet in spite of these obstacles many immigrants did acquire land and did well in America. What accounts for their success in an environment where "succeeding" was becoming increasingly difficult?[6]

Money was one answer. German-speaking immigrants writing home to a land of scarcity emphasized in their letters that land, natural resources, and freedoms were abundant in Pennsylvania, but that one needed to bring a lot of money in order to succeed in America. A year after his arrival in Philadelphia in 1751, a clever Swiss immigrant from Canton Bern penned a few lines to his friends and family at home which illustrate this point. The city council of Bern published his poem as part of their campaign to stem the tide of emigration from their territory to Pennsylvania.

> Whoever wishes to go to the New World
> Should be sure to take a sack of money
> And also a strong stomach
> So he can withstand the demands of the ship.[7]

Samuel Güldin, a Reformed minister who had emigrated from Canton Bern in 1710, described Pennsylvania as a place with abundant land, wildlife, and other resources. Güldin, who acquired 800 acres in Strasburg Township, Lancaster County, in 1714, and left his son 400 acres in Oley Township, Berks County, after his death in 1745, wrote that even early on land was expensive. Those who did not bring a great deal of money and faith with them, and who did not work hard after arriving, would plunge unavoidably into poverty. Johann Michael Wagner, of Schwaigern, in the northern Kraichgau, wrote, "Things are not as good in this place as many people say, but whoever brings plenty of money—he will have it good. For whoever brings in money can buy a piece of land."[8]

Not surprisingly, many immigrants who succeeded in Pennsylvania, and then wrote the most glowing accounts of the colony, were already relatively wealthy when they arrived in Philadelphia. Mark Häberlein has documented a direct relationship between wealth among Baden-Durlachers prior to emigration and the amount of land they possessed years later in Pennsylvania: Those who had more at home attained more in Pennsylvania.[9] Many immigrant letters also substantiate this. Durs Thommen, who emigrated from Canton Basel with his large family in 1736 and by October 1737 owned a 435-acre farm with livestock and several buildings, sent back several positive reports to the city council in Basel. Yet this family left Basel with £425 (3,187 *Basler Pfund*) after paying emigration fees. Thommen purchased his farm in Lebanon Township, Lancaster County, privately for £360—probably nearly all he had left after arriving in Philadelphia, and much more than the average immigrant could afford.[10] Peter Lohrmann, a Schwaigerner who settled in Germantown, wrote home describing his bountiful harvests and a barnyard filled with livestock. Things were going so well for Lohrmann, in fact, that he wrote "ich leb ale tag so gut als der Wuchere."[11] But Lohrmann, who purchased several servants from Schwaigern as they arrived in Philadelphia, brought significant wealth with him. He left Schwaigern in 1737 with 1,296 guilders, while most Schwaigerners left with less than 200 guilders.[12]

But many immigrants did not do well in Pennsylvania, and often their troubles were associated with the voyage to the colonies and its immediate aftermath. The worst scenarios involved those who died on the way, either during the journey down the Rhine, the wait in Rotterdam or Cowes, England, or during the long ocean crossing. Some also died shortly after arrival, either from illnesses contracted during the voyage or in the new environment. But letters home show that many newcomers who were struggling could not pay their debts upon arrival and were sold as servants—about half of all German-speaking immigrants. One Swiss immigrant who arrived in 1750 could not pay his debts and had to serve "the worst master in all of Pennsylvania" for three years. Luckily, two friends discovered his plight and purchased him from his master after only fourteen months of his term had been served. But the immigrant continued to struggle and was unable to buy land because it was so expensive. He despised Pennsylvania and told those at home not to come. Johann Georg Rüdel of Schwaigern was able to purchase land deep in the backcountry very quickly, but when he wrote home in 1750, he told others not to come because the voyage was too difficult and land was expensive and hard to find. Poorer immigrants who couldn't pay their debts upon arrival, didn't have a chance in the colony, according to Rüdel. They were sold and had to work at hard labor for four to ten years.[13]

Since most immigrants were not wealthy—they were among the poorer inhabitants of their often struggling villages—they had to find other ways to become established in their new world. A closer look at immigrants from the Kraichgau reveals how they did it.

Almost all of the nearly 2,000 northern Kraichgauers who landed in Philadelphia had left subsistence agrarian communities of nuclear villages like Hoffenheim and Ittlingen, or small market towns like Schwaigern and Eppingen, and most had left the Kraichgau with other families from the same village. But to what extent did the immigrants from one village actually settle together and live in the same township in Pennsylvania? Answering this question is an important step toward establishing the degree to which the old village community affected how the immigrants settled.

The experience of the Kraichgauers indicates that the entire immigrant population from one village rarely settled in one township in Pennsylvania, settling instead in several, sometimes widely scattered townships. For example, 152 Ittlingers emigrated to the colonies, and they settled in more than forty locations from Philadelphia to the North Carolina backcountry. From Hoffenheim, 102 landed in Philadelphia and then settled in more than thirty locations, also ranging from Philadelphia to North Carolina. This pattern was typical for virtually all fifty-three northern Kraichgau parishes. The immigrants left their villages in groups, and when they arrived in the New World they scattered across dozens of large counties and hundreds of townships within Greater Pennsylvania.

There were several characteristics of Greater Pennsylvania that prevented all the immigrants of one village from settling in one colonial community. For example, not all villagers arrived together, as they had often done in the first two phases of German emigration to America. Immigrants arriving in the later phase could not always get land in or near the township of their fellow villagers. Also, many of the Kraichgauers could not pay their debts upon arrival and became indentured servants, living wherever their master lived. Lastly, the vastness of the landscape—hundreds and hundreds of miles stretching from Philadelphia to the Alleghenies, and then southward to the North Carolina backcountry—offered a wide variety of opportunities for those in a position to make a move from Philadelphia on their own. The villagers simply responded to the lure of the landscape in different ways.

Yet this general pattern of dispersion and apparent lack of village orientation in the New World conceals the ways in which the home village did influence where many immigrants settled. A closer look at the Kraichgauers reveals that many from a single village did settle together in Greater Pennsylvania. For example, thirty-nine Ittlingers (21 percent of all immigrants from that village) settled in Lancaster; thirty-three Hoffenheimers (26 percent) settled in New Hanover; and twenty-two Eppingers (27 percent) located in Upper Hanover. Furthermore, an additional 18 percent of Ittlingers settled in New Hanover, while 11 percent of the Hoffenheimers remained in Philadelphia, and 17 percent of the Eppingers went to Milford, Pennsylvania. In other words, while the village as a whole did not settle in one Pennsylvania township, many of the immigrants from any given village did cluster in certain townships. In fact, more than half of immigrants from any given Kraichgau parish settled in three or fewer townships in Greater Pennsylvania.[14]

Even when Kraichgauers did not settle with large numbers of fellow immigrants from their home parish, they often stayed in touch with each other and with the home village. The immigrants from Schwaigern, for example, clustered less than most of the Kraichgauers (the largest number to settle in any one township was twenty-six, or only 20 percent, in Lancaster), yet they created and maintained a large network of communications and contacts in Pennsylvania and with their home parish. Their letters reveal how extensive the network was, and how important it was to remain a part of the network in order to succeed in Greater Pennsylvania.

In 1739, Peter and Margaretha Lohrmann, a Lutheran family from Schwaigern living in Germantown, wrote a long letter home that illustrates the workings of their dispersed village. The Lohrmanns had emigrated with their three daughters and seven others from Schwaigern two years earlier, landing in Philadelphia on October 8, 1737, on the *Charming Nancy*, along with a large number of Amish immigrants.[15] In their letter the Lohrmanns discuss the arrival of large numbers of Schwaigerners on different ships, how they settled, who they married, and where they lived. Sebastian Dieter and his wife and children, Marcel Schneider and his wife and children, Christoph Schaber, and Jerg Gebert, all survived a shipwreck in 1738 before reaching Philadelphia. The Lohrmanns had recently spoken with Martin Boger, who arrived in 1731 and had just received a letter from Mathes Beringer in Schwaigern telling of difficulties there. One of the Lohrmann's daughters had married Martin Schwartz, who came from Schluctern, an adjacent village. They had heard news from Schwaigern that Matthes Graßauer's wife and son had died. The Lohrmanns suggested that someone tell Graßauer to remarry a young woman, have several children, and then move to Pennsylvania, where he could become rich. Further, their friends in Schwaigern should tell Mathes Beringer that his son had been indentured to an English preacher. Martin Reißinger, one of several tailors who had emigrated to Pennsylvania, was living with the Lohrmanns and had remarried. Reißinger's daughter had married as well. They had heard nothing about Peter Heinrich's daughter, but Hannes Kober's daughter, Maria Barbara, had arrived in the country and her husband had died in Philadelphia. After this they heard nothing more of Maria Barbara. (Her fate will be discussed later.)

The Lohrmanns were a wealthy family, and they served as the financial center of the Schwaigern "community" in Pennsylvania. When two fellow Schwaigerners, Sebastian Marcel and Jerg Gebert, landed in Philadelphia, Peter Lohrmann rode into the city and purchased them for four pounds, five shillings. This saved the new arrivals from the normally difficult, sometimes devastating experience of the servant auction, which could potentially lead to divided families, an oppressive master, and the permanent loss of the chance to get good land and become well established in the colonies. Later, Lohrmann purchased Hans Dieter's daughter, Anna Maria, and Mathes Gräßle, both from Schwaigern. He also conducted a business deal with Jerg Dieter (brother of Sebastian), who lived twenty-five miles away.

Perhaps by virtue of their financial connections and wealth (the Lohrmanns left Schwaigern with nearly 1,300 guilders), this family also served as the communications hub for the dispersed community. When Jerg and Wendel Heinrich, who had emigrated in 1731 and 1737 respectively, rode into Germantown in 1743 to buy provisions, they went first to Peter Lohrmann's house to exchange news about Schwaigern and Schwaigerners, both at home and in the colonies. Lohrmann was the unofficial mailman for the community. By arrangement, Schwaigerners received their mail from home at the Lohrmanns' house, and they dropped off letters (as the Heinrichs did that day) that Lohrmann then forwarded home in batches.[16]

Many Kraichgauers and other German immigrants maintained their dispersed communities even as they moved from Pennsylvania into the North Carolina piedmont. Susanne Mosteller Rolland discovered that kinship, acquaintanceship, and religious networks, especially among northern Kraichgauers, influenced migration and settlement from Germany to Pennsylvania, and from Pennsylvania to North Carolina. The Germans may have settled in a "series of clusters" instead of in isolation or in a single colony. She found considerable networking among extended families moving from Pennsylvania to the region beyond the Catawba. The southward migrants, many of them second-generation Europeans, followed friends and relatives to this frontier area and settled near them. In short, they brought their dispersed community with them.[17]

Many other German communities kept in close contact with emigrants by way of letters routed to specific persons designated to handle the transatlantic exchange. Antoni Müller, an apprentice cabinetmaker from Lettweiler in the Palatinate, received a letter from home through two other Lettweilers, Henrich Mießener and Andreas Seyß. When Johann Conrad Scherer, an immigrant from Dörnigheim in Wetteravia living in Pikeland Township in Chester County, exchanged letters with his father at home, they discussed other villagers who had already come to Pennsylvania or who were planning to do so soon. Peter Wachner, who lived at the Kaiser's Mill in Pikeland Township, received Scherer's mail. Durs Thommen, an immigrant from Niederdorf, Canton Basel, who settled in Lebanon Township, Lancaster County, wrote the city council in Basel that everyone wishing to contact him should send their letters to Caspar and Johannes Wistar in Philadelphia. Barbara Börlin, an immigrant from Bennwill, Canton Basel, who settled first in Conestoga Township and later in Lebanon Township, Lancaster County, received her letters through Johannes Wister as well. The Thommen family was part of a large group migration in 1737. After this group's arrival, Hans Georg Gerster began writing open letters from Germantown to Niederdorf, informing everyone of the whereabouts and fate of the group.[18]

This kind of financial and communications network became crucial to the new immigrants' struggle to establish themselves in the New World. The emigrants had left their strong, cohesive communities in small groups, and all reports from previous travelers indicated that life in the New World would be a difficult undertaking, so staying in touch with the "community" would be important. Just making it as far as Philadelphia left many indebted and virtually all in ill health. If the villagers knew where to go after disembarking, or better yet if friends of family members from the home village, such as Peter and Margaretha Lohrmann, had heard of their pending arrival and met them on the docks, paid their debts in the form of a loan, and took them in, then the new immigrants stood a good chance of becoming one of the success stories described in letters to the home village.

But what happened to those who could not stay connected with the dispersed village, and either by choice or circumstance had to make a go of it alone? Unless someone they knew "redeemed" them, that is, paid their debts to the ship's captain, they became indentured servants and had no choice as to where they might settle. If their contract was long and their master lived far away, indentured servants would often disappear from the dispersed community networks, which could mean that life in America would be a long, difficult ordeal. Such was the case with Maria Barbara Kober, of whom Peter and Margaretha Lohrmann "heard nothing more" after the death of her husband in Philadelphia in 1738.

Kober told her story in a letter to her brother in Schwaigern in 1767— twenty-nine years after her arrival and disappearance in Philadelphia. During this long interval, her family and friends in Schwaigern thought she had died. Instead, as she wrote from Philadelphia after her reappearance, she had been living in the backcountry with the "English" who had purchased her on the docks of Philadelphia many years before. In May 1738, just three months after her marriage to the twenty-four-year-old weaver Elias Beringer, Kober had left Schwaigern for Philadelphia with her newborn son, Johann Michl, and twenty-eight others. Her son died on the way from Rotterdam to Cowes, England. After a difficult transatlantic voyage lasting sixteen weeks, the group landed in Philadelphia on the *Elizabeth* on October 30, 1738.

Kober and her husband were redemptioners. That is, after their arrival in Philadelphia, they were given a short period of time to search for some friend, relative, or other person who would pay their debts—if they were lucky, in the form of a gift or loan. For three weeks they lived on the ship while they wandered through the streets of Philadelphia, searching for some opportunity to meet their financial obligations and get started in Pennsylvania. Having no luck in this endeavor, Kober, on the advice of her husband, indentured herself for four years to some "English" ("unter lauter Englische") who lived about twenty-six miles from Philadelphia. She then left her husband on the ship, never to see him again. Even as she wrote home twenty-nine years later, she did not know what Peter and Margaretha Lohrmann had discovered: that her husband had died soon after she left him on the ship in Philadelphia.

In 1742, after working off her debts, Kober returned to look for her husband or some indication of what had happened to him. Seeing no prospects of finding him or making a life for herself in Philadelphia, she returned to her former master and acquaintances and continued living and working with them for twenty-three years. She finally married a linen weaver from Saarbrücken, Heinrich Probst, in 1761. Five years later, her husband decided that he no longer wanted to live among the English ("unter puren Englischen"), so they moved to Philadelphia to be near other Germans.

By returning to Philadelphia Kober reentered the network of communications and contacts with other Schwaigerners, in both Pennsylvania and the home village, and this enabled her to at least attempt to improve her financial situation. In 1766, she met Gottlieb Böckle and Paul Kober on the docks. They had originally emigrated in 1764, then returned to Schwaigern, and later, once again, recrossed the Atlantic. Böckle and Paul Kober (probably a distant relative) informed Maria Barbara Kober that her mother and father, her brother Johannes and her sister Margaretha had died. Her brother Johann Adam (to whom she wrote), her sister Maria Catharina, and another brother, Paul, were still living. She immediately wrote home to inform her family of her circumstances, but the ship carrying the letter was lost at sea. She wrote again the following year (1767), and told her story. Kober was motivated by more than just a suddenly recovered affection for long-lost relatives, however: Hearing that both her parents had died, she wanted her inheritance. At the conclusion of her story she informed her brother that she was sending her husband to Schwaigern with a power of attorney to collect the inheritance. Kober, now a member of the Schwaigern community in Pennsylvania, began to use the connections with the home parish that so many others had used before her to improve her standing in America.[19]

In fact, many immigrants kept in close contact with events in their home village in order to recover inheritances and other property. In 1753 Georg Sehner, a cabinetmaker who had immigrated to Pennsylvania in 1749 and settled in Lancaster, wrote his brother in Schwaigern and enclosed an English-language letter from the authorities in Lancaster with a German translation. Martin Offner, who had immigrated from Schwaigern in 1749, and Hannß Martin Reisinger, who had arrived with Peter Lohrmann in 1737 on the *Charming Nancy*, signed for Sehner as witnesses. Sehner requested his inheritance, which he calculated as $107\frac{1}{2}$ guilders, and appointed a friend in Schwaigern, Dieterich Schopff, to collect it for him. In spite of the tremendous distances involved, the immigrants maintained these legal-financial connections with their home villages. In fact, Heinrich and Peter Miller, two German-language printers in Philadelphia, sold power-of-attorney forms (one of which Maria Barbara Kober used) to meet the tremendous demand. Throughout the eighteenth century, Pennsylvania Germans successfully made claims for their inheritances even when they had emigrated illegally. The legal-financial interests were an important strand in the web of overlapping, transatlantic connections between the clusters of villages in the Kraichgau and their respective dispersed communities in Pennsylvania. Clearly, whatever the inheritances were, they had not been enough to hold the emigrants in the Kraichgau.[20]

These examples of village and family financial and communication networks indicate that the bonds of community, which had been growing stronger during the decades of recovery and rebuilding in southwest Germany, remained important even after the villagers immigrated into Greater Pennsylvania. Many who had crossed the Atlantic together also settled together, and those who did not settle in the same township as many of their village neighbors nevertheless lived with their families in the region and stayed in touch through the networks established by the village. Those who, like Maria Barbara Kober, neither settled with fellow villagers nor connected with the village network often faced long ordeals in colonial America.

Yet the traditional "communal model" for early American settlement

does not entirely explain the German immigrant experience. By leaving
the community to try and improve their fortunes in the dispersed, capitalist environment of Greater Pennsylvania, German emigrants in some ways
took the ultimate step toward becoming model upwardly mobile, self-
interested individualists.

German-speaking immigrants in Pennsylvania, however, seem to have
exhibited characteristics of both "communal" and "individualistic" behavior. Perhaps as they found themselves in an environment hostile to the
formation of closed, nuclear villages, they realized that the best way to
succeed as individualists was to maintain extended-family and village connections. True individualists who did not maintain such connections were
likely to join the growing ranks of the impoverished classes in the colony.
Thus to behave as much as possible as a communal peasant was to behave
in the immigrants' own rational economic self-interest. Within the framework of migration, community and individual interest may have been
complementary, not contradictory strategies. A successful immigrant indi-
vidualist needed to remain a community-oriented peasant to whatever degree the new environment would allow.[21]

Ethnic Settlements

The immigrants relied on "Old World" factors such as extended family and
village connections to get settled, but the "New World" phenomenon of
ethnicity played a critical role in determining where within the landscape
they settled.[22] The German-speakers came from a wide variety of political,
linguistic, and cultural backgrounds in Europe. The origins of the vast majority lay within a region stretching 250 to 300 miles from the highlands in
Canton Bern (Switzerland) to the middle Rhine. The rest came from virtually every other region of central Europe.

The German-speakers were well aware of their diverse backgrounds—
more so than their new neighbors were—but these differences paled in
comparison to those between them and the English, the Scots-Irish, Scots,
and others. For most, an ethnic character developed that became the source
of at least part of their identity. Other Americans called them "Palatines"
when the context was immigration (regardless of whether they came from
the Palatinate) and "Dutch" in most other contexts.[23] Some of their spokesmen referred to them all as the "Germans," the "German people," or the

"German nation," both in political exhortations and often in casual correspondence.

An ethnic identity manifested itself not only among the leadership of the "German" community, but also among the general populace, which demonstrated a strong tendency to settle in areas inhabited by large numbers of other German-speakers. In Pennsylvania a clearly defined "Pennsylvania German" landscape existed by 1760, within which virtually all German-speakers of the colony lived, regardless of whether they were recent arrivals or descendants of immigrants from three-quarters of a century earlier.

Most Pennsylvania Germans lived in the heavily German upper parts of the three older counties in the colony (Chester, Philadelphia, and Bucks), or in Northampton, Berks, and all but the western portions of Lancaster County. In fact, Lancaster, Northampton, and especially Berks were so heavily populated with German-speaking people that they were essentially German counties. In 1790, 72 percent of the white population of Lancaster County was ethnic German, while Northampton County was 63 percent German, and Berks and Dauphin counties together (until 1785 Berks included this entire area) were 73 percent German. York County was 49 percent German, and Montgomery County, which was formed in 1784 from most of the back parts of Philadelphia County, was about 57 percent German. On the other hand, only 11 percent of Delaware (eastern Chester during the colonial period), 16 percent of Chester, and 17 percent of Cumberland were German. Only those German-speakers who lived in or near Philadelphia and a few other scattered areas mixed significantly with other ethnic groups.[24]

Demographers have developed an "Index of Dissimilarity," that measures the degree of segregation in residence patterns among ethnic groups. The index measures the difference in the distribution of two population groups in the same area and indicates the minimum proportion of either group that would have to be shifted in order to achieve an equal distribution for both groups. For example, if 15 percent of the population of Pennsylvania in 1790 was Scots-Irish and 15 percent of every *county* in Pennsylvania was Scots-Irish, then the Index of Dissimilarity would be 0.0, meaning that the way Scots-Irish settled was the same as that of the non–Scots-Irish population at the county level. A high Index of Dissimilarity means that the Scots-Irish pattern was so "dissimilar" to the non–Scots-Irish pattern that large percentages of either the Scots-Irish or the non–Scots-Irish

TABLE 3.1   The Index of Dissimilarity: Ethnic Segregation in Pennsylvania
by County in 1790.

ETHNIC GROUP*	% OF WHITE POPULATION	INDEX OF DISSIMILARITY
Germans	38.0	.431
English	25.8	.271
Scots-Irish†	15.1	
Scottish†	7.6	.308
Irish	7.1	.269
Welsh	3.6	.274
Dutch	1.3	.394
French	0.9	.368
Swedish	0.6	.410
	100.0	

* Each group as opposed to all others (Germans versus non-Germans, etc.)
†Purvis was unable to distinguish Scots-Irish names from Scottish ones, thus those groups
must be taken together when figuring the Index of Dissimilarity. He estimated that the
Scots-Irish equaled about two-thirds of the total.

Source: Purvis, "Patterns of Ethnic Settlement in Late Eighteenth-Century Pennsylvania,"
115.

population would have to be moved in order for the Scots-Irish to live in
a "similar" pattern to the others. The importance of the index, which is
based upon a surname analysis of male heads of household in the 1790 Federal Census, may depend in part upon the degree of ethnic intermarriage,
which was low for Germans (see Chapter 6).[25]

Table 3.1 shows the Index of Dissimilarity for each ethnic group versus the rest of the population in Pennsylvania. A measure of 0.0 means that
both distributions in a given test were exactly equal (that is, there was no
segregation), and a measure of 1.0 means both groups resided completely
separate from one another.

Table 3.1 shows that there was significant segregation in residence by
county for all ethnic groups in Pennsylvania in 1790. After a long century
of immigration, Pennsylvania had become a society in which much of the
population lived in segregated ethnic enclaves. In order to make the residence patterns of Germans and non-Germans equal, at least 43.1 percent of
either group would have to be shifted. For Scots-Irish and Scots, 30.8 percent of the group would have to be shifted, and for English 27.1 percent.

But high levels of ethnic segregation were not unique to Pennsylvania. In western Maryland, German immigrants tried to buy land where

TABLE 3.2   Ethnic Segregation in New York, New Jersey, Pennsylvania, and
Maryland by County in 1790 for Selected Ethnic Groups.

	INDEX OF DISSIMILARITY			
Ethnic Groups	New York	New Jersey	Pennsylvania	Maryland
Germans vs. non-Germans	.310	.370	.431	.672
Germans vs. English	.341	.394	.447	.709
Germans vs. Scots-Irish/Scots	.306	.305	.466	.623
Germans vs. Dutch	.267	.604	.481	.875

Note: Ethnic residences for Maryland are based upon Purvis's analysis for 1800.

Sources: Purvis, "The National Origins of New Yorkers in 1790"; "European Origins of
New Jersey's Eighteenth-Century Population"; "Patterns of Settlement in Late Eighteenth-
Century Pennsylvania"; and his unpublished manuscript on the northern Chesapeake in 1800
(for Maryland).

they could get the best deal, but they also tried to settle with other Germans. In the Shenandoah Valley and piedmont of Virginia, distinct ethnic
enclaves of Germans existed by 1750, and most Virginia Germans lived in
such enclaves. In the North Carolina piedmont, Germans lived in distinct,
though small and scattered communities. The Index of Dissimilarity in the
states for which it is measurable for 1790 reflects significant ethnic segregation in most cases; in Maryland it is even higher than in Pennsylvania (see
Table 3.2).[26]

Other factors, such as population pressure and the location of markets and political centers, also played a role in the settlement patterns of
Germans and others in Greater Pennsylvania, but in many ways these factors were overshadowed by that of ethnicity.[27]

If population pressure was the most important determinant of where
immigrants settled, then there must have been a gradual expansion of the
boundaries of settlement as immigration increased. Succeeding waves of
immigrants should have settled ever farther westward and southward, and
not in established areas of southeastern Pennsylvania. Those who arrived
in the late 1740s and 1750s should have settled farther west than those who
came in the late 1720s, 1730s and early 1740s.

Yet this was not the case. The naturalization records for Pennsylvania, which indicate place of residence, suggest that German immigrants
arriving in the 1730s and especially the 1740s and 1750s lived in both
newly established and older areas of settlement. These are the residences of

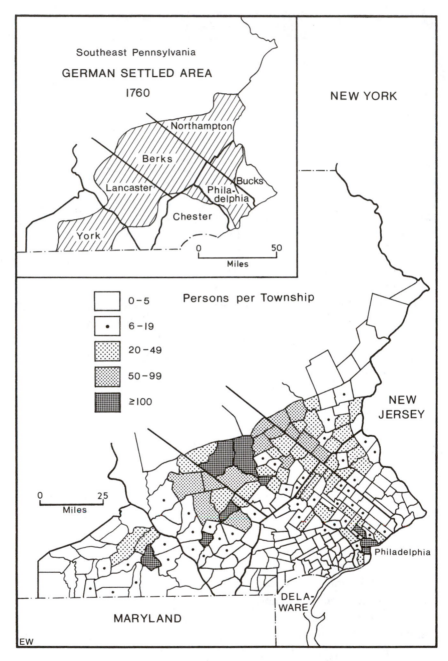

Map 3.1. Township of Residence of German Immigrants Who Were Naturalized in Pennsylvania by the Terms of the 1740 Act of Parliament, 1761–1765. *Source*: Compiled from Giuseppi, *Naturalizations of Foreign Protestants*.

foreign-born German-speakers after they had settled down—by law at least seven years after their initial arrival in Philadelphia, but in reality about thirteen years later. Map 3.1 shows the location by township of those who were naturalized from 1761 to 1765, the large majority of whom arrived between 1740 and 1755, especially during the peak period of immigration from 1749 to 1754. Of the 4,443 adult men who are represented, only 1,413 (32 percent) lived in areas settled after 1730. For the majority, then, something other than population pressure or the availability of land on the frontier influenced their place of residence.[28]

This pattern of immigrant settlement in older as well as newer areas of settlement extended throughout Greater Pennsylvania. From about 1730 until nearly 1770, during which the majority of German (and other) immigrants arrived, the boundaries of Greater Pennsylvania remained largely the same. With the exceptions of southwestern Virginia and the North Carolina backcountry, which were not opened up until the 1740s, immigrants arriving in Philadelphia in the 1750s and 1760s could and did settle where those who arrived in 1730 had settled. By 1730 (somewhat earlier in the Shenandoah Valley), Europeans had already established a loose, far-flung network of settlements among, and sometimes west of, Native American populations in Greater Pennsylvania. Settlement had already reached the Alleghenies, beyond which it would not expand until the late 1760s. Indeed, itinerant Moravian missionaries encountered Europeans living fifty miles west of the Shenandoah as early as 1744, and these settlers had already been there "a number of years." The early settlers established the boundaries within which the masses of later immigrants would settle, in what Louis De Vorsey calls a "dynamic zone of interaction" between European and Native American inhabitants.[29]

Thus the some 50,000 Germans who arrived in Philadelphia during the 1730s, 1740s, and early 1750s had many choices as to where they could settle and resettle. They could have remained in Philadelphia because either they were attracted by the opportunities the city offered or they could not escape the environment of disease, death, and debts. They could have settled in the three older counties of Pennsylvania (Chester, Bucks, and Philadelphia), where private land eventually became more scarce and more expensive than in the backcountry, but where demand for labor was high and opportunities for skilled artisans were many. Or they could have settled deep in the backcountry, in the new counties of Northampton, Berks, Lancaster, York, and Cumberland, or in Frederick, in Maryland. Whatever their choice, the immigrants tended to settle near other Germans.

The naturalization records also indicate that the location of markets and county seats, in and of themselves, did not determine the Germans' settlement patterns. The Kraichgauers, Württembergers, Badeners, Alsatians, Swiss, and others often did settle in or near commercial centers and county seats, but, with the exception of Philadelphia City and parts of lower Philadelphia County, they located in or near such nodes of settlement only when they were largely German in their ethnic makeup. Few Germans settled in or near Chester or Bristol, the county seats of Chester and Bucks counties, respectively. And few settled in other market towns of these largely "English" counties, except in the northern areas of each county, which were clearly part of the Pennsylvania German landscape. Furthermore, few Germans settled in western York or Cumberland counties, yet there were market towns and a county seat there.

In short, a desire to settle near other German-speaking peoples—regardless of their region of origin in central Europe—played an important role in shaping settlement patterns. Many late-arriving immigrants did move to the farthest boundaries of Greater Pennsylvania, but many others stayed in the older areas of settlement. Most settled in or near commercial centers and county seats, but, with the exceptions visible in Philadelphia, Germantown, and other nearby areas, they did so only if the areas were largely *German* commercial centers and county seats. The desire to be near other people who spoke the same language (even if it was a difficult dialect) and who, when compared to the English, Irish, and others, appeared to have similar customs and ways of life, should not be overlooked as a factor shaping how and where Germans settled.[30]

The Role of the Church

Only a small percentage of the Germans emigrated because of religious persecution or experimentation; their experiences were different from that of the majority of German immigrants in that religion was the foremost shaping factor in almost all of their endeavors (see Chapter 4). With few exceptions, Lutherans or Calvinists from a given village did not emigrate to America and exclusively settle one community with their own church, but religion was important to the immigration and settlement of the Lutheran and Calvinist (or Reformed) majority in a different way. Whether emigrating to the east or the west, southwest German and Swiss inhabitants inquired about the religious situation in the destination lands. Their primary concern was whether they would be able to practice their religion

13. The Lutheran church built in 1768 at New Hanover in upper Philadelphia (now Montgomery) County, Pennsylvania. (Courtesy of the Lutheran Archives Center at Philadelphia.)

freely. Many letters and official recruitment notices addressed this issue, assuring them of tolerance, if not complete freedom of religion.

Although it may not have been the primary cause of their emigration, many Lutheran and Reformed immigrants had complained about the hardening church order developing in southwest Germany in the eighteenth century—even in areas where their own religion was the official state religion. The lack of an overbearing religious establishment in North America was appealing to some, including the wealthy farmer who proclaimed to a Lutheran churchman in Pennsylvania that a manure pile was his God—a proclamation that would have led to blasphemy charges in Germany.[31]

On the other hand, many immigrants lamented the absence in the colonies of a strong establishment, as had existed in their home villages, and they worked hard to bring in more pastors and erect more church buildings. This led to conflicts over the nature of the establishment they did create and over who should control it—controversies central to the German Great Awakening.[32]

Regardless of whether they were "awakeners" promoting the further

14. The Augustus Lutheran Church at Trappe, in Upper Providence Township in upper Philadelphia County. The minister Henry Melchior Muhlenberg and his family are buried here. (Courtesy of the Lutheran Archives Center at Philadelphia.)

establishment of the Lutheran and Reformed churches, or whether they were disgruntled with the existing establishment in Europe or America, most Lutheran and Reformed immigrants settled in some kind of church community in Greater Pennsylvania or helped build one shortly after settling. Without traditional nuclear villages, churches often became the focal points of the dispersed rural communities of Greater Pennsylvania. Sometimes pastors helped new arrivals get started, just as family and fellow villagers often did, but few communities had a regular preacher, relying instead on an itinerant who visited them every few weeks or months or on appointed lay leaders or "irregular," non-ordained pastors. Many communities did not have a church building for years, meeting instead in private homes, barns, public buildings, or in the open. Nevertheless, it was usually not long after initial settlement before some kind of church community was established wherever Germans settled throughout Greater Pennsylvania (see Table 3.3).[33]

For members of the Lutheran and Reformed churches, religion and

TABLE 3.3   German Reformed and Lutheran Churches in Greater Pennsylvania, 1776.

COLONY	LUTHERAN	REFORMED	TOTAL
New York	13	0	13
Pennsylvania	126	123	249
New Jersey	10	9	19
Maryland	17	19	36
Virginia	15	16	31
North Carolina	15	12	27
Total	196	179	375

Note: Glatfelter (*The History*, 149) estimates that there were about seven Roman Catholic congregations in Pennsylvania in 1776, most of whose members were German.

Source: Glatfelter, *The History*, 144. For North Carolina see note 33.

ethnicity became important, mutually supporting aspects of immigrant culture in their new communities. Most Calvinists and Lutherans maintained distinct identities in religious matters, yet for each the church played an important role in establishing their community and distinguishing it from the non-German population. Even in the union churches, where the two groups shared the same building, they consciously kept their services and other aspects of their religious lives separate. In Pennsylvania, Henry Melchior Muhlenberg could easily cooperate with Swedish Lutherans because their number was so small: his own Lutheran parishioners felt "secure" in their church community because of their majority status. The Reformed minister Michael Schlatter had to work with the Dutch Reformed hierarchy in Amsterdam because help from the German authorities simply was not forthcoming. Yet deep in the heart of Pennsylvania German country there was never any question whether "German Reformed" culture was secure, and both religion and ethnicity were central to that culture.

The propensity of early church communities to attract later immigrants who had left Europe for secular reasons underscores the importance of the church in immigrant culture. Any given community may have contained immigrants from throughout southwest Germany and Switzerland, and it may or may not have been located in or near a market town or county seat. But the church communities continued to attract a diverse lot of German speakers who chose to settle there rather than in some non-

15. The Reformed church in Reading, the county seat of Berks County, Pennsylvania, erected in 1761. (Courtesy of the Evangelical and Reformed Historical Society of the United Church of Christ, Lancaster, Pennsylvania.)

German community. This point is demonstrated in comparisons of Map 3.2 and Map 3.1. Map 3.2 shows the location of Lutheran and Reformed churches in Pennsylvania in 1748, just before some 30,000 German immigrants began to arrive in the colony over the course of a five-year period. The map shows the townships in which the immigrants could have settled if they wished to locate in or near a church community. Map 3.1 shows where many immigrants who arrived after 1748 settled. The close resemblance of the two maps suggests that the newcomers settled in or near previously existing church communities.

Even in the North Carolina backcountry, deep within Greater Pennsylvania and hundreds of miles from Philadelphia, a large number of Lutheran and Reformed communities developed in spite of the extreme

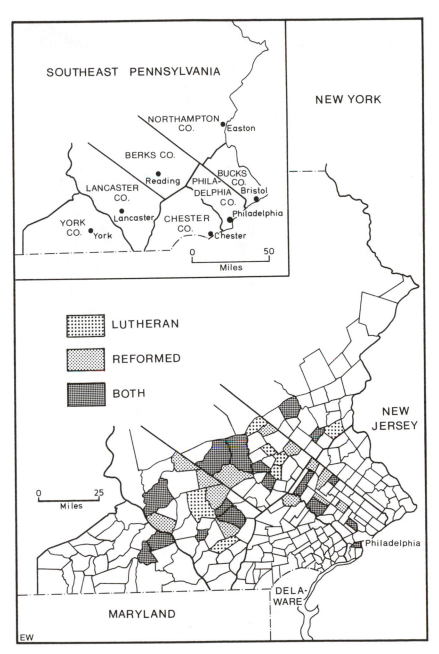

SOUTHEAST PENNSYLVANIA

NEW YORK

NORTHAMPTON
CO.
● Easton

BERKS CO.

BUCKS
CO.
● Bristol

LANCASTER
CO.

● Reading

PHILA-
DELPHIA
CO.

YORK
CO.
● York

● Lancaster

CHESTER
CO.

● Philadelphia

● Chester

0   50
Miles

LUTHERAN

REFORMED

BOTH

NEW
JERSEY

0   25
Miles

● Philadelphia

DELA-
WARE

MARYLAND

EW

Map 3.2. Pennsylvania Townships with Lutheran and German Reformed Churches Established before 1748. *Source*: From Glatfelter, *The History*, 154–155.

16. Organ Lutheran Church, near Salisbury, North Carolina. Begun in 1774 and completed in the 1790s. (Photographed by James P. Barringer, Jr., of the *Salisbury Post*.)

shortage of ministers, and most German settlers lived in or near those communities. By 1760 there were eighteen Reformed and Lutheran communities; by 1770 there were twenty-four; and in 1780 there were thirty. Yet only one Lutheran minister served in North Carolina before 1773, and by the outbreak of the Revolutionary War there were only two. There were two Reformed ministers in the backcountry in 1760, only one in 1770, and two again in 1780. These figures attest to the importance the Lutheran and Reformed populace attached to establishing and living in church communities, regardless of whether they had a regular minister. In the vast, heavily populated expanses of the North Carolina backcountry, where there were no cities and few towns, the church was often the center of the German community.[34]

Stable Ethnics

Once established in the rural ethnic enclaves of the backcountry or in the relatively mixed areas of the city of Philadelphia and lower Philadelphia County, did the immigrants stay put, or did they move on? Until recently, historians tended to associate strong communities and low geographic mobility with New England, while individualism and a high degree of geographic mobility characterized the middle colonies. New Englanders settled in nuclear communities and for the most part stayed put, while colonists of the middle colonies lived in dispersed settlements, where, among other things, a high degree of geographic mobility hindered the development of stable towns and communal values.[35]

Much of the recent literature emphasizes the complex and changing nature of mobility patterns in colonial America. Virginia DeJohn Anderson, for example, argues that a pattern of "short-run mobility followed by long-run persistence" characterized New England settlement. New arrivals generally spent their first year or two moving about the region before choosing a home near the center of a newly founded community, where they remained for the rest of their lives. James Horn emphasizes a high degree of geographic mobility and argues that kinship and friendship ties were important factors in persuading early planters to move to new sites within the Chesapeake Bay area.[36]

Most historians are still inclined to accept the notion of high geographic mobility in Pennsylvania, and they often link this phenomenon to the high levels of immigration into the colony in the eighteenth century. Even though studies of other colonies are coming back to the proposition that Germans were more geographically stable than other ethnic groups, especially Scots-Irish, many still believe that immigrants into Pennsylvania, including German-speaking immigrants (the largest group), landed in Philadelphia and then began a wandering existence within the colony or perhaps in Greater Pennsylvania.[37]

If it were true that immigrants brought these on-the-move, get-ahead attitudes to Pennsylvania, then they should have been the most mobile people in the population. All the immigrants began in Philadelphia, where they landed, and many remained there until they died. Most moved at least once, but did they continue to move about within or outside the colony, or did they soon settle down? If there were high levels of geographic mobility in eighteenth-century Pennsylvania, and if the origins of this nomadic behavior lay in the success-oriented mindset of its European-born people, of which Germans were the largest group, then German immigrants should have moved from Philadelphia not once or even twice but several times before dying.

But they did not. Table 3.4 shows the number of times immigrants relocated from one township to another. In the case of the "secular" immigrants (those from the northern Kraichgau), their first move from Philadelphia is counted. For the Moravians and New England immigrants, the first move is the one they made after initial settlement in their respective colonies. The large majority of the secular immigrants and those who came as part of small religious groups either never left Philadelphia or moved only once to another township and remained there. These figures represent minimal mobility for the immigrant population.

There are some biases in the data, but the available evidence indicates that mobility among European-born immigrants was very low. A bias toward stability is built in because it is easier to find and record people who move less. Sometimes, then, the data below reflect a minimum number of moves. But there are enough immigrants for whom complete movement history is known to establish a pattern of low mobility, which is corroborated by the evidence available for the remainder. For example, 14 percent of the immigrants from the six northern Kraichgau parishes never left Philadelphia, and 79 percent either never left or moved only once: from Philadelphia after their arrival to some other township where they remained until they died. Nineteen percent moved to a township outside of Philadelphia and then moved again to a second township, remaining there until they died. Only 2 percent moved twice after leaving Philadelphia, and none from the six sample parishes moved as many as three or more times. In short, the Kraichgauers did not move a lot.[38]

The plausibility of this remarkably high level of stability is confirmed by the religious-group migrations of the Amish and the Moravians, for whom there is more complete data. Table 3.4 indicates that the Amish were slightly more mobile than the secular immigrants: only 2 percent remained in Philadelphia (as opposed to 14 percent), and only 60 percent made at most one move (as opposed to 79 percent). However, the Amish settled in groups, primarily in upper Berks County initially, and had never intended to settle in Philadelphia. (The four persons who never left Philadelphia actually died there shortly after their arrival.) After their initial settlement (the first move), 58 percent never moved again, and 29 percent moved only once more. The Amish lived in dispersed, rural, but nevertheless tightly

TABLE 3.4   Mobility of German Immigrants in Pennsylvania by Religious Group (1717–1775), Compared to Pre-1650 New England Immigrants.

	RELIGIOUS GROUP							
	Secular*		Moravians		Amish		Pre-1650 New England immigrants	
No. of moves	n	%	n	%	n	%	n	%
0	52	14	142	27	4	2	2,946	46
1	237	65	178	33	132	58	1,996	32
2	66	19	80	15	66	29	1,039	16
3	8	2	39	7	24	10	276	4
≥4	0	0	93	18	3	1	103	2
Total	363	100%	532	100%	229	100%	6,360	100%

	CUMULATIVE							
No. of moves	Secular		Moravians		Amish		New England	
0	52	14	142	27	4	2	2,946	46
1	289	79	320	60	136	60	4,942	78
2	355	98	400	75	202	89	5,981	94
3	363	100	439	82	226	99	6,257	98
≥4	363	100%	532	100%	229	100%	6,360	100%

*"Secular" refers to the northern Kraichgau immigrants from the six sample parishes who had emigrated for secular reasons.

Sources: See note 38.

knit communities, the locations of which are well known. Although the entire movement history of only a few Amish immigrants is known for certain, most of the missing data for this religious group is the result of their unwillingness to keep church books for these few colonial communities, and not because they moved around so much that later genealogists and historians could not track them.

The records of the Moravians are so comprehensive that the movement data for that group can be accepted as quite accurate. On the surface, their movement history appears somewhat ambiguous: They have the highest percentage among the German groups of those who made no moves (27 percent), yet they also have the highest percentage of those who made four or more moves (18 percent). Those who made no moves went directly to a prearranged destination, usually their headquarter communities in Bethlehem or Nazareth, Pennsylvania, and remained there until death. Virtually all of those who moved at least four times were clergy (staid ministers, itinerant preachers, and missionaries) and their families. In fact, many from this group moved seven or eight times—even more—as they ranged up and down the North American continent and the Caribbean, preaching to Native Americans, African slaves, and European colonists. When the unusually large number (157) of the clergy are factored out, the record of the remaining Moravians even more closely resembles that of the other groups: 33 percent never moved, 72 percent moved no more than once, and 89 percent moved no more than twice before death. Even including the clergy, the record of the majority of all Moravians (60 percent) resembles that of other immigrants—they either remained in their initial place of settlement or moved only once thereafter.[39]

The case of Johannes Schlessmann and his family demonstrates on a personal level what the data on the Kraichgauers, Moravians, and others suggest was typical. Shortly after his arrival in the autumn of 1753, Schlessmann wrote a letter to three individuals in three different locations in his home territory of Wertheim and described his family's situation. (Immigrant letters were typically intended to be read by many, perhaps the entire village, or even members of several villages.) Schlessmann's brother-in-law, who was from Oxford, just north of Philadelphia, had met the family at their ship and taken them in. Schlessmann also met his son in Oxford. He and his family planned to move soon to Germantown to spend the winter with a "rich man" named Türks Keyser. In the spring they would move inland and look for land.

Another letter home written by Schlessmann sixteen years later reveals that his family never left Oxford. This time Schlessmann wrote to his wife's family (addressing her brother, his wife, and their children, as well as brothers, sisters, and other in-laws). Instead of moving about in the backcountry of Pennsylvania as they had planned, Schlessmann bought a "middling place" in or near Oxford. In his letter he gave news about all their acquaintances, who lived "far scattered from each other," but remained in touch. He enclosed a power of attorney for his brother-in-law in Wertheim to be used to collect an inheritance. They should send all correspondence to the Schlessmanns through Christopher Saur in German-town. Apparently, the Schlessmanns had not only stayed put, but also stayed in touch and attained the ranks of the "middling sort," which they hoped to improve upon by retrieving an inheritance from their home village.[40]

So the story for German immigrants of all sorts is not one of extreme mobility but rather one of how the majority made a single move before settling down, and how a minority made a second move sometime later. For most of the northern Kraichgauers, the first move from Philadelphia proved to be their last. When they finally left the city and settled in the Pennsylvania German countryside, they tended to follow others who had gone before them. They had come a long way to set themselves up, live, work, and die in some largely German corner of the colony.[41]

Christopher Saur, the pharmacist-turned-printer from Wittgenstein who came in 1724 and settled in Germantown, captured the mood and motivations of many of these immigrants who were moving out of Philadelphia and searching for a place in which to settle. He observed the astounding number of German-speaking immigrants who were overwhelming the city in the late 1740s and early 1750s and began to print advice literature for the new arrivals. Saur's newspapers, almanacs, and broadsides circulated widely in the Pennsylvania German areas.

In late 1750 Saur began to print in his yearly almanacs (or "calendars") a long series of fictional dialogues between a well-settled German inhabitant, or *Einwohner*, and a newly arrived immigrant, a *Neukommer*. The *Einwohner*, who represented Saur himself, was older, wiser, and sought to give advice to new immigrants so that they might be as successful as he had been. The *Neukommer* was young and came from a small, agrarian, nuclear village such as those in the Kraichgau.[42]

In the first year, the *Neukommer* encounters the *Einwohner* somewhere in the Pennsylvania German countryside. The *Neukommer* is looking for a comfortable place ("einen beqemen Platz") to settle, but is unfamiliar with the surroundings and seems to be suffering from a touch of culture shock: When the *Einwohner* asks him how he likes it here, the *Neukommer* replies, "One spoke of the New World in my country, and it is indeed a *new world* to me, for everything here is completely different than from where I came."[43] The *Neukommer*, who comes from the Palatinate, goes on to say what he likes so far about Pennsylvania: freedom of movement (without fines or fees), generous and helpful inhabitants, no tithes, no forced labor or feudal dues (*Frohnen*)—in short, the absence of an oppressive state and local aristocracy are what please him most about the colony.

I remember all the dues and fees I had to pay in the Palatinate, just so the sovereigns and bureaucrats could direct and exploit their great state. Then I see how the older settlers [*Einwohner*] here in this country live like nobles, indeed better than some nobles in Germany, for some who are worth in the neighborhood of 10–20,000 guilders only pay [in taxes] 5–10 guilders per year, and in some years nothing at all. And they pay only one guilder or maybe two for a poor tax, to help the poor and prevent them from showing up at the door as beggars.[44]

But there were also many things about Pennsylvania that the *Neukommer* did not like, especially the dispersed nature of settlements and the resulting social consequences. Most people lived relatively great distances from the nearest church, doctor, veterinarian, or school, and there were not enough preachers. The *Neukommer* came from a nuclear village with all these services. The village or parish had only one or two different churches, and perhaps a very small number of Mennonites or other small nonconformist religious groups. He found it a bit overwhelming that so many different religious groups lived dispersed yet intermixed throughout the countryside in which he had been wandering for several weeks. All of these problems, together with the increasing scarcity and high price of good land, were making it very difficult and time consuming for the *Neukommer* to find "einen bequemen Platz."

After describing this dilemma, the *Neukommer* summed up his entire experience since leaving Germany by stating what he was trying to do:

I made the difficult move across the sea so that I could improve my situation and establish for myself a peaceful life, as I once had had. To this end I have searched this land for the best place I can find and yet afford. While I can still work, I hope to set myself up in order that I shall have saved enough so that by the time I am old and can no longer work, I shall not need to. Thereafter I want to serve GOD so that I might be blessed in death.[45]

The *Neukommer* had been through a great deal and was willing to patiently search the Pennsylvania German countryside—for a long time if necessary—in order to find just the right place to settle. There he hoped to live, prosper, and die. But the country was vast and unfamiliar, and he knew that he could not make it alone, so he sought advice from a fellow countryman who had successfully maneuvered through the same process years earlier. He knew what he was looking for before leaving home, and his search for one place in which to finally settle down was the last stage of a single, hopeful journey that had begun when he walked or rode out of his village in the Palatinate.

*   *   *

The experiences of the Kraichgauers and others in colonial America suggest that German immigrants may have been stable ethnics rather than mobile individualists. This high level of stability, remarkable especially for a "migrant" population, facilitated the maintenance of the village and extended-family networks that were so critical in getting many immigrants settled and established within the rural, ethnic enclaves as well as the cities and towns of Greater Pennsylvania. Religion and ethnicity played important, mutually supportive roles in establishing the character and identity of the Reformed and Lutheran majority in the fledgling, scattered church communities throughout the colonies, but for the radical pietists—a small but influential minority—religion and the social organizations resulting from their religious beliefs played an overwhelming role in shaping the character of their migrations, settlement, and community in North America. The next chapter examines how the collective strategy of these groups led to unprecedented success in commercial-capitalist Greater Pennsylvania, where cultural cohesion and economic rationality could be and often were mutually supportive.

4

The Radical Pietist Alternative

ON OCTOBER 2, 1766, A GROUP MADE UP OF twelve girls (aged thirteen to seventeen years), four single women, one married woman whose husband was already in North Carolina, a single man who apparently accompanied the group without permission, and an English preacher and his wife bade an emotional farewell and departed Bethlehem, Pennsylvania, the headquarters community of the Moravian church in North America. Traveling with a large wagon, tents, supplies, and nine horses, this "choir," or living group, of girls (Moravians divided their communities into living groups separated by gender, age, and marital status) began a long migration to the Moravian colony called *die Wachau* (Wachovia), in North Carolina.[1] (A second wagon accompanied them as far as the Susquehanna River.) One of the travelers, a sixteen-year-old girl named Salome Meurer, wrote a fascinating journal while on the trail which reveals a great deal about the conditions of migration within Greater Pennsylvania for Moravians and others in the 1760s, as well as about the character of the people they encountered along the way.[2]

It did not take long for those in the surrounding countryside to realize that this was a very unusual party of migrants: eighteen teenage girls and women and only two men. In nearly every town they passed through from Pennsylvania to North Carolina, crowds of men gathered to watch, crack jokes, make passes at them, demonstrate their talents for consuming alcohol, or provide gentlemanly assistance. Sometimes these encounters took on a more serious tone. Drunks hung around the Moravians' tents at night, whistling and hooting. In the Virginia wilderness, some of the girls strayed off the trail and stumbled onto some "bad company" — six men who tried to kidnap them. For reasons to be explained further below, Moravian prejudices against Virginia had become well entrenched by this time: Salome Meurer disliked the colony intensely. Several other incidents in the colony did nothing to change her mind. The river crossings were frequent and dangerous, and torrential downpours often kept the travelers drenched for days on end. Wild geese and sometimes aggressive, unenclosed pigs running through the forest disturbed their camps and made off with their provisions. One night three Irishmen came to their camp and harassed them. One insisted that he be allowed to take a wife from the group and was chased away only with great difficulty. Meurer displayed extreme dislike for the slaves she encountered, especially those who ferried them across the rivers, until one night six slaves came to their campfire and visited with them for awhile. Thereafter, her references to slaves became more positive.

While the colony of girls and women made its way south, the Moravians in Bethabara, the headquarters community in Wachovia, prepared for their arrival. On October 6, a relief wagon went north to meet them halfway. After dropping off supplies and exchanging mail with the southbound column, the relief wagon continued on to Bethlehem. On October 24, Matthaeus Schrobb and Gottfried Grabs rode to meet Schrobb's wife coming down the trail. While in Corbintown (Hillsborough), North Carolina, they met his wife, Anna Maria Schrobb, Meurer, and a couple of others who had gone ahead of the main party. A celebration ensued, after which Richard and Sally Utley (the English couple) and the Schrobbs rode on to Bethabara, ahead of the others, arriving on October 30. The following day, October 31, the main party reached Bethabara as the band played "God Bless Thy Arrival" ("Euren Eingang segne Gott"). A love feast (a community meal consisting of tea and bread to celebrate special occasions) and singing followed, and the girls were shown their new quarters in the community house (*Gemeinhaus*).[3]

The Moravians were one of a large number of radical pietist immigrant groups in eighteenth-century America. Numerically, these groups made up only a small portion of the total German-speaking immigration into the thirteen colonies, but they were influential beyond their numbers, and by 1776 they constituted more than one-fourth of all German congregations. For them the religious community, not the home village, was the focal point of their collective strategy, and for some Moravians the process of migration itself played a special role in building their ideal communities.[4]

Radical Pietist Migrations

The radical pietists were small, dissenting religious groups, sometimes called "sects," that had contributed greatly to the diversification and "multiplication" of religions in central Europe since the Reformation (in some cases earlier) and in Pennsylvania since the late seventeenth century. They were not the "Pietists" who made up the large movement *within* the Lutheran and German Reformed churches during the late seventeenth and the eighteenth century. In fact, many Lutheran Pietists, such as Gottlieb Mittelberger, the organ player who reached Pennsylvania in 1750, condemned the proliferation of religions in the colony and attributed social ills there to the "blind zeal of the many sects." The peculiar ways of the radical pietists and their group migrations and settlements made them highly visible to contemporaries and later historians.[5]

The radical pietist alternative became attractive to some southwest Germans in the late seventeenth and early eighteenth centuries. After witnessing decades of religious warfare, persecutions, and the destruction of their society, many simply lost faith in the ability of the traditional churches to provide for their spiritual needs. As had happened in England, in Germany a large number of seekers, wanderers, and seers roamed the devastated southwest, gaining followers. Many older, relatively well-established radical pietist movements also experienced a rebirth or growth during this period.

Religious persecution and the search for purity or perfection motivated the emigration of these groups to both eastern Europe and North America. The Mennonites from the Palatinate and the middle and lower Rhine regions were the largest group leaving for either destination. Another large group, the Moravians, maintained communities throughout central Europe, as well as in England and Sweden, but their heaviest concentrations were in Saxony and Wetteravia. The Swiss Brethren came primarily from Germanic Switzerland and the Palatinate, while an offshoot from that movement, the Amish, came from those two regions and Alsace. The Church of the Brethren, also known as the Dunkers, the German Baptist Brethren, and other names, came from the Schwarzenau, Krefeld, Friesland, and the lower Neckar and Rhine regions. The Schwenkfelders came from Saxony and Silesia. Lastly, the Waldensians came from Württemberg.[6]

The reputation of the German-speaking radical pietists of Pennsylvania was great, and their efforts at proselytizing other German speakers were often quite successful, but the number who actually emigrated from Europe to the colonies was relatively small. Table 4.1 lists the major groups of radical pietists who emigrated before 1776.[7]

Table 4.1 suggests that the radical pietists accounted for less than 10

TABLE 4.1   German-Speaking Radical Pietist Immigration into the Thirteen Colonies.

	TOTAL IMMIGRATION IN PERSONS
Mennonites	1,536–4,200
Moravians	700– 750
Amish	265– 300
Dunkers	260– 300
Schwenkfelders	206
Waldensians	110
Total	3,077–5,550

Note: The figure for Mennonites also includes the Swiss Brethren, who had different origins than the Mennonites and came from different parts of Europe but are not distinguished in the source providing these figures. The Moravians were originally called the *Unitas Fratrum*, and they still use this name. About 140 Moravian immigrants were not from German-speaking lands and thus are not included in the table. The Dunkers were known by several names, the preferred one in English being the Church of the Brethren.

Sources: See note 7.

percent of the entire German-speaking immigration. The table does not include European- or American-born persons who converted to one of these groups in the colonies, nor does it include radical pietist groups such as the cloister at Ephrata, Pennsylvania, or the Weberites in South Carolina, both of which were formed in the colonies. There were a few other religious groups, and even individuals such as the Separatist printer Christopher Saur, who were radical pietist immigrants, but their total numbers were very small and grew larger only after arrival in the colonies. Estimates for the Dunkers, Waldensians, Moravians, and especially the Schwenkfelders are more accurate than for others. The figures in the left column represent a minimum number of immigrants, while the figures in the right column represent a rough estimate of maximum immigration. The range of 3,077 to 5,550 is only 3.6 to 6.5 percent of the total German-speaking immigration (about 85,000 immigrants).

From the beginning, most radical pietists migrated in groups, often constituting the majority if not all passengers on their respective ships. Franz Daniel Pastorius led forty-two Quakers and Mennonites to Philadelphia on the *Concord* in 1683. The following year about twenty-five Rosecrucians arrived, and, in 1694, Johannes Kelpius led a group of forty people to the wilderness near Germantown. Almost all of the Church of the Breth-

TABLE 4.2 Immigration of German-Speaking Radical Pietists into the Thirteen Colonies by Year, 1717–1775.

YEAR	AMISH	MORAVIANS	MENNONITES	DUNKERS	SCHWENKFELDERS	WALDENSIANS	TOTAL
1717	2		300				302
1719				44			44
1722				22			22
1725				1			1
1727	1		160				161
1728			35				35
1729				130			130
1731			17		1		18
1732			140	1			141
1733	6		70	2	11		89
1734		2			170		172
1735		8		2	1		11
1736	2	24	40		8		74
1737	49		120		14		183
1738		3					3
1740	10	7					17
1741		9					9
1742	45	71	75				191
1743		115					115
1744	12	5	70				87
1745		5					5
1746		11					11
1747		1					1
1748		22					22
1749	24	110	149				283
1750	40	94	120			9	263
1751	3	21	60			23	107
1752	15	35				6	56
1753	5	34				63	102
1754	1	87	180			9	277
1755	5						5
1756		19					19
1758		1					1
1761		46					46
1763		11					11
1764		2					2
1765		3					3
1766		4					4
1767	7	1					8
1768		3					3

TABLE 4.2   Continued

YEAR	AMISH	MORA-VIANS	MENNO-NITES	DUNKERS	SCHWENK-FELDERS	WALDEN-SIANS	TOTAL
1769	2	3					5
1770	3	17					20
1771		4					4
1772		1					1
1773		7					7
1774		3					3
Unknown	33	41		58	1		133
Total	265	830	1,536	260	206	110	3,207

Note: The Swiss Brethren are included with Mennonites. The Moravian total includes those not from German-speaking lands.

Sources: See sources for Table 4.1.

ren came on three ships: Forty-four arrived in Philadelphia in 1719 and twenty-two in 1722; in 1729 all 130 passengers on the *Allen* belonged to that group. In 1734, 170 Schwenkfelders arrived on the *St. Andrew*. Over half of the Amish arrived on five ships, including at least forty-nine on the *Charming Nancy* in 1737 and forty-five on the *Francis & Elizabeth* in 1742. About sixteen Waldensians reached Philadelphia on the *Patience* in 1751 and sixty-three on the same ship two years later. The Mennonites migrated in relatively large numbers, usually in large groups over a long period of time, forty-five came on the *Molly* in 1727, and thirty-two arrived on the *Samuel* and seventy on the *Samuel & Plaisance* in 1732. A list of arrivals of the radical pietist immigrants indicates the clustered nature of their migrations (see Table 4.2).[8]

After arriving in Philadelphia, most of the radical pietists moved into the Pennsylvania German countryside and settled in separate townships. The Mennonite, Moravian, Church of the Brethren, Amish, and Schwenkfelder immigrants (probably well over 90 percent of all the radical pietists) established congregations in ninety-three Pennsylvania townships, and of these seventy-three contained only one of the groups and seventeen contained two. Only Tulpehocken in Berks County and Upper Milford in Northampton contained three of the pietist groups, and only German-town contained four. In other words, while these immigrants chose to settle within the larger boundaries established by all German immigrant

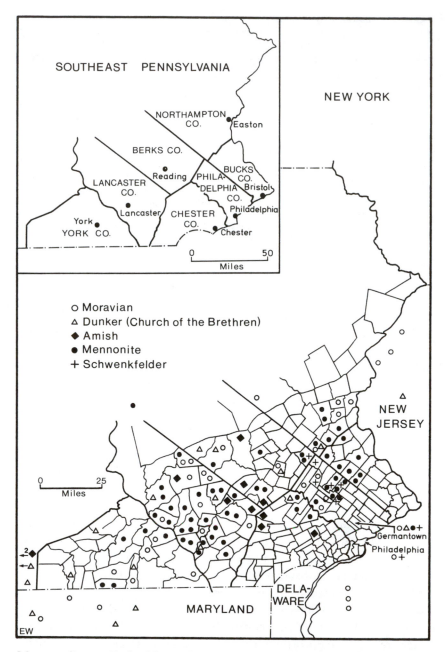

Map 4.1. German Radical Pietist Immigrant Congregations in Colonial Pennsylvania, New Jersey, and Maryland. *Sources*: See sources for Table 4.1. For the Mennonites, see also Cappon, *Atlas of Early American History*, 38.

groups, individual radical pietist groups tended not to mix with other pietist groups (see Map 4.1).[9]

At first glance the radical pietist congregations appear to be scattered throughout the Pennsylvania German countryside, but in reality, many were concentrated in certain areas. The Mennonites, Moravians, and Church of the Brethren scattered the most, but the majority of the Moravian immigrants settled in two closed communities at Bethlehem and Nazareth in Northampton County, and a significant number settled in the closed community at Lititz, in Lancaster County. The Mennonites were concentrated in central Lancaster County and in the upper portions of Chester, Philadelphia, and Bucks and southern Northampton counties.

The Amish and especially the Schwenkfelders settled not only in distinct townships, but also in clusters of townships occupying relatively small corners of southeastern Pennsylvania. The Amish began settling in upper Berks County during the 1730s. Later, many began moving into southern Lancaster and northern Chester counties. It was not until the late 1760s and early 1770s that they began expanding into western Pennsylvania. The 200-plus Schwenkfelder immigrants concentrated in upper Philadelphia, lower Berks, and southern Northampton counties. In fact, 87 percent of the 157 Schwenkfelder immigrants for whom place of death is known died in the adjacent or nearby townships of Macungie (Northampton County), Hereford (Berks), Upper Hanover, Lower Salford, Towamencin, Worcester, and Frederick (all in Philadelphia County).

Thus many radical pietist immigrants settled in distinct enclaves that dotted the Pennsylvania German countryside. A closer examination of the overseas and internal migrations of one extremely well-documented group, the Moravians, reveals the dynamics of this process.

The Case of the Moravians

The Moravians were a small, pietistic religious group descended from the radical wing of the fifteenth-century Hussite movement in Bohemia and Moravia that eventually came to be known as the *Unitas Fratrum*. They placed heavy emphasis on biblicism and revelation. After their reorganization and renewal, officially proclaimed in 1727 on the Saxony estate of their new leader, Count Zinzendorf, the Moravians entered into a militant, ecumenical, expansionist phase, and simultaneously began to develop an unusual form of spiritualism that soon permeated their liturgy, as well as their social organization and lifestyles.[10]

Yet the Moravians were not subsistence-farming, localist sectarians trying to remove themselves from the world in order to practice a pure, exclusive religion. Instead, they were a highly organized, tolerant, ecumenical, even cosmopolitan church. Though their numbers were small, the Moravians tried to maintain close contacts with the surrounding religious world. From their European headquarters in Saxony, and later Wetteravia, they reached out to persecuted radical pietist groups such as the Schwenkfelders and offered them shelter and support—which aroused suspicion among many adherents of the state church. On the other hand, the Moravians tried to maintain amicable relations with the Lutheran state church, and during Zinzendorf's lifetime (up to 1760) they insisted that they were a part of that church. They played an important role in an ecumenical movement that developed among radical pietists in Pennsylvania in the late 1730s and early 1740s. Rather than isolating themselves within subsistence economies as the Amish had done, the Moravians became skillful at debt-financing to cover the expenses of their expanding, worldwide network of closed communities, congregations, and missionary outposts, which included the construction of thriving industries and centers of commerce. Moravians placed heavy emphasis on education and literacy for all of its members and on university education for its clergy.

The explanation for this seemingly contradictory lifestyle which combined extremely pietistic, spiritualistic religiosity in a small group of true believers—some would call them a "sect"—with a cosmopolitan, ecumenical *Weltanschauung*, lies in a pietist concept called "separating to unite." In the late seventeenth and early eighteenth centuries many pietists, especially those within the Lutheran church, articulated and attempted to implement this principle.[11] Pietists believed in a "true" church, which consisted of those living in intimate communion with Christ, and a false, or fallen church, which they associated with the confessional churches of their times. There were true believers or regenerate souls in the midst of the larger, corrupt, confessional churches and among the smaller sects. They hoped the truly regenerate could separate themselves from the unregenerate and make themselves visible, so that they could unite according to true Christian principles. Although they would still retain membership in their formal church, they would meet with each other separately and reform the entire Church; in other words, they sought to finish the Reformation. The Moravians reflected the quintessence of this concept, whose development in German-speaking lands is associated in the Lutheran church with the movement known as "Pietism," led first by Philipp Jakob Spener and later by August Hermann Francke. But the Moravians were not a recognized church and had to struggle to maintain their existence and identity, even when they claimed to be part of the Lutheran church. From these difficult beginnings (or new beginnings) in the 1720s and 1730s, they launched a worldwide missionary program, and, under the principle of separating to unite, they hoped to unify all Protestant territorial churches and denominations into a single religious confederation under their leadership.[12]

Part of the reason contemporaries and later historians thought of the Moravians as a "sect," or an exclusive religious group that regards itself alone as the true Church, was because their unusual social organization in some ways resembled that of other radical pietist groups, some of which were more or less sectarian. In the 1730s, when Moravian theology and spiritualism began to undergo major changes, Zinzendorf developed an ideal of "community marriage," in which the community of Moravian believers was divided, cloisterlike, into living groups, or choirs, based upon age, sex, and marital status. He based this ideal on a "metaphysics of gender" (*Metaphysik der Geschlechter*). There were important differences, but in their choir system the Moravians resembled the hermetic cloister at Ephrata, in Lancaster County, which was extremely sectarian and isolationist.[13]

The choir system, developed in Germany and transplanted to North America, was central to the organization and direction of Moravian society. Moravians compartmentalized themselves into living, economic, and religious groups determined by their gender and status in life: single women, married women, single men, married men, and so forth lived, worked, and worshipped in separate groups. Such measures were most strictly observed during the period known as the "General Economy," which lasted roughly from the late 1730s to, in some communities, as late as the 1770s. Some features of the choir system continued for many years thereafter. Each choir had its own leadership, kept its own diary, and organized its own work schedule and religious life. Even in death, the choir system predominated. Moravians buried their dead in straight rows and columns, each in chronological order of death, and separated by gender and status in life. Not all Moravians lived in these exclusive, compartmentalized, and gendered communities, but their headquarters and a few other communities in both Europe and North America were so constructed, and the majority of the pre-1776 immigrants to North America eventually settled and died in such communities.

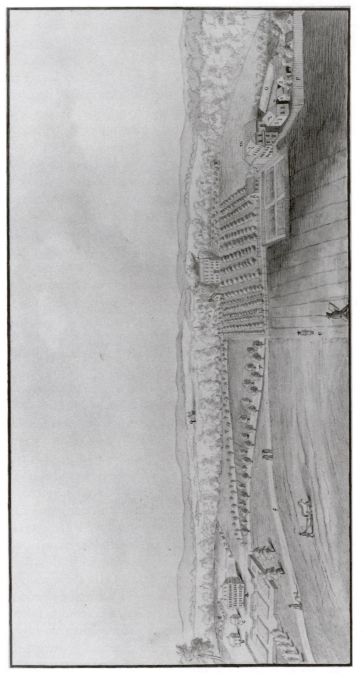

17. Nicholas Garrison's 1761 view of the Moravian community at Nazareth, in Northampton County, Pennsylvania. The Manor House, is the large building on the left. The large building in the center is the Whitefield House. These buildings, and many others from the colonial period, are still standing in Nazareth. (Courtesy of the Moravian Historical Society.)

In general, the Moravian choirs and the rest of their society in the eighteenth century were oriented and directed from the top down. With only a few hundred members and limited financial resources the Moravian leadership became masters of organization and planning in order to establish and maintain their huge networks of missions and communities. During the period of the General Economy, the church regulated all economic activity, and a system of collective ownership of the means of production was implemented. Moravians living in the General Economy received no wages for their work and were provided housing (separately, by choir), food, and other provisions by the church.

At the head of the rapidly expanding network of closed communities, open congregations, and missionary outposts in North America was a huge cadre of clergy and nobility. The immigrant church contained an incredibly high ratio of clergy to lay members—a ratio no other German church in the colonies could match. Of the 830 known Moravian immigrants who arrived in North America by 1775, 170 (20 percent) were either ministers (that is, ordained clergy) or very high church officials who did at least some preaching and evangelizing, either to Native Americans or to Germans and other colonists. In 1753 a Moravian census enumerated just over 1,600 white members in the North American colonies. (By then 648 of the 830 immigrants had arrived.) These figures do not even include the large number of men and women who held lesser church offices or some of the other positions within the community hierarchy, such as the choir leaders. In stark contrast, about 80,000 German Reformed and Lutheran immigrants had arrived in the colonies by 1776, yet only some eighty Reformed and eighty-six Lutheran ministers had served this population and their descendants, and many of these were lay ministers, much less "qualified" than the Moravians.[14]

The presence of large numbers of nobility in their ranks is further evidence of the top-heavy nature of Moravian society.[15] In addition to the leader of the Moravian church, Count Zinzendorf, there were at least seventeen other families of noble birth living in the North American colonies at one time or another, and many occupied important leadership positions. Frederic Wilhelm von Marschall, for example, was an aristocrat from Saxony who held the most powerful post in Wachovia (*Oeconomus*) from 1763 until his death in 1802. The residence the Moravians built in Nazareth for Zinzendorf symbolizes the aristocratic influence in Moravian society. Begun with pomp and circumstance in 1755 and completed the following year, this enormous structure (which still stands) may very well have been

18. A nineteenth-century view of the Manor House, or Nazareth Hall. Built as a residence for Count Zinzendorf in 1755–1756, this enormous structure may have been the largest residence constructed for a single person or family in colonial America. Zinzendorf never occupied the dwelling, however, and it was used to house missionaries. The community chapel lay in the center section of the first two floors. (Courtesy of the Moravian Historical Society.)

the largest residence built for a single person or family in British North America, though Zinzendorf never occupied it. The nobility and clergy played crucial roles in planning, organizing, and carrying out the Moravian overland migrations in the colonies, just as they had for the overseas migrations.[16]

Migration and the Moravian Community

The way the Moravians migrated reflects many aspects of their community. For most German and other voluntary immigrants in the American colonies, the purpose of migration was to leave difficult circumstances in Europe in order to find a better life in America, but for the Moravians, there were additional purposes. In both their overseas and internal migrations Moravians sought to escape persecution, begin or help sustain their ecumenical and missionary efforts, provide the necessary labor and skills to help run the General Economy, and construct their ideal closed community in the "proper way." Planning and decisions about who would make overseas or overland journeys took place until 1738 in Herrnhut, the original headquarters in Saxony. When the Saxon court banished Count Zinzendorf from that state, he transferred the center of Moravian operations to Herrnhag, in Wetteravia. In 1749, Count Büdingen began ejecting Moravians from his estates in Wetteravia, and Zinzendorf once again moved his headquarters, this time back to Herrnhut, where the Saxon government had agreed to tolerate them once again. One of the consequences of this kind of planning and organization, and of the adept financing that accompanied it, was that the Moravians were able to safely transport hundreds of their members across the North Atlantic and to establish them in communities in North America.

The machinery of Moravian migrations was set into motion at meetings and in discussions of the church's leaders at their various headquarters communities in Germany, Pennsylvania, and North Carolina. First the elders considered the needs of the communities—whether they were proposed new communities or established communities that had asked for more people. Then the planners asked for volunteers, conducted careful screenings of all persons available for the enterprise, and used the Lot (the customary mode of deciding questions in Moravian church councils and conferences) to sanctify their decisions. Thereafter the church leadership informed members of their selection and departure dates, often on very short notice. They did not force anyone to go, but in general church members could not emigrate unless they had been selected. The conferences and committees planning the migrations then sent instructions to the Moravian colonies established on the primary routes of travel: in Zeyst on the Rhine (in Holland), Rotterdam, London, New York, and Bethlehem for the Pennsylvania migrants, and in Wachovia for those traveling to that colony. Instructions to the colonies indicated when and how many migrants they should expect to meet, take care of, and send along to the next station.[17]

The experience of Johann Philipp Meurer reflects the nature of the planning and organization of Moravian overseas migrations.[18] Meurer was the father of Salome, the young woman who migrated with the group of girls and women from Bethlehem to Wachovia in 1766. He was a shoemaker from Alsace who became acquainted with the Moravians in Strasbourg in 1737. He went to Herrnhag with two others in 1740. According to his diary, he was asked on November 9, 1741, if he wanted to go to Pennsylvania, and he felt flattered and honored that he had been chosen. On November 22 church officials confirmed that he would go. From December 9 to December 19, the Moravians from Herrnhut who would travel with Meurer's group arrived in Herrnhag, while Meurer himself received instructions and advice. On December 19, everyone going to Pennsylvania gathered together for the first time in nearby Marienborn and held a love feast. Thereafter they were divided into seven choirs (four for married persons and three for single persons); Meurer led a group of five single brethren. The next day the bishop, David Nitschmann, spoke with Meurer's group, reminding members that they should be going voluntarily and that anyone who wished could stay behind. He also reminded them that no one should leave with anything weighing upon their heart, or it could be the death of them.

On December 20, 1741, just six weeks after Meurer's initial notification that he might be going to America, the emigrants began their journey, each group, or choir, traveling separately. On December 30 Meurer's group reached Heerendyk, the Moravian colony on the Rhine near Utrecht (in the Netherlands) that served as one of the gathering and provisioning points for the overseas voyage. (The colony in nearby Zeyst would take over this function in 1746.) By January 4, 1742, all seven groups had arrived in Heerendyk. They tarried there for a month, making preparations and holding conferences. By February 2, three individuals experienced a change of heart and returned to Marienborn. On February 6 they finally departed—the brothers walked in three groups to Rotterdam, while the sisters went by ship. Two others from Amsterdam joined them, and on February 8 some of the emigrants boarded an English ship, the *Samuel and Elizabeth*, bound for London, where they arrived on February 24. Members of the London congregation took them in the following day, and on February 26, August Gottlieb Spangenberg, the highest official in the church next to Zinzendorf, formed them into the "sea congregation," so called because they became a religious community of choirs and continued to worship during the ocean crossing.

On March 16, 1742, the First Sea Congregation sailed down the Thames on the *Catherine*, passing a sunken ship along the way—a sobering reminder of the risk they were taking by sailing while Britain was at war with Spain. After being chased by a Spanish privateer and enduring a stormy crossing of the North Atlantic, they reached Long Island Sound on May 21 and weighed anchor at New London, Connecticut, two days later. The "stirred-up," or awakened, state of the many visitors to the ship and the people who followed them around New London encouraged the Moravians. They preached every day to standing-room-only crowds. They then sailed to New Haven, where crowds gathered to greet them and hear them preach, and where a group of Yale students came to debate doctrine with them. Continuing through Long Island Sound, they reached New York on May 30. After a difficult trip down the coast and up the Delaware River, the First Sea Congregation arrived in Philadelphia on June 6.

Several Moravians, including Count Zinzendorf, greeted Meurer and the other new arrivals on board the *Catherine* in Philadelphia. For the first few days, while Moravians already in Pennsylvania made preparations for them in Bethlehem and Nazareth, the new immigrants lived on shipboard, supported and visited by the small Moravian contingent living in Philadelphia. They were also trying to keep a low profile by staying on the ship. In contrast to the enthusiastic greetings they received from the crowds in Connecticut and New York, the Great Awakening in Pennsylvania had taken a decidedly anti-Moravian turn. The count's ecumenical synods, in which most of the German religious groups initially participated, were going badly, and tensions were high when the First Sea Congregation docked in Philadelphia. On June 15 the first group finally departed for Bethlehem. Most of the members of the First Sea Congregation went to Bethlehem, but the English Moravians went to Nazareth. Meurer's group departed Philadelphia and stopped in Germantown and New Hanover, where they met other Moravians. On June 21 they reached Bethlehem, thus ending their long journey.

Meurer's journey from Marienborn in 1741–1742 down the Rhine to

Rotterdam, across the English Channel to London, and then across the North Atlantic to Philadelphia was a typical one for most German immigrants insofar as the route and timing are concerned, but otherwise there were few similarities. In addition to being part of a colony with a religious mission, Meurer was also part of the first relatively large Moravian migration to North America (forty-five members were on the *Catherine*) in which the leadership of the church established a pattern of careful planning and organization. Whether later immigrants landed in New York, Philadelphia, or Charleston, South Carolina, most traveled along routes established by preceding parties and received support from Moravian communities along the way, as was the case with Meurer's group in 1742.

In the end, Meurer and the other members of the First Sea Congregation avoided most of the difficulties that other immigrants encountered in Rotterdam, in England, and upon reaching Philadelphia. Rather than struggling to pay off their debts in the often exploitative and unhealthy environment of the city, Meurer's group was able to move fairly quickly to their prearranged backcountry communities of Bethlehem and Nazareth, thus bypassing the difficulties so many other immigrants before them had experienced.

The missionary and ecumenical impulses heavily influenced where Moravian planners decided to locate their expanding network of closed communities, open congregations, and mission outposts in North America. The location of other Germans and Native Americans, among whom they hoped to proselytize, and the resistance of some religious groups (especially the Lutherans) were crucial factors in shaping Moravian settlement patterns. The leadership in Herrnhut, Herrnhag, and especially in Bethlehem chose the locations of new Moravian settlements and congregations based upon scouting reports of explorers or itinerant ministers that indicated where the best prospects of awakening or converting other Germans might be. Further migrations of choirs established new closed communities, while itinerant preachers roamed the countryside to establish small congregations of the converted among other German communities, and missionaries traveled alone or in small groups to set up outposts among the Native Americans. As these networks became more extensive, the Moravians migrating overland among these communities received better support along the way.

Because the Moravians hoped to settle near other Germans and preach to them, their general settlement patterns corresponded closely to those of German immigrants as a whole. The large majority settled initially in

Pennsylvania (although most arrived in New York, not Philadelphia). Most settled in the backcountry of the Pennsylvania German areas, and some helped settle Greater Pennsylvania (see Map 4.2).

The Moravians had begun their first settlement on the North American continent at Savannah, Georgia, in February 1735, following in the wake of other German-speaking immigrants. A group of Lutherans from the Archbishopric of Salzburg had begun settling in Savannah the previous year, and a large number of German-speaking Swiss immigrants arrived on the *Two Brothers* with the ten-man Moravian party led by Spangenberg in 1735. Later that year, David Nitschmann led twenty-four Moravian men and women to Savannah on the *Simmons*. (Among the other passengers on this ship were John and Charles Wesley, and the governor of Georgia, James Oglethorpe.) [19]

The Moravians abandoned the Georgia settlement, however, and in 1740 and 1741 began moving into Pennsylvania, which by that time had once again become the destination of the large majority of German immigrants. While in Georgia they had been under pressure to fight against the Spanish, but the primary reason for their move was that Zinzendorf wanted to center the Native American mission in Pennsylvania and at the same time begin a worldwide ecumenical movement among the Germans in that colony. The Moravians quickly built two closed communities, Nazareth and Bethlehem, in Northampton County, and open congregations in Philadelphia and Oley (in Berks County). They then began extending their network of communities throughout the Pennsylvania German countryside and into New York, eastern New Jersey, and western Maryland.

When the Moravians attempted to move into the Shenandoah Valley of Virginia in the mid- and late 1740s, however, they encountered resistance, and their expansion in Greater Pennsylvania ground to a halt. The resistance came from German Lutherans in the Valley, but its origins lay in the Moravian-Lutheran conflict in Pennsylvania and even in Europe.

The Moravian plan to unite all the German religious groups in Pennsylvania had failed by the summer of 1742, but bitter feelings remained, especially among Lutherans, as they and many others resented what they perceived to be a blatant attempt by the Moravians to impose their order on all the Germans of Pennsylvania. It was at this time that the Moravians began immigrating in large numbers, bringing their proselytizing clergy and missionaries into a colony heavily populated with German Reformed and Lutheran inhabitants who had almost no clergy or church organi-

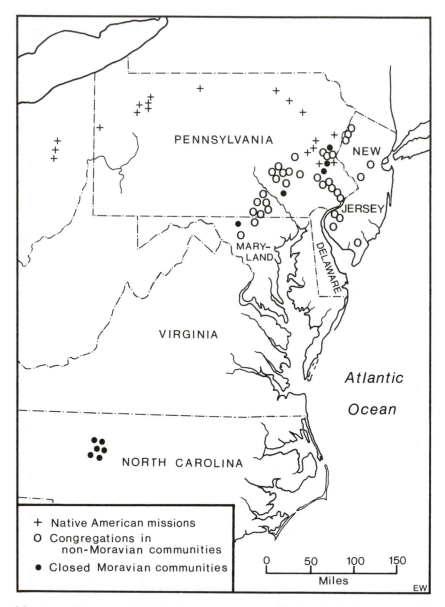

+ Native American missions

O Congregations in
  non-Moravian communities

● Closed Moravian communities

Map 4.2. Moravian Communities in Greater Pennsylvania. *Sources*: Abraham Reincke, "A Register of Members of the Moravian Church between 1727–1754," *Transactions of the Moravian Historical Society*, 1 (1873), 283–426; burial and other church records; and *General-Catalogus von denen Seelen die in der Brüder Pflege sind in America zu Anfang des Jahres 1753* (Moravian Archives, Bethlehem).

zation of their own. Further, the Moravians were just then reaching the height of their new mystic spiritualism, which Lutheran pietists in Germany had already condemned.

For the outnumbered Lutheran clergy, their worst nightmare began to unfold in 1742, as the Moravians turned their attentions away from the failed ecumenical movement and toward the Lutheran population. That summer, Zinzendorf established himself as the head of the Lutheran church in Philadelphia and began to direct Moravian-Lutheran activities from there. This was intolerable to the Lutheran pietists in Halle (in Saxony), who despised the Moravians for their extreme spiritualism, predestinarian teachings, militant expansionism, and for the pompous behavior of their count. Halle had already sent a young minister, Henry Melchior Muhlenberg, to the colonies to undermine Zinzendorf's efforts. Muhlenberg arrived in Philadelphia in November 1742. He was eventually able to wrest control from the count and began organizing the Lutherans in the colony along the pietistic lines acceptable to the Halle leadership, but this took time.[20]

Meanwhile, the sparks of the Moravian-Lutheran conflict scattered throughout the colonies, as rumors and anti-Moravian pamphlets circulated, and Muhlenberg and other Lutheran clergy implored their flocks to "beware." Muhlenberg disliked the Moravians and Zinzendorf as much as the Lutheran leadership in Halle did. He had known them since 1739, when he received an appointment from Halle to administer a school and later to pastor the Lutherans on Zinzendorf's estate in Groß Hennersdorf, in Saxony. In 1751 Muhlenberg wrote, "The true church of Jesus Christ had never since the time of the Apostles had a more harmful, dangerous, and sly enemy as the Zinzendorfian sect."[21] This kind of statement from the normally cool-headed Muhlenberg reflects the intense emotions the Moravian-Lutheran conflict generated as the Moravians made their first rapid moves to extend their network throughout Greater Pennsylvania in the early days of settlement.

This intense anti-Moravian sentiment among Lutherans reached the Shenandoah Valley by the mid-1740s, and was so strong that it prevented the Moravians from ever gaining a foothold there, or anywhere in Virginia, despite their efforts.

In the 1740s several Moravian missionary scouts based in Pennsylvania began roaming up and down the Shenandoah Valley and even west of the Valley, into the mountains. They sought out German settlements there, none of which had regular pastors, and preached to them. Early on, they

concentrated their efforts in the lower Shenandoah Valley and the German settlements east of the Blue Ridge at Germanna, Germantown, and
Little Fork. This entire region had been heavily settled by Germans, so the
missionaries had little trouble finding German communities. Most of the
inhabitants there saw a minister only once every three or four years and
so were happy to receive communion from the Moravians or to have their
children baptized. They usually lodged the Moravian ministers and gave
them directions to the next German settlement. In late 1742 one missionary reached Patterson's Creek, fifty miles west of the Shenandoah.[22]

But nearly everywhere the Moravian scouts encountered hostility, and
eventually the project was abandoned. When Leonhard Schnell and Robert
Hussey passed through Virginia and the Carolinas on their way to Georgia
in 1744, they heard strange anti-Moravian stories and rumors, including
one about a new religion in Pennsylvania (Moravianism) that promoted
rituals in which people were given a magic potion to drink so that they
would adhere to the sect and turn over all their possessions. Sometimes
the missionaries were forced to deny that they were Moravians in order to
escape difficult situations. Moravians often had some success at the beginning of their tours in the lower Valley, and then moved on to preach in
the upper Valley or in the mountains. But as they passed through the Valley again, on their way home to Pennsylvania, they encountered problems.
On several occasions Lutherans and others had been spreading rumors
and circulating anti-Moravian tracts during their absence. When Leonard
Schnell and Vitus Handrup returned to Fredricktown (now Winchester)
after a long tour in the upper Valley, settlers warned them about the Virginia governor's report forbidding their activities. They chose to remain
there overnight, however, and the next day hurried across the Potomac,
just eluding the Fredericktown justice of the peace.[23]

The failures in Virginia in the 1740s and the renewed pressures on
the church in Germany led the Moravian leadership to bypass permanent
settlement in that colony and to begin making plans for moving into North
Carolina. In 1749, Count Büdingen informed Zinzendorf that he would no
longer tolerate the Moravian presence on his estates in Wetteravia. Shortly
thereafter, the Moravians began making plans to move many of the nearly
3,000 members living there to a new settlement in North Carolina, Wachovia. By 1753 abandonment of the Wetteravian settlements was nearly complete. Also in that year the first settlers from Pennsylvania reached the
100,000-acre tract that the church had purchased deep in the backcountry
of North Carolina.[24] A large emigration from Wetteravia to North Caro-

TABLE 4.3 Moravian Immigration into Wachovia, 1753–1771.

YEAR	N	YEAR	N
1753	11	1763	1
1754	9	1764	21
1755	37	1765	1
1756	12	1766	42
1757	6	1767	2
1758	11	1768	12
1759	9	1769	8
1760	4	1770	5
1762	17	1771	13
Total: 221 persons			

Source: From Fries, *Moravian Records*, I, 484–492.

lina never materialized, but more than 200 European- and American-born Moravians did migrate to the colony by 1771. Most traveled in groups, and many in separate choirs (see Table 4.3).

The Moravian internal migrations to North Carolina demonstrate how the church leadership used migrations to provide labor and skills as well as other components of their ideal communities. Like their overseas migrations, the Moravian migrations from Pennsylvania to North Carolina were well planned, well organized, and well financed. Columns of migrants left Bethlehem heading southward only after the Moravian leadership in Herrnhut, Bethlehem, and Wachovia had decided what the settlement's requirements were—in numbers and in the skills of men, women, boys, and girls. After the migrants were chosen and financial arrangements were made, the committees responsible sent advance instructions to the communities along the trail, telling them how many travelers to expect and when.

The first colony of Moravians to migrate from Pennsylvania to North Carolina left Bethlehem on October 8, 1753.[25] Fifteen single brethren with a large wagon and a tent followed the trail of the earlier missionaries through western Maryland and up the Shenandoah Valley, on the so-called Great Wagon Road.[26] After a very difficult trip, in which they were often lost and had to traverse many steep mountains, tying a tree to the wagon and locking the brakes on the downward slopes to maintain control, they sighted Pilot Mountain (just across the North Carolina border), which helped guide them toward the 100,000-acre tract they had purchased from the Earl of Granville.[27]

When subsequent columns of Moravians migrated overland to North Carolina, they received a great deal of support from their fellow members who lived along the trail. Indeed, most were able to stay overnight at the homes of other Moravians nearly every day of the journey—except while in Virginia. Salome Meurer and many other Moravians like her, who migrated through Greater Pennsylvania to Wachovia, disliked Virginia because of the lack of support networks there. Perhaps they had also heard stories about the itinerant preachers who had worked there in the 1740s and encountered such strong anti-Moravian sentiments.[28]

A series of three group migrations to Wachovia in 1766 reflect the dynamics of Moravian planning and organization. In August 1765, the Unity Directors in Herrnhut informed the Elders' Conference in Bethabara, North Carolina, that they were sending one married couple and eight single men to their community to assist in their efforts. Most of the emigrants were already in Zeyst (Holland), preparing to travel to London. In addition, the directors included biographies of the emigrants, descriptions of their capabilities, and general instructions as to how they should be employed, though the Elders' Conference in Bethabara would have the final say in that matter. They also sent a thirteen-point memorandum to the emigrants, giving them travel tips and advising them about how to get along with each other, especially since some were English and did not speak German. In the autumn of 1765, the Reverand John Ettwein in Bethabara received word that new immigrants would arrive soon and sent Jacob Steiner to Charleston to meet them and pick up supplies.[29]

On January 30, 1766, the first group (the married couple and the eight single men) reached Bethabara, thus meeting the immediate requirements for the single men's choir, but Bethabara still needed boys and girls, as well as more men. In April, the Elders' Conference wrote to the Provincial Synod in Bethlehem, asking for a half-dozen boys and two more men with a taste and aptitude for farming. They also asked for a dozen older girls, some craftsmen (for example, a hatter, a dyer, a turner, and several carpenters and masons), and a surgeon (to replace Dr. Schubert, who had disliked life in Bethabara and had left the community). The synod advised Bethlehem not to send the new settlers until the autumn, however, because the Bethabara community would be unable to provide the necessary guides, food, and other necessities until then.[30]

In June, Frederic Wilhelm von Marschall, still in Bethlehem, replied to Bethabara's request for help. He informed them that Jacob Bonn (a resident of Wachovia since 1758) was to become their new surgeon. Further-

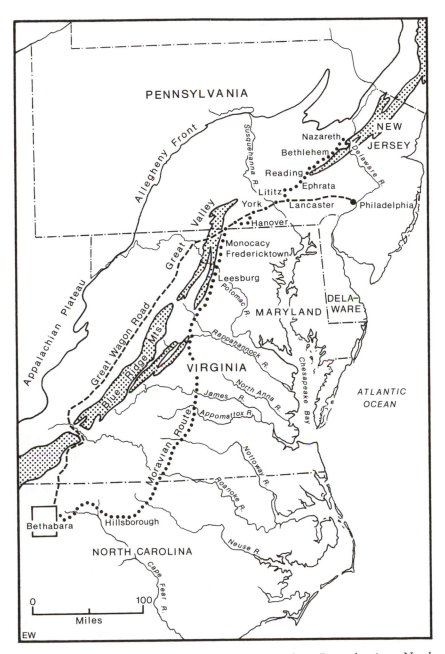

Map 4.3. The Primary Moravian Migration Route from Pennsylvania to North Carolina. *Sources*: Published and unpublished Moravian travel journals (see note 24).

more, the Pennsylvanians were planning to send a second and a third group from Bethlehem to Bethabara to meet the settlement's remaining requirements.[31]

The second group, a choir of eight boys just then completing their apprenticeships and their adult supervisors, arrived in Bethabara on October 11 and received a warm greeting from the brass band ("unter fröhlichen Schall der Trompeten"). Only one boy had misbehaved; two days later at a meeting, the elders decided to put the boy in question to work in the community kitchen. On October 15, the boys visited the new community of Salem, which would soon become the headquarters of Wachovia. Shortly after their return to Bethabara, each received his permanent assignment.[32]

The third and last group to migrate to Wachovia in 1766, a choir of girls and their supervisors, included the sixteen-year-old Salome Meurer, whose tale has already been told.

"Now Bethabara is a complete community with all its choirs," proclaimed the minister who kept the community diary when the girls and women in Salome Meurer's party arrived in North Carolina on October 31, 1766.[33] This statement, appropriately made by a minister in this top-down–oriented society, reveals the final priority in building the Moravian community: It was not enough to have skilled craftsmen, farmers, businessmen, housewives, children, and ministers in the community. Nor was it enough to achieve economic self-sufficiency, for Bethabara had accomplished this by 1758.[34] To build a "complete community" one had to construct and compartmentalize it the correct way—"with all its choirs." This the Moravians did by planning and organizing a series of migrations that, one after another, systematically provided the components of the community. At the close of 1766, 130 Moravians inhabited Bethabara. The same minister listed the 130-member community by its components in the diary:[35]

18 married couples	36
Widowers	3
Widows	4
Single Sisters	3
Older Girls	12
Younger Girls	5
Single Brethren	36
Older Boys	20
Younger Boys	11
Total	130

Soon the new town of Salem would replace Bethabara as the focal point of Moravian society in North Carolina. The leadership placed it in the middle of their large tract so that it would be roughly equidistant to all the other communities and act as a centripetal force, attracting the inhabitants inward, rather than toward the non-Moravian community. By 1772, the entire Wachovia project was complete.[36]

* * *

What did all this lead to, this commitment to the religious community above all else? To what extent did religion as the focal point of a collective strategy facilitate the migration, settlement, and establishment of the small minority who chose the radical pietist alternative in Europe and then pursued its callings to British North America? In a word: success, especially in surviving the journey and establishing themselves in the colonies.

Indeed, the radical pietists enjoyed tremendous success in emigrating to and settling within North America because they employed the methods of the most successful secular immigrants: utilizing good financing and/or a collective strategy toward finding their way across the ocean, through the bureaucratic, often corrupt and disease-ridden environment in Philadelphia, and into the increasingly crowded, expensive backcountry. The Mennonite, Amish, and Schwenkfelder migrations were exceptionally well organized and financed. The Dutch Mennonite Commission for Foreign Needs sponsored these groups, providing them with money, guidance, and information. In addition, many early Mennonite and Amish immigrants who had done well in the colonies paid the passage for later immigrants so that the newcomers could avoid indentured servitude. These immigrants, in general, maintained the pious character of their communities as they migrated and settled in groups; this strategy led directly to their relative success in an increasingly turbulent immigrant society where many succeeded and many failed.[37]

But the Moravians, with their unusual combination of spiritualism, collectivism, and engaging, cosmopolitan *Weltanschauung* were the most successful of all. With few exceptions they used their own ships and crews to bring over their flock, thus avoiding the exploitative ship captains, crews, and merchants that Gottlieb Mittelberger and others so harshly condemned. They also avoided the auction block, involuntary separation from family and friends, and other uncertainties of the redemptioner and indentured servant systems. These factors, combined with extensive, strategically located support networks on both sides of the Atlantic, and good plan-

ning and financing, led to a phenomenal survival rate and better health for
Moravian passengers: Only one of the 830 Moravian immigrants (0.1 percent) died during passage from Europe to North America. This figure was
sixteen times less than the death rate of the northern Kraichgau immigrants
and thirty-eight times less than that of all German-speaking immigrants
who arrived in Philadelphia. Indeed, many observers commented on the
relative good health of the Moravians upon their arrival in the colonies.[38]

What the Moravians and many other radical pietist and secular immigrants discovered after having immigrated and settled down in their ethnic-
religious enclaves was that they had transplanted themselves into a large,
diverse immigrant society with growing political problems—from within
and from without. If they wished to consolidate and build upon their successes so that their children might do even better, they could not merely
withdraw into their ethnic enclaves and passively observe (or ignore) the
growing crisis in colonial America. At the appropriate time they would
have to take to the streets, as many other colonials did, and act.

5

Germans in the Streets: The Development of German Political Culture in Pennsylvania

FOR A FEW DAYS IN LATE SEPTEMBER and early October 1765 there was a great deal of excitement on the streets of Philadelphia. More than 2,600 German-speaking immigrants from near and far descended on the city to be naturalized during the September Supreme Court session. This was more than one-fourth of all naturalizations in all thirteen colonies during the colonial period, ten times the number in Pennsylvania in 1764, and thirty times the number in the previous court session in April. The future citizens so overwhelmed the court that the officials had to extend their proceedings for more than three weeks into October. The clerk of the court apologized for the delay in writing to his father in England because he was overwhelmed with the paperwork.[1]

The Moravians seemed to be the only ones to keep the situation under control. Years before, they had developed a do-it-yourself "naturalization kit," which included German translations of all the appropriate declarations of loyalty the candidates would be called upon to affirm (not swear) before the court. In typical Moravian fashion, they planned in advance who needed to be naturalized, presented them with the kit, notified their fellow Moravians in Philadelphia when to expect the visitors, and sent them off. The entire affair lasted five days, including the 120-mile trip from Bethlehem to Philadelphia and back.[2]

But it was more than just naturalization that brought Germans and other inhabitants of Pennsylvania onto the streets of Philadelphia. The pending election for the Pennsylvania Assembly had become even more hotly contested than in 1764, and both sides were canvassing the streets, begging, bribing, and threatening violence to secure votes before elec-

19. This anonymous, anti-Franklin political cartoon, which appeared in Philadelphia in 1765, depicts some of the activities and excitement when many Germans and others took to the streets of the largest city in British North America. Note the crowd of Germans in the background waiting to vote at the steps of the courthouse. The angel proclaims, "The Germans are Victorious." (Courtesy of the Library Company of Philadelphia.)

tion day, which was October 1. Members of the Proprietary Party planned to arm their supporters in mostly German Lancaster County, crash into the courthouse during the election, and "thrash the Sheriff every Inspector Quaker & Menonist (Mennonite) to Jelly" should they show the least sign of partiality and not insure that all German voters were naturalized.[3] The primary issue of the election, as it had been in 1764, was whether or not Pennsylvania should become a royal colony or remain a proprietary colony owned by the Penn family. The voters and others followed Benjamin Franklin's moves in London closely as he tried to gain approval for the petition to make Pennsylvania a royal colony. Rumor had it that Franklin himself hoped to be made royal governor of Pennsylvania.[4]

Furthermore, many church activities brought people onto the streets. Internal dissension racked some of the Lutheran and German Reformed churches in and around Philadelphia. And the divided congregation at St. Michael's, pastored by Henry Melchior Muhlenberg, anxiously awaited the proprietor's approval of their new charter. The proprietor, Thomas Penn, finally approved the charter, hoping that by doing so he would win the Lutherans' votes in the election. Six hundred people met at St. Michael's the evening before the election to discuss the proposed charter, and two days later they all went together to the courthouse to vote. In early October, there were also several funerals that drew large crowds of Germans to the streets of Philadelphia.[5]

Muhlenberg administered communion (required for naturalization) to hundreds of Germans and then signed the certificates they would present at the Supreme Court. He wrote in his diary that there was "excessive hubbub and running in and out" of the city, while the newspapers in the country reported that new stamp duties would raise the price of naturalization as much as a hundred times—from two shillings to nine or ten pounds.[6]

The day after the election, the ship carrying the stamps from London appeared in Philadelphia harbor as the city's bells tolled solemnly. Thousands gathered at the State House while leading lawyers and merchants harangued them, and the people echoed with yeas and nays. The atmosphere on the streets was so tense, according to Muhlenberg, that "a single spark would have been able to kindle and set the whole dry, inflammable mass in flames and the houses of the stamp-master and others would have been demolished and not one stone left upon another."[7]

Thus at any given time in late September and early October 1765, literally hundreds of Germans from the countryside and Philadelphia wandered about the streets, waiting to be naturalized, voting, and otherwise contributing to the already excited atmosphere of the city. Those few days and weeks were a time of crowds, rumors, political action, anxieties, and fears in this, one of the largest cities in the British Empire. Mixed in with the familiar topics of the election, Franklin's petition for a royal government, and the Stamp Act crisis was this little known but extraordinary event of more than 2,600 Germans migrating to Philadelphia to be naturalized in the space of a few days.

What was happening? How were all these events connected, if connected they were? These events were part of the German immigrants' collective struggle for success, their struggle to maintain the foothold they had gained since arriving in Philadelphia and making their move into the countryside. Their return to the city—or, for those who had never left, their simultaneous reappearance in the streets with those who had—was in some ways the last act of a drama begun when they chose to leave Europe years earlier to try and make a better life in America.

The immigrants' struggles to overcome the obstacles awaiting them on the docks upon arrival and then acquire land in the countryside had long been issues in colonial politics. But now, in the mid-1760s—by which time German-speaking immigration had slackened considerably from the record levels of 1749–1754—the struggles of many earlier immigrants to protect the gains they had made were linked to the larger political issues of the day in new alliances and in a different kind of ethnic voting bloc. The colonial German political culture that had developed by this time was largely the product of their Old World communal tradition of defending their property and other rights whenever challenged by their rulers (see Chapter 2) and by their experiences in America as non-British immigrants. These two factors, rather than officeholding and the traditional factional politics of the colony, give form and meaning to German political activity in Pennsylvania.

Indeed, the events that involved so many Germans (and others) in the streets of Philadelphia during those autumn days of 1765 were symptomatic of the birth of not one but several new political orders in Pennsylvania: one represented by the Penns and the majority of the so-called "church" Germans, one by Franklin, and another, newer one, represented symbolically by the opposition to the Stamp Act, which would ultimately prevail. This chapter will follow the various threads of the story and then reassemble and explain these crowds in the streets of Philadelphia during those early autumn days of 1765.

Germans and Pennsylvania Politics

Many recent historians have rejected the long-held notion that Germans were passive in colonial politics or that they played at most a "supportive" role.[8] New studies point toward German activism in Pennsylvania politics, whereas most others have emphasized religion, class, and other components of that involvement.[9] Earlier historians held that ethnic political behavior only became important during the Revolutionary Era and the 1790s.[10]

But the surge of ethnic political activity during Pennsylvania's "internal revolution" of 1776–1778 and later did not spring from a void, nor were its progenitors merely the religious and other issues of late colonial America that happened to have affected a people called "German" or "Dutch." Instead, it followed a generation of German political activism that occurred during the period of peak immigration and settlement. This activism was a part of the collective strategy that many German-speakers adopted during the process of migration and settlement. As with the other elements of their strategy, its origins lay both in Europe and in the new conditions of immigrant America.

Two historians have emphasized the European origins of German political ideas and behavior in the colonies. Richard MacMaster's study of the Mennonites in colonial Pennsylvania shows how the pacifist principles developing within this group since the sixteenth century were transplanted to America by immigrants in the century before the Revolution. Pacifist principles shaped their involvement in colonial political affairs. Although colonial Mennonites were by no means united on all religious and political matters, most refused to hold office because of their religious scruples, not because they were apolitical. They asserted themselves politically in other ways, namely by stubbornly clinging to their pacifism in war and peace, and by voting overwhelmingly for those pacifists who had no qualms about officeholding, the English Quakers.[11]

A. G. Roeber's study of German-speaking Lutherans explores the concept that eighteenth-century villagers and clergy in central Europe may have transplanted aspects of their own political culture to the colonies. Roeber suggests that Lutheran immigrants transplanted their own concepts of "liberty" and their traditional concerns for inheritance and property rights, which were central to village life in Europe. By the 1760s in Pennsylvania, their concepts of liberty and property solidified into a political culture that was articulated by the German-language press. More and more German speakers associated liberty with the protection of property.[12]

In addition to traditions of pacifism among the radical pietists and concepts of liberty and property among Lutherans, another European source of colonial German political culture lay in the former villagers' long struggles with the German nobility and the growing state apparatus. Patterns of noncompliance or resistance to new encroachments by the state or local nobility into village affairs were part of the immediate past of many immigrants (see Chapters 1 and 2). In short, the absence in southwest Germany and Switzerland of democratic institutions in the Anglo-American sense did not mean that the immigrant population in the colonies was inclined toward political inertness.

But the question still remains: What was the basis for German involvement in colonial political affairs? When Benjamin Franklin, Thomas Penn, and other leaders of colonial political factions plotted, bribed, and schemed to gain the "Dutch" vote, how did this appear to the objects of their schemes? How did this appear to the majority of German-speaking colonists, who struggled to succeed in largely ethnic enclaves of the Pennsylvania German countryside, where Old World bonds of extended family, village, and religion remained important?

A close look at the German political experience reveals that this ethnic group—by far the largest in the colony—had their own interests at stake when dealing with the political apparatus of the colony, whether it was in the proprietor's apparatus for enforcing land policy, or in the assembly.

The immigrants' first ceremonial brush with the authorities came shortly after their arrival. City officials boarded each immigrant ship and summoned all males sixteen years and older who were well enough to disembark. Carrying a passport and a letter of recommendation from their pastor, they appeared before two clerks at separate desks, usually at the courthouse on High (now Market) Street, between Second and Third streets. There they swore or affirmed their allegiance to the Crown and signed in. Thereafter, half of the group had to go through the difficult process of selling themselves as servants, a process regulated by colonial authorities and laws. In fact, the entire immigrant shipping trade was regulated to some extent. When the trade became extremely abusive at midcentury, Christopher Saur warned the governor of grave political consequences if the government did not take steps to protect German immigrants from the exploitation of the Philadelphia merchant and maritime community. In 1764, immigrants formed the German Society of Pennsylvania, which

TABLE 5.1   Naturalizations by Ethnic Group in the Thirteen Colonies during the Eighteenth Century.

COLONY	GERMAN		OTHER		TOTAL	
	N	%	N	%	N	%
Pennsylvania	6,919	95	100	5	7,019	100
Maryland	1,173	96	52	4	1,225	100
New York	716	61	458	39	1,174	100
New Jersey	511	100	0	0	511	100
North Carolina	102	100	0	0	102	100
South Carolina	2	6	30	94	32	100
Virginia	25	93	2	7	27	100
New England	0	0	23	100	23	100
Georgia	0	0	0	0	0	0
Total	9,448	94	665	6	10,113	100

Note: The table includes naturalizations by acts of the colonial assemblies and by the 1740 Act of Parliament. "German" refers to those from German-speaking lands, as determined by surname analysis when not so identified in the records. All figures are approximate, and in some cases represent the minimum. Georgia was covered by an ambiguous general naturalization law.

Sources: Pennsylvania: see Table 5.2; Maryland: Wyand and Wyand, *Colonial Maryland Naturalizations*; New York: Richard J. Wolfe, "The Colonial Naturalization Act of 1740, with a List of Persons Naturalized in New York Colony, 1740–1769," *The New York Genealogical and Biographical Record*, 94 (1963), 132–147, and James H. Kettner, *Development of American Citizenship, 1608–1870* (Chapel Hill: University of North Carolina Press, 1978), 104n; New Jersey: Rosalind J. Beiler, "*Gemeinschaft* or *Gesellschaft*? Germans in Colonial New Jersey" (unpublished typescript, University of Pennsylvania, 1989); North Carolina: Lorena S. Eaker, "The Germans in North Carolina," *The Palatine Immigrant*, 6 (1980), 3–34, found 101—I found one additional in the district supreme court records in Raleigh; South Carolina: Giuseppi; New England: Kettner, 100, and 104n; Virginia: Wust, 22, and Giuseppi; Georgia: Kettner, 101–103, and Roeber, 160.

pressured the government to correct abuses in the immigrant trade. German immigrants formed similar societies in Charleston (1766), Baltimore (1783), and New York (1784). Saur was an unusual case of a politically active immigrant, but he makes an important general point: Almost all Germans came into the colony through the port at Philadelphia and experienced the treatment (good or bad) of the authorities and the merchant community. It was an experience none of them would ever forget.[13]

Years after their arrival, many German-speaking immigrants returned to the scene of their initial contact with colonial authorities in order to become naturalized. In fact, more than 10,000 immigrants were naturalized in

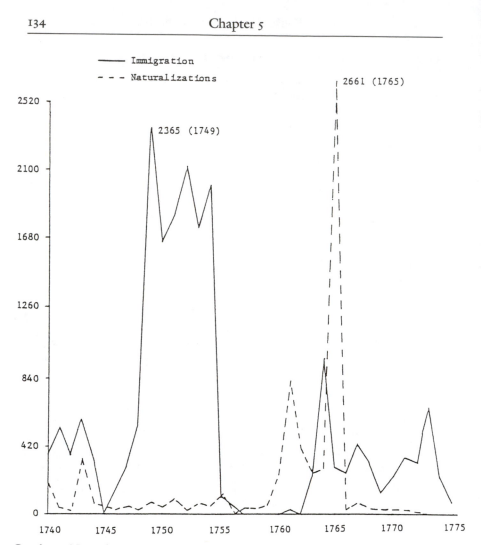

Graph 5.1. Naturalizations and German Immigration in Pennsylvania, 1740–1775. *Note*: Immigration refers to males aged sixteen years and older. Naturalizations reflect almost without exception adult males. *Sources*: Strassburger and Hinke, *Pennsylvania German Pioneers*, for German immigrant males aged sixteen and older, and Table 5.1 for naturalizations.

the eighteenth century, and about 94 percent were from German-speaking lands. Thus the Germans were the only numerically significant "alien" immigrant group during this period. About one-third, perhaps more, of eligible Germans were naturalized (see Table 5.1).[14]

German naturalizations in all colonies peaked during the years 1760 to 1765 due to the large wave of immigration that began in 1749 and suddenly ceased after 1754, when war broke out, but this does not explain the extraordinary increase in Pennsylvania during the autumn of 1765, especially since there were only ninety-three naturalizations during the April Supreme Court session. Something happened between April and September that caused over 2,600 German-speaking immigrants to suddenly realize that they ought to become naturalized (see Graph 5.1).[15]

This unique aspect of the German immigrant experience was connected to a large web of interests and motivations that had been developing for at least a generation. It is only one of many examples of how German interests and political culture manifested themselves during the three most important periods of political conflict in Pennsylvania during the generation before the Revolution: the early 1740s, the mid-1750s, and the mid-1760s.

Thomas Penn and the Germans

In 1732 Thomas Penn reached his majority and went to Pennsylvania to reorganize the land system, which he believed had not been serving the best interests of the proprietary Penn family. He set up a land office with a secretary, surveyor general, and three to five commissioners of property. He extended the "manor system" under which the proprietor kept one-tenth (usually the best one-tenth) of each new tract of land for his own use—either for speculating or renting to tenants. He also regulated the procedure for warranting and purchasing land and collecting quitrents. Perhaps most significantly, Penn raised the price of one hundred acres of vacant land from ten pounds sterling to fifteen pounds ten shillings—the highest price it would reach during the colonial period—and he also doubled quitrents.[16]

But the new system did not work. Many immigrants had encountered this kind of pressure from their lords before, whether in the Kraichgau, in other German-speaking regions, in Ulster, Ireland, or in Scotland. Now, in the vast spaces of America, where there was no local aristocracy and little state apparatus to enforce a rent offensive from their new lord, and when many new arrivals were still short on cash, there was little reason to comply. By 1740, the Land Office had issued 4,000 warrants, but only 500 patents. People were settling on the land and having it surveyed, but simply were not paying either the purchase price or the quitrents.[17]

Thomas Penn's changing land policies and the European wars beginning in 1739 provided the backdrop to the political turmoil in the colonies during the early 1740s, and the Germans played a key role. In 1739 and 1740 naturalization of German immigrants increased significantly, thereby providing more voters in these crucial election years (see Table 5.2). The defense issue with the Quakers was the biggest debate. The pacifist, radical pietist Germans who dominated the early migrations supported the Quakers, who were against raising troops or funds to support the British war effort. But many of the later-arriving "church" Germans—that is, Lutheran and Reformed immigrants—also supported the Quakers. On election day, October 1, 1740, there was a "great tumult" in Philadelphia, as the "Protestant country people" (Germans) successfully resisted Penn's attempts to oust the Quaker majority in the assembly. According to the Reformed minister John Philip Boehm, Penn was extremely angry with the Germans for not supporting his ticket.[18]

In 1741 several events occurred that illustrate the connections between Thomas Penn's land policy, naturalization, and the assembly elections. The Germans' reactions to these events reflect important aspects of their developing political culture.

In 1741 Penn enlisted the aid of John Philip Boehm in getting "church" Germans naturalized so that they might support the proprietary cause against the Quakers. He provided Boehm with German translations of the oaths required by the new naturalization law of 1740, and Boehm distributed them among the Germans. Boehm and more than 200 other Germans were present at the Supreme Court session of April 10–11, 1741, in Philadelphia, and the court rejected all but a handful of applicants because they had not obtained the required communion certificates.[19]

Next, Thomas Penn, now back in England, instructed his new Secretary of the Land Office, Richard Peters, to put pressure on squatters, tenants, and others who refused to pay. Peters had a list drawn up of "some of the most notorious Dilinquents [sic] in every County" who were to be ejected if they did not pay up. He circulated 350 notices of the pending ejectments in the countryside, hoping to frighten others into reporting to the Land Office. Just before the Supreme Court session in late September and the election in early October, Attorney General John Kinsey prepared ejectment papers.[20]

The election for sheriff in the fall of 1741 was as important as the assembly elections, because it was the sheriff who was responsible for serving ejectment papers to settlers who had not paid for their land or quitrents. In the tense campaign, both sides vied for the German vote. On Septem-

TABLE 5.2   Naturalizations in Colonial Pennsylvania by Act of Assembly or Act of Parliament.

1691	62	1746	26	1760	239
1709	57	1747	48	1761	835
1724	3	1748	29	1762	392
1726	7	1749	68	1763	258
1730	113	1750	42	1764	280
1731	98	1751	84	1765	2,661
1735	74	1752	25	1766	35
1739	172	1753	67	1767	73
1740	184	1754	47	1768	37
1741	29	1755	126	1769	29
1742	8	1756	10	1770	28
1743	356	1757	33	1771	29
1744	66	1758	35	1772	21
1745	46	1759	65	1773	6

Note: Includes all who were naturalized in Pennsylvania, a very small minority of whom were not from German-speaking lands.

Sources: William I. Hull, *William Penn and the Dutch Quaker Migration to Pennsylvania*, Swarthmore College Monographs on Quaker History, vol. 2 (Philadelphia: Patterson & White, 1935), 418–421; James T. Mitchell and Henry Flanders, eds., *The Statutes at Large of Pennsylvania from 1682 to 1801* (Harrisburg: Clarence M. Bush, 1896–1902); Giuseppi, *Naturalizations*.

ber 20, 1741, Conrad Weiser, a German immigrant who served as one of Penn's agents dealing with Native Americans, published a pamphlet in support of the proprietor. Weiser suggested to the church Germans that the Quakers, with Christopher Saur's help, had duped them into believing that the French threat was minimal; the new naturalization law had made it easier for Germans to protect themselves and to vote, now they must do so by voting for the proprietary ticket. On September 29, just before the election, a pamphlet (probably written by Saur) that attacked Penn appeared; it claimed that Penn was trying to make slaves of them all and was actually trying to prevent the pacifists from becoming naturalized because, while they would affirm their allegiance to the Crown, they would not swear an oath. In the end, the Quaker Party won the assembly seats, and they also won the sheriff's election in Philadelphia County, where more people voted for that office than for the assembly. Peters blamed the defeat on the last-minute publication and distribution of the anti-proprietary pamphlet, which cost them the German vote.[21]

Although Penn's candidates had lost the election, the land offensive continued. Richard Peters began cracking down on corrupt and inefficient surveyors, and he placed Nicholas Scull, who had just lost the sheriff's election, in charge of making new maps to assist their efforts. He also had new quitrent rolls made, and he considered opening an escheat office in the lower counties (Delaware) and appointing an escheat master, who would identify escheatable lands to be sold. When the assembly tried (according to Governor George Thomas, in a blatant attempt to gain favor and votes from the Germans), to pass a bill allowing the lands of aliens who died unnaturalized to devolve to their children, Peters informed Penn of the threat to his right of escheat, and the bill failed. Also, Attorney General Kinsey circumvented the county courts (and sheriffs) and provided Peters with a list of names of those who were delinquent in their payment of the purchase price and quitrents on land. Peters then diligently pursued the ejectments, hoping that this would "have a good Effect and make Business for the Receiver General." Initially, he had some success.[22]

But Penn realized that he must use something other than fear to motivate German and other settlers to pay up. He directed Peters to print hundreds of mortgage forms to be issued by the General Loan Office. Since the 1720s, paper money issues in Pennsylvania had been used overwhelmingly for the purpose of lending money through the Loan Office to people trying to buy or improve land. If settlers were going to begin streaming into the Land Office to pay for purchases and quitrents, they would first have to stop at the Loan Office to borrow the money. Thus paper money became a central issue in the colonists' struggle to gain secure title to their lands.[23]

In 1742 and 1743 Penn and Peters continued their coercive tactics, which were publicly and privately linked to naturalization, escheat, and the issues of the annual assembly elections. After the election in 1742, Peters claimed that the Proprietary Party lost because some of the German leadership, including the pacifist printer Christopher Saur, Caspar Wistar, and others, had been telling the Germans that the militia the proprietor was trying to raise to defend the frontier was really intended to help serve ejectments against Germans, a charge that may have seemed believable after the actual measures implemented by Penn since 1741. Furthermore, according to Peters, sailors who had started a riot in Philadelphia by attacking "about 500" Germans waiting to vote that year had been in league with the proprietary ticket; they rioted because so many naturalized and unnaturalized Germans had shown up in town the day before that they threatened to tip the balance in favor of the opposition. Not coincidentally, a record number of German heads of family were naturalized in 1743 (356), which protected them from escheat and allowed them to vote legally in the fall election (see Table 5.2).[24]

What Thomas Penn and Richard Peters did not understand was that it was more than Christopher Saur's propaganda that cost them the all-important German vote—among both the "sects" and the "churches." From the German point of view—as alien immigrants who had left their homelands primarily because of acute land scarcity, as peasant immigrants who had left their villages in groups to get some of the land they had heard was available in the New World, as survivors of a long, difficult, and expensive voyage who had made one move into the countryside to establish themselves—acquiring and protecting their land had become as important as the issue of religious toleration (perhaps more important) in influencing their political behavior. The radical pietists continued to support the pacifist Quakers, but they were no longer the majority. The Lutheran and Reformed majority and the radical pietists supported the Quakers in the critical election years because they were against Penn, who had made himself their enemy by implementing coercive measures in his land policy, the kind of coercive measures many immigrants from southwest Germany had been resisting for years in their home villages. Penn was able to win over some German elites, such as John Philip Boehm and Conrad Weiser, who disagreed with Saur and the Quakers for religious and other reasons, but most Germans—radical pietists and "church" people alike—supported the Quaker Party out of self-interest in the contentious political years of the early 1740s.

German Political Interests

While Penn was trying to create and maintain an efficient, profitable land system, the Germans were trying to successfully immigrate, settle, and prosper in Pennsylvania. The last generation of immigrants before the Revolution became increasingly concerned with defending their property against the colonial government's threats of foreclosure and escheat.

Initially, Germans came to Pennsylvania because of the religious tolerance practiced there, and this remained an important issue for later immigrants, but the vast majority of colonists who came during the third phase of immigration chose Pennsylvania because of its reputation in central Europe as a decent place to live that offered abundant opportunity. By the mid-eighteenth century new German immigrants wanted to settle with or near other Germans—even if it meant paying Penn's higher prices and getting land that was perhaps not as good as land available farther south.

To make a go of it in Pennsylvania, German immigrants needed, among other things: (1) plenty of land (facilitated by an aggressive policy of acquiring land from Native Americans); (2) an efficient land office, to keep speculators at bay and give individual settlers a chance to get good land; (3) a means of financing purchases of the expensive land (that is, paper money, issued through the General Loan Office); and (4) security for their property (from the French and Indian threat, fraud, foreclosure, and escheat), for which frontier defense and naturalization were critical issues.[25]

German support, which was crucial in all of the important elections, waxed and waned for the various political factions depending on who the German immigrants thought could help them achieve their goals. Many English- and German-speaking spokesmen (printers, pamphleteers, and others) urged Germans to become naturalized in order to protect their land, and then to vote for the party that would help them acquire, pay for, and protect their own land.

Although many Germans, church and sect alike, continued to vote for the Quaker Party in the 1740s and early 1750s, they threatened to challenge both Penn and the Quaker Assembly in the mid-1750s, when war erupted on the frontier. In 1755, while the assembly and Penn were gridlocked over another paper money issue through the General Loan Office and the defense of the frontier after Braddock's defeat, word began reaching Philadelphia that the patience of many colonists in the backcountry, who were bearing the brunt of the Delaware offensive, was wearing thin. On November 24, at a meeting of the Provincial Council, the councilmen discussed a letter from Col. William Moore to Governor Morris, which warned that 2,000 inhabitants from Chester County were preparing to come to Philadelphia to compel the governor and the assembly to pass laws necessary for the defense of the colony. Several other rumors warned that large numbers of Scots-Irish and Germans from Cumberland, York, and Berks counties were also planning marches on Philadelphia to make similar demands.[26]

By now the issue of self-defense had "lost its abstract character" and became a matter of life and death for thousands of Pennsylvanians. First the Delaware offensive, launched a few weeks earlier, and now threats from their own outraged colonists threatened to force the issue with both Penn and the assembly.[27]

On Tuesday evening, November 25, 1755, large numbers of Germans from Berks County (fifty miles away) marched into Philadelphia to make good on their threats. They carried several corpses that had been mutilated by Indians to dramatize their plight. According to newspaper reports, about 600 men came to demand that their plantations, wives, children, and religion no longer be held hostage between the murderous Delaware Indians and an impotent government, whose duty it was to protect them. The next day the crowd found the governor and demanded action. Governor Morris convinced them that the proprietor had done all he could and that the problem lay with the assembly. When the crowd marched to the assembly, then in session, and repeated their demands, they were promised that something would be done. The next day the governor signed a bill raising 60,000 pounds for defense.[28]

Although German support for the Quakers weakened in 1755 over the defense issue, many still had every reason to be against Penn and his party. In the preceding five years, 30,000 new immigrants—twice the population of the city itself—had poured into Philadelphia. It was becoming increasingly difficult for them and others in the colony to get and secure land. As prices for privately owned land escalated and the Delaware offensive temporarily rolled back the entire frontier, Penn continued to push his rigorous enforcement and ejectment policies of the early 1740s.

During this difficult time, Christopher Saur best articulated what many Germans—pacifists and nonpacifists alike—wanted and how Penn seemed to be obstructing their efforts. In 1755 he published a series of articles in his widely circulated newspaper, *Pennsylvanische Berichte*, and in his annual almanac, *Der Hoch-Deutsch Americanische Calender*, in which he advised German immigrants on how to buy land and on the importance of naturalization. He also warned them of the dangers of fraud, foreclosure, and escheat. He blasted Penn for closing the General Loan Office and advised the new wave of immigrants to look for land in Virginia or North Carolina, because it was no longer affordable in Pennsylvania.[29]

To persuade his readers, Saur used political rhetoric easily understandable to many Germans, who had struggled against state and aristocratic encroachments into their communities only a few years earlier. He claimed that Penn was trying to get Germans to protect his land for nothing—just as the feudal lords had in Germany. Penn wanted to subject them to *Frohnen* (feudal dues) and make *Lehens-Leute* (vassals) out of them all. A real lord, according to Saur, pays for everything and leads his people to war, but their present lord expected them to pay while he remained safely behind the front lines.[30]

While condemning Penn and his policies, Saur linked the critical issues of acquiring and protecting land to naturalization and the major political issues of the day. He urged Germans to become naturalized to help protect their land, and he urged them to vote for the party that supported paper money and other programs needed to help them succeed in Pennsylvania. If their government did not support them, then they would have no choice but to leave Pennsylvania and go south, as thousands were already doing.[31]

Thus after 1755, at the end of the period of peak immigration, it seemed that Penn was the biggest obstacle to the German immigrant's successful establishment in Pennsylvania. Penn would not lower the price of land, and he closed the General Loan Office, the mechanism that made it possible for many Germans to acquire land.

Saur died in 1758. His son, also named Christopher Saur, took over the newspaper, and in 1759 he and others, including the German printers Peter Miller and Ludwig Weiss, praised the governor and the assembly for passing an £80,000-paper money bill, a general naturalization bill allowing the children of deceased aliens to inherit their property and avoid escheat, and a bill to set up a survey office, which would help eliminate corruption and inefficiency in land deals. The printers continued to emphasize the importance of naturalization, however, because the bill regarding inheritance only applied retroactively to deceased aliens (that is, in the future the proprietor could still seize the property of unnaturalized immigrants after their death). Saur, Miller, Weiss, and many other inhabitants of Pennsylvania received quite a shock the following year when they discovered that the king had repealed all of these acts, at Thomas Penn's request.[32]

Penn's New Policy and the German Response

Both the Germans and the Penns had pursued their separate, sometimes antithetical, goals for decades, and there were many political expressions of this struggle, including the Germans' overwhelming support for the Quakers and Franklin at the polls; but in the mid-1760s their aspirations became linked to one another and to the growing imperial crisis. For the first time, the German vote in the assembly elections split significantly, with many voting for the Proprietary Party. For Germans, this development reflected their increasing sensitivity to issues involving securing their newly acquired property from the Native American threat, from the government, and from other colonists. By 1765 it seemed to many Germans that Penn was no longer an obstacle but a steppingstone to their pursuit of prosperity.

The assembly election of 1764 was one of the most hotly contested in the history of Pennsylvania. Pontiac's War had begun the previous year and frontier defense once again became a critical issue. The "Paxton Affair" began in December 1763 when a crowd in Lancaster County descended upon a settlement of Christian Indians, killing all they found. When authorities transferred those who escaped to the Lancaster jail for their own safety, another crowd attacked the jail and murdered them. In February the famous march on Philadelphia occurred—this time the Scots-Irish played the dominant role, though many Germans participated.[33]

Franklin's moves to transform Pennsylvania into a royal colony further exacerbated an already explosive situation. Many colonists associated his efforts with the Quaker Party and its reluctance to defend the frontier. In an intense propaganda campaign, each side attacked the other with caustic broadsides, pamphlets, and cartoons. To a large degree the Germans were central to the rhetoric, and land issues, naturalization, and escheat played prominent roles in the debates. In order to win, Franklin's party realized that it must go to extraordinary ends to keep the German vote, by far the largest ethnic bloc in the colony. On the other hand, the Proprietary Party correctly sensed that this time they finally had a chance to crack the German bloc vote that had frustrated proprietary designs at the polls since the early 1740s. In the end the crucial German vote split, and Franklin and many others in the Royal Party lost their seats. While most of the radical pietists voted against the proprietor (as usual), many of the German Reformed and Lutherans voted for the Proprietary Party for the first time. Franklin fumed after losing his assembly seat, claiming that his enemies had stolen the German vote from him. Later, Thomas Wharton informed Franklin that the opposition had used unnaturalized German voters against him.[34]

While contending with the election issues of war and defense and the move to make Pennsylvania a royal colony, Germans became increasingly concerned with securing their property. New World immigrants were highly conscious of property and its significance. They maintained close ties with their home village for many reasons—one of which was to recover inheritances. They studied English and colonial laws to protect themselves against those who would use the courts against them. In 1752 Henry Melchior Muhlenberg traveled to New York and saw how badly English lawyers had cheated Lutherans out of their land and church buildings. When he returned to Pennsylvania he initiated a long process to acquire a charter of incorporation for St. Michael's Lutheran Church in Philadelphia, which he hoped would protect them from a similar fate. Muhlenberg, Conrad Weiser, and Emmanuel Zimmerman requested that David Henderson, a young lawyer from Berks County, write a legal handbook for the Germans, explaining the essential English and colonial laws. The German printer Henry Miller translated and published the book, whose central theme is property rights, in Philadelphia in 1761. In addition, the German press and church ministers began to emphasize writing wills in America.[35]

But for most rural Germans, who had immigrated from villages pressured by acute land scarcity and by either local lords or the renewed demands of a growing state apparatus, the central issues remained what they had been for a generation or more. Germans had heard stories in their crowded home villages about the large tracts of land available in the New World. Although many had failed to escape the perils of the voyage and the increasingly abusive redemptioner and indentured servant system, those who had come with some wealth or who were well-connected with family, other villagers, or a church community, succeeded in making their move into the countryside and acquiring land. Now, a few years later, they struggled to protect their gains from the French and Indian threat and from Penn's policies.

In the early 1760s Penn steadfastly defended his land rights. These included escheat and tax exemption for his personal lands. Further, he refused to accept paper money in payment for land purchases or quitrents. But Penn also realized that he needed to make some changes in his land policy. In thirty years he had not been able to reap the financial rewards he thought Pennsylvania land could yield, though he had achieved some limited successes. His advisors were telling him that immigrants had been going south in large numbers since the end of the French and Indian War because of abuses in the Land Office that allowed speculators to monopolize frontier lands. Thus, if he did not act quickly, he could lose much of his population, which would make it even more difficult to take in the level of income he desired from Pennsylvania. And perhaps Penn realized, in the face of Franklin's offensive, how badly he needed German support at the polls.[36]

Penn began changing his tactics and shifting his allegiances: Rather than trying to force settlers to pay his high prices with threats of ejectment or foreclosure, he tried to induce them to pay by making it easier for them to acquire land. Penn's first move was to temporarily close the Land Office because it had become so inefficient and corrupt under the recently appointed secretary, William Peters. Then, in 1762, he created the Survey Office and appointed John Lukens the new Surveyor General. Lukens closely monitored the deputy surveyors and attacked corruption and inefficiency in the surveying department. In 1763 Thomas Penn sent his nephew John to Pennsylvania to monitor his land policy, appointing him governor.[37]

By the summer of 1765 Thomas Penn was ready to implement a sweeping new land policy. He lowered the price of 100 acres of land from fifteen pounds ten shillings to five pounds, and he doubled the quitrents (from four shillings two pence to eight shillings four pence per 100 acres). Further, he recognized improvements made on the land and gave occupiers of "vacant" land (that is, squatters) the first chance to buy it at the reduced rate, thus undercutting many speculators who had some claims to such lands. This and other measures taken to restrict speculation were an overt attempt by Penn to make his land policy work to the benefit of settlers (as well as the Penn family) at the expense of the speculators. Nearly full-page announcements explaining the new land policy in great detail appeared in German- and English-language newspapers and in a handbill issued by the Land Office.[38]

Penn expanded and revamped his apparatus to enforce the new policy. He created a Board of Property, which met once a month to handle disputes. He had more surveyors deputized, and he brought them under strict control. He appointed a new Receiver General to collect incomes, and in 1769 he appointed an Auditor General. In September 1765, Penn instructed the Land Office to favor "poor settlers" in disputes but to enforce escheat, a proprietary right he refused to give up. By the end of the year he replaced the Secretary of the Land Office, William Peters, who had been the source of much incompetency and corruption, with James Tilghman.[39]

Now Penn was virtually at war with speculators, rather than with the German immigrants and other settlers. He correctly judged that settlers were willing to pay the purchase price of land if it was low enough and if corruption and inefficiency were eliminated so that they would not be wasting their money. People were willing to do this, even if it meant paying double quitrents. The Germans—increasingly concerned with securing their property rights—were willing to pay the new low price, and to become naturalized, in order to get clear, permanent title to their land. They did so in extraordinarily large numbers the very next chance they had—in late September–early October 1765.

Acquiring land, protecting property rights, and acquiring the right to vote were becoming critical steps for immigrants as the imperial crisis escalated in 1765. The Proclamation of 1763, the Currency Act (1764), and the Stamp Act (1765) led many to believe that the British Parliament had become an obstacle to their prosperity. With no western land available, no paper money, and stamp taxes on legal documents, it would become even more difficult to establish oneself in the New World. (This situation did not bode well for Benjamin Franklin and his party: he was in London at that very moment, petitioning the king and Parliament to take over the government of Pennsylvania.) On the other hand, Penn now seemed to be assisting Germans and others in achieving their goals, though he still maintained the power of escheat.

Thus the time had come to be naturalized. In those few critical days in late September and October 1765, 2,600 Germans who had been living in Pennsylvania for an average of thirteen years flooded the streets of Philadelphia. They lined up outside Henry Muhlenberg's door by the hundreds for his signature on their communion certificates. They flocked to large German funerals. And if they were not too late, they voted in the assembly election. Afterward, some probably took part in the Stamp Act demonstrations. When they went home, they continued to pursue prosperity, many achieved it and many did not, but almost all thought that by becoming naturalized they had taken a significant step in the right direction.

As for Thomas Penn, it seemed that his new plan worked—for a while, anyway. In the late 1760s proprietary income from land sales and quitrents increased significantly, and in the 1770s it skyrocketed, making the Penns one of the richest families in England (see Table 5.3).

Penn had company in his success, for in the second third of the eighteenth century many European aristocratic families began to successfully enforce their claims to land rights (especially quitrents) that they had possessed in theory since the seventeenth century. Lord Baltimore was receiving more than 30,000 pounds per year from his Maryland lands in the 1760s. Until his death in 1763, the Earl of Granville collected 5,000 pounds per year in quitrents alone from his tract in North Carolina. By 1768, Lord Fairfax was receiving 4,000 pounds in yearly quitrents from his estate in the Northern Neck of Virginia, as well as revenue from manor rents, land sales, and other sources. The lords of several manors in New York each

TABLE 5.3   Penn Family Income in Pounds Sterling from Land Sales, Interest, and Quitrents for Their Lands in New Jersey and Pennsylvania, 1701–1778.

DATES *	POUNDS STERLING	DATES	POUNDS STERLING
1701–1709	823	1767	22,677
1712–1732	721	1768	12,235
1732–1738	8,220	1769	9,562
1738–1743	9,992	1770	15,447
1743–1751	12,714	1771	10,428
1751–1762	10,352	1772	21,138
1762	24,939	1773	51,261
1763	19,217	1774	67,731
1764	9,673	1775	28,338
1765	17,158	1776	18,171
1766	18,147	1776–1778	5,591

* Figures for 1701–1762 represent average annual income.

Source: Compiled from Edmund Physick, Pennsylvania Cash Accounts, 1701–1778, Penn Papers, HSP.

began returning roughly 1,000 to 2,000 pounds a year. The East Jersey proprietors also clamped down on tenants in Newark and Elizabeth.[40]

In the mid-eighteenth century there were enough incidents of aristocratic families finally making successful claims to their old land rights, especially quitrents, to begin calling it a movement—an "aristocratic offensive"—that extended from New York to North Carolina. This was, in fact, part of a larger movement in eighteenth-century Europe that extended from Scotland and Ireland to the Kraichgau and to France. Thomas Penn's aristocratic offensive, and those of many other families in the colonies, ended during the Revolution, when Penn lost his land, and quitrents were abolished forever in Pennsylvania.[41]

*   *   *

Thus from 1740 to 1765 the collective strategy that had served German immigrants so well during the process of migration and settlement also began to shape their political behavior. Given the immigrants' immediate background in Europe and all that they had gone through to get to America, their activism should not be surprising, nor should the basis of that activism be surprising: their struggle to make secure what they had

acquired in their *Neuland*. In the turbulent prerevolutionary years of immigrant America, they shared many of the problems and anxieties (and
political candidates) of other immigrant strangers, like the Scots-Irish; but
as aliens the Germans were even more vulnerable, and they had to take even
further steps, including naturalization, to secure their interests. In Pennsylvania, the issues connected with acquiring and securing land—Penn's
policies, the introduction of paper money, frontier defense, naturalization,
and escheat—were the issues of greatest concern to the Germans. These
concerns largely shaped their participation (which may have been higher
than that of non-Germans) in the elections.

In essence the Germans, many of whom had arrived between 1748
and 1755, were not an established people: In the face of difficult conditions and policies, they and their children were still a people striving for
success. But many were becoming unified around their culture, leaders,
and institutions. They could act decisively, and they did so. The Germans
had been presented with a choice of "old regimes" in the New World.
Acting out of self-interest, they chose to side with the Penns in prefer-
ence to Franklin, whose old regime included not only himself as governor
but, unfortunately for him, imperial restrictions on settlement and paper
money that would have blocked the Germans' struggle for success. The
irony was that the opposition to these imperial measures and to the Stamp
Act, which Franklin nimbly joined, soon swept aside *all* visions of an old
regime society in America. Germans and non-Germans alike were swept
into a new age. Once this happened, the Germans' ascendant political behavior and bloc voting would prove more lasting than the object of their
support had been. The Penns went under, and ethnic interest blocs rose
into normalcy.

6

The Structuring of a Multi-Ethnic Society

IN THE LATE COLONIAL PERIOD and throughout the Revolutionary Era, even as immigration slackened, German society and culture in North America began to flourish rather than dissipate into the larger "American" culture. By 1790 much of the German population still lived in rural, ethnic enclaves—in counties where large portions of the population, if not the majority, were German. Moreover, they continued to speak German, at home and in public. During the Revolutionary Era, the German-language press expanded dramatically in Pennsylvania and Maryland. German printers produced newspapers, almanacs, broadsides, and books that were among the most important in America. This flood of printed matter included political and religious materials, advice to new immigrants on how to get settled and adjust to New World conditions, and general news—all in their own language. German churches (Reformed, Lutheran, Catholic, and radical pietist) grew and prospered during this period. By the late 1760s and 1770s, the German Reformed and Lutheran churches in Pennsylvania were training their own ministers in substantial numbers, and by the time of the Revolution, their dependence on Europe was nearly broken. This development led to further growth of German religious culture in America; the Reformed and Lutheran congregations received more pastors, who organized more churches. Continuing to speak German in their services, the pastors and churches played critical roles in building and maintaining German communities. Lastly, as immigration became a less important source for the development and maintenance of German or German-American culture, endogamy helped maintain ties within this large ethnic community. In fact, before the nineteenth century, German-speakers—even of the third and fourth generations in America—rarely married non-Germans.[1]

This is not to say that the Germans developed and maintained a separate culture by isolating themselves economically and politically from other colonists. Rather, the immigrants' connections with extended family, the home village, and the church were often the critical factors that helped them succeed in the growing commercial economy of Greater Pennsylvania. Those who did not remain in such networks often lost out during the difficult last generation before the Revolution.

In fact, Germans played a crucial role in all the contentious elections in Pennsylvania from 1740 to 1765. The major contestants in all parties realized that they could not win without the all-important "Dutch vote." Representation of German-speakers in the assembly increased significantly in the 1760s, even though they were hindered by disproportional representation (the counties where most Germans lived received fewer assembly seats) and statutory restrictions on voting and officeholding (see Graph 6.1). By the 1770s, Germans began to push for equal representation and for increased numbers of German officeholders. In June 1774, the Philadelphia radicals proposed adding seven mechanics and six Germans to the list of nominees for the Philadelphia Committee of Nineteen, the principal organization of the resistance movement. In 1776, German representatives made up the largest ethnic component in the new assembly, constituting 38 percent of the total. When underrepresentation became a problem again in the 1780s, Germans responded in the explosive campaign of 1788 by electing "every candidate they could find" of ethnic German origin on the Federalist and Anti-Federalist tickets in Pennsylvania. In the 1790s, ethnic politics dominated the rural elections, as German-speakers struggled for more community autonomy through the creation of new counties with German administrators, magistrates, and juries.[2]

But the real basis for the politicization of the German populace during the colonial period lay not in the realm of the traditional politics of officeholding, consistent voting for a faction or party, or fighting wars for empire and independence. For the German immigrants, instead, politicization was linked to the entire process of migration from Europe and settlement in the countryside of Greater Pennsylvania. When the emigrants chose to leave their crowded clusters of peasant villages and towns in a world marked by change, scarcity, and growing pressures from the state and local nobility, they took a calculated risk. Word had it that if they survived the voyage to Pennsylvania and the immediate aftermath with few or no debts, they stood a good chance of procuring a tract of land a fourth the size of their entire parish at home. Moreover, the new lands contained huge forests teeming with game, and there were few or no restrictions on who could harvest it. It was only after they had begun their journey that

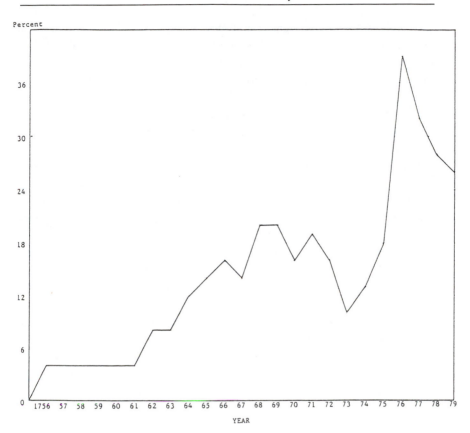

Percent

YEAR

Graph 6.1. Percentage of Pennsylvania Assemblymen of German or Swiss Ethnic Background, 1755–1779. *Source*: From Bockelman and Ireland, "The Internal Revolution in Pennsylvania," 159.

the emigrants realized how many obstacles they would have to overcome before they might find themselves clearing and plowing their own large field in the colonies.

German-speaking immigrants supported whomever they thought could help them in this pursuit of land, prosperity, and security, and they resisted those they perceived to be blocking their efforts. The immigrants' long-range goals remained constant, but the individuals who had the power to help or hinder them were subject to the whims of traditional factional politics. To many politicians, such as Benjamin Franklin, the actions of the Germans seemed incongruent, shifting, and contradictory because they were not always true to any particular party. One might oppose the Penns and their faction not because they refused to allow their lands to be taxed (the usual reason for those involved in assembly politics), but because they would not reform the Land Office or allow paper money to be printed. German immigrants (and other colonists) needed an efficient land office to acquire legal title to their lands, and they needed paper money to pay for it and for quitrents. With a corrupt land office that served only the interests of speculators, and with the recall of paper money, it became extremely difficult for many immigrants to get started in the colony, thus the Germans opposed Penn in the 1740s, 1750s, and early 1760s. During the struggle between the royal and proprietary parties in the mid-1760s, the issue for many immigrants and others was not who should run the government, but which regime would support their goals of acquiring and securing land. When Penn instituted his reforms in 1765, it became clear to many that they should throw in their lot with him.

When the Germans flooded the streets of Philadelphia during the autumn days of 1765, they were participating in politics on their own terms. Their struggles to secure land for themselves and their children had become part of larger issues, including, eventually, the imperial crisis. In 1765 and in other cases when it seemed necessary, the German-speaking immigrants, continuing their collective strategy, took political action to keep their lands. This, after all, had been the primary reason they had left central Europe just a few years earlier.

*   *   *

Throughout the long process of migration, settlement, politicization, and through the rearing of the next generation, German-speaking and other immigrants in the eighteenth century were becoming "Americanized." This is not to say that they were becoming like the people who had already settled there: Half the population of 1776 was immigrant or descended from eighteenth-century immigrants, and in the 1790s German culture was still strong, though it had become a New World German culture. When ethnic voting became connected to the issue of equal representation, instead of merely to acquiring and protecting property rights vis à vis the lord or proprietor, the politically active Germans became part of the *American* Revolution. Being German in 1790 meant participating in American public affairs, but speaking and reading German, going to a German church, marrying a German, and living with other Germans. So in a sense, America became them. But for them "Americanization" meant learning how to succeed in the very pluralistic, diverse America they had helped to create—a place with a large, multi-ethnic immigrant population, parts of which lived in segregated rural enclaves and parts of which lived in areas of integration. The survival strategies of these many ethnic and religious groups, former villagers, families, and individuals varied, but all tried to succeed somehow.

Over the course of the immigrants' search for prosperity and security, many succeeded and many failed. Those who succeeded often came to the country with significant wealth, or had family, friends, fellow villagers, or members of their religious group to support them along the way. For those who arrived with few or none of these advantages, it was much more difficult, though not impossible, to make a go of it. Some—convicts and especially African slaves—took no calculated risk or made no conscious choice to cross the ocean and begin this endeavor in America. Forced to go either by their judicial system or slave hunters, they had to make do as best they could after arriving in the colonies. By 1776, with the rhetoric of equality and liberty in the air, a far-flung, ethnically diverse collection of immigrant societies had nearly displaced the Native American populations east of the Appalachians. Here, among the hundreds of thousands of voluntary European immigrants and their descendants, were the many success stories that provided the basis for the rhetoric of 1776, but there were also many stories of people who never quite made it. At the same time, involuntary immigrants—the slaves—became the largest immigrant group of the eighteenth century. Success and failure, freedom and slavery: Such were the components of the immigrant society America had become when independence was achieved.

Appendices

Appendix 1. Methods and Sources Used for Demographic Calculations in the Thirteen Colonies

Proportion of Immigration to Total Population

THE FIGURE FOR TOTAL IMMIGRATION IN Table I.1 (585,800) may seem low—indeed, it is only as good as the secondary sources upon which it is based—but even if one were to use this figure as a minimum, it is clear that immigration in eighteenth-century America was extremely high and that it had a tremendous impact on the overall demographic growth of what was one of the fastest-growing populations in the world. The sheer demographic impact of the immigrants and their progeny can be approached by several indices. The simplest "immigration index" is arrived at by dividing the number of immigrants in a time period by the total population at the beginning of the time period (see Table A.1).[1] This gives a crude measure of the impact of immigrants in proportion to the initial size of the society. In the case of mid-eighteenth-century America, the base population of 466,185 in 1720, and the immigration of 328,700, yield a ratio, or index, of 0.71 (see Table A.1). The index reaches a high point of 0.74 for the years 1730–1769; which suggests a very dramatic impact. Comparing it, for example, with the same index for 1840–1879 (0.53) or 1880–1919 (0.47)—periods generally seen as having exceptionally high levels of immigration—one can see that the overall demographic impact of immigration on American society was actually higher in the eighteenth century than it was in the nineteenth and early twentieth centuries. Table A.1 shows the immigration index for selected forty-year intervals.

TABLE A.1   Immigration Index in the United States in Selected Forty-Year Intervals.

(A) INTERVAL	(B) POPULATION *	(C) IMMIGRATION	(D) INDEX (C ÷ B)
1700–1739	250,888	130,000	0.52
1720–1759	466,185	328,700	0.71
1730–1769	629,400	464,500	0.74
1740–1779	905,563	460,800	0.51
1760–1799	1,593,625	471,300	0.30
1780–1819	2,780,369	667,500	0.24
1800–1839	5,308,483	1,027,683	0.19
1820–1859	9,638,453	4,908,774	0.51
1840–1879	17,069,453	9,065,289	0.53
1860–1899	31,443,321	13,766,260	0.44
1880–1919	50,155,783	23,492,630	0.47
1900–1939	75,994,575	19,544,653	0.26
1920–1959	105,710,620	8,350,761	0.08
1940–1979	131,669,275	10,834,556	0.08

*Population at the beginning of the interval.

Sources: Historical Statistics of the United States, vol. 1, 105–106; U.S. Bureau of the Census, *Statistical Abstract of the United States, 1992* (1992), 8 and 10; and Table I.1. Immigration figures for Africans, 1780–1810, are from Fogel, Galatine, and Manning, *Without Consent or Contract*, 55; those for 1810–1820 are from Allan Kulikoff, "Uprooted Peoples: Black Migrants in the Age of the American Revolution, 1790–1820," in Ira Berlin and Ronald Hoffman, eds., *Slavery and Freedom in the Age of the American Revolution* (Charlottesville: University Press of Virginia, 1983), 143–171, 149 and 152. Estimates for Europeans during the same period are from Hans Jürgen Grabbe, "European Immigration to the United States in the Early National Period, 1783–1820," in Susan E. Klepp, ed., *The Demographic History of the Philadelphia Region, 1600–1860*, Proceedings of the American Philosophical Society, vol. 133, n. 2 (June 1989), 190–214.

The immigration index is misleading for the seventeenth century, and is therefore not included in the table: The population doubled due to "immigration" as soon as the second man disembarked at Jamestown. By the mid-eighteenth century, however, colonial American society had become more developed, and the index becomes a more meaningful measure of the relationship of immigration to the base population. Indeed, the *increase* in the index from the early to the mid-eighteenth century suggests that the era of the extraordinarily high, skewed indexes of the early colonial period had passed. Beginning in the eighteenth century, the index better indicates the relative importance of immigrants to the makeup of the population at the end of various intervals.

Calculation of the proportional impact of immigration at the end of each decade from 1700 to 1775 suggests that immigrants at any given time made up a large proportion of the population and that they may have made up the highest proportions at mid-century[2] (see Table A.2).

TABLE A.2   Recent Immigrants as a Proportion of the Total Population in Colonial America, 1700–1775.

(A) INTERVAL	(B) POPULATION *	(C) IMMIGRANTS	(D) PROPORTION (C ÷ B)
1700–1709	331,711	11,500	.035
1710–1719	466,185	20,300	.044
1720–1729	629,445	22,000	.035
1730–1739	905,563	76,200	.084
1740–1749	1,170,760	110,000	.094
1750–1759	1,593,625	120,500	.076
1760–1769	2,148,076	157,800	.073
1770–1775	2,500,000	67,500	.027

*Population at the end of each interval.

Sources: For the population figures, see Historical Statistics, vol. 2, 1168. Figures for immigrants are from Table I.1.

Population Projections

A glimpse at the hypothetical level of population at the outbreak of the Revolution, had there been no immigration in the preceding seventy-five years, reveals the impact immigration had on population growth. Some formulas used by demographers to project populations can help us roughly estimate how much lower the population would have been without immigration.

Once the continuous annual growth rate in the eighteenth century without immigration is approximated, it is possible to project the population of 1700, using this rate to see how large it would have been in 1775. Such a projection allows us to determine how much of the population in 1775 was either immigrant or descended from eighteenth-century immigrants, as opposed to having descended by natural increase from the seventeenth-century population—a more accurate measure of the total impact of immigration (see Table A.3).

TABLE A.3   Percentage of the Population of the Thirteen Colonies in 1775 Who Were Immigrants or Descendants of Eighteenth-Century Immigrants (Populations in Thousands).

(A)	(B)	(C)	(D)	(E)	(F)	(G)
			HYPO-	IMMI-		% IMMI-GRANTS AND DESCEN-
		CAGR OF	THETI-CAL	GRA-TION	ACTUAL	DANTS
	1700	1700	1775	1700–	1775	1775
REGION	POP.	POP.*	POP.†	1775	POP.	POP.**
All colonies	251	.023	1,408	586	2,500	44
Middle/South	158	.022	823	575	1,817	55

*Continuous Annual Growth Rate of the 1700 population, excluding immigrants and their descendants.
†Projected population in 1775, excluding immigrants and their descendants.
**Percentage of the actual 1775 population that was either immigrant or descended from eighteenth-century immigrants.

Sources: Historical Statistics, vol. 2, 1168, and Table I.1.

The continuous annual rate of natural increase for the population from 1700 to 1775 was approximately 2.3 percent. At this rate of increase, the population of about 250,000 in 1700 would have increased only to about 1,400,000 by 1775 (instead of 2,500,000) had there been no immigration. Thus nearly half (1,100,000 or 44 percent) of the population in 1775 was either immigrant or descended from eighteenth-century immigrants. That is, only about 56 percent of the population resulted from the natural increase of the base population of some 250,000 in 1700.

Immigration to New England in the eighteenth century was minimal. Some Scots-Irish and Germans, for example, did settle in Maine, New Hampshire, and Massachusetts. With slight adjustment of the immigration figures to take this and other factors into account, it follows that only 45 percent of the population of the middle and southern colonies in 1775 was descended from the base population living there in 1700, and the majority

(55 percent) was either immigrant or descended from eighteenth-century immigrants.

The method for computing population projections based on continuous annual growth rates is as follows:

Population in 1700	250,888
Population in 1775	2,500,000
Immigration 1700–1775	585,800

$$r^* = \ln(P_t/P_0) \div t$$
$$P_t = P_0 \times e^{r^*t}$$

Where r^* is the continuous annual growth rate; t is the length of time of the projection in years; P_t is the population at the end of the time period; and P_0 is the population at the beginning of the time period.

The actual r^* for the period 1700 to 1775 is as follows:

$$r^* = \ln(2,404,233 \div 250,888) \div 75 = .030$$

Thus the continuous annual growth rate from all causes, including immigration, was 3.0 percent, which means the natural rate of increase of the base population in 1700, without immigrants and their descendants, was less than 3 percent. Given the limited amount of data for the eighteenth century, it is difficult to establish how much of the population was descended from immigrants and thus to determine what the r^* for the 1700 population would have been. One could estimate this rate by figuring the growth rate in each decade without the immigrants and then calculating a weighted average of these rates. (A weighted average is needed to take into account the various population levels growing at different rates in different decades.)

This method is reasonably accurate only if fertility and mortality among new arrivals were minimal before the end of the decade. It is very difficult to measure either of these factors with data available on eighteenth-century immigrants, but neither factor should be overestimated.

Fertility for Africans (nearly one-half of the total) shortly after arrival was very low, as it was for convicts. Because of the dislocations and economic hardships associated with indentured servitude, it also may have been low for servants initially, and nearly half of the European immigrants were servants. In addition, many of the immigrants were children, and many others were single. Many immigrant women arrived in the middle or later years of each decade and went through a period of illness and dislocation that reduced the time for childbearing before the end of the decade. Thus the immigrant population likely to have large numbers of children shortly after arrival is limited to free European couples who came early in a decade—a very small portion of total immigration.

"Gateway" mortality or "seasoning" was certainly a significant factor that distorts the results of the hypothetical population projection, but it was not always as high as one might think. Farley Grubb estimates the First Year Immigrant Crude Annual Death Rate for Germans in Philadelphia in the years 1738–1756 at 61 per thousand, while the rate for the "established resident" population was only 37. Yet the first-year rate for the northern Kraichgau cohort of German immigrants (1717–1775) was only 35 per thousand (N = 227), and the annualized rate for the first five years was 14 per thousand.[3]

The fertility and mortality of immigrants in their early years do distort the population projections, but these two factors tend to cancel each other out. The following tables present data with exaggerated precision, but it should be understood that the final result (expressed in a percentage) is intended to be a very rough measure of the overall impact of immigration on eighteenth-century population growth.

DECADE	P_t	I_t	W	R^*	$W \times R^*$
1700–1709	250,888	11,500	.033	.024	.000792
1710–1719	331,711	20,300	.044	.030	.001320
1720–1729	466,185	22,000	.062	.026	.001612
1730–1739	629,445	76,200	.084	.028	.002352
1740–1749	905,563	110,000	.121	.016	.001936
1750–1759	1,170,760	120,500	.156	.023	.003588
1760–1769	1,593,625	157,800	.213	.022	.004686
1770–1775	2,148,076	67,500	.287	.025	.007175
	7,496,253	585,800	1.000		.023461

P_t: population at the beginning of the decade
i_t: immigration during the decade
w: P_t/P (P = the sum of all P_ts)
r^*: continuous annual growth rate for each decade, excluding immigrants

Thus the weighted average of r^* for the entire period for the 1700 base population, excluding immigrants and their descendants was, approximately 2.3 percent (the sum of all $w \times r^*$). This allows the following computation to be made.

$$P_{1775(\text{hypothetical})} = 250,888 \times e^{.023(75)} = 1,408,109$$

The hypothetical population is only 56 percent of the actual (1,408,109 ÷ 2,500,000 = .56). The immigrants and their descendants thus make up the remaining 44 percent.

This method for calculating the "natural" growth rate per decade only excludes immigrants arriving during that decade, which means that the fertility and mortality of immigrants who arrived in previous decades is counted toward "natural" growth during that decade. This factor, too, distorts the final result, thus creating a bias in favor of the natural growth rate; calculations for decadal natural growth rates should therefore be treated as maximums. This means that eighteenth-century immigrants and their descendants made up a slightly larger percentage of the 1775 population than indicated in column (g) of Table A.3.

After making slight adjustments for immigration into New England, which was minimal in the eighteenth century, the same calculations for the middle and southern colonies yield the following results:

$$r^* = \ln(1,817,289 \div 158,125) \div 75 = .033$$

The rate for the base population in 1700 was thus less than 3.3 percent. Weighted averages can again be used to approximate the growth rate:

DECADE	P_t	I_t	W	R^*	$W \times R^*$
1700–1709	158,125	11,300	.030	.026	.000780
1710–1719	216,617	19,800	.042	.024	.001008
1720–1729	295,292	21,000	.057	.028	.001596
1730–1739	412,094	74,700	.079	.027	.002133
1740–1749	615,859	108,000	.118	.013	.001534
1750–1759	810,749	118,500	.155	.023	.003565
1760–1769	1,143,991	155,800	.219	.021	.004599
1770–1775	1,567,038	66,000	.300	.022	.006600
	5,219,765	575,100	1.000		.021815

The continuous annual growth rate for the base population in 1700 for the middle and southern colonies was 2.2 percent, which allows the following calculation:

$$P_{1775(\text{hypothetical})} = 158{,}125 \times e^{.022(75)} = 823{,}341$$

Thus only 45 percent of the population in the middle and southern colonies in 1775 descended from the natural increase of the population in 1700 $(823{,}341 \div 1{,}817{,}289 = 0.453)$.

Appendix 2. Volume and Timing of Legal Emigrations from Southwest Germany, 1687–1804

The following table of legal emigrations of families (not persons) by decade from four areas of southwest Germany (Baden and the Breisgau, the Lower Neckar, the Bishopric of Speyer, and the Territories of the Imperial City of Ulm) demonstrates that significant levels did not exist until the middle third of the century. This was true for the emigration to British North America and to other lands:

DECADE	TO 13 COLONIES/USA		TO OTHER DESTINATIONS		TO ALL DESTINATIONS	
	N	%	N	%	N	%
1687–1689	0	0	172	1	172	1
1690–1699	0	0	120	1	120	1
1700–1709	0	0	13	0	13	0
1710–1719	3	0	135	1	138	1
1720–1729	59	5	224	1	283	2
1730–1739	249	18	383	2	632	4
1740–1749	262	19	1,634	11	1,896	11
1750–1759	566	42	1,989	13	2,555	15
1760–1769	131	10	2,868	19	2,999	18
1770–1779	48	4	2,397	16	2,445	15
1780–1789	28	2	2,410	16	2,438	14
1790–1799	10	0	2,271	15	2,281	14
1800–1804	4	0	675	4	679	4
Total	1,360	100%	15,291	100%	16,651	100%

The four regions chosen represent those investigated by Werner Hacker from which numerically significant emigrations to the thirteen colonies occurred. See Werner Hacker, *Kurpfälzische Auswanderer vom Unteren Neckar, Rechtrheinische Gebiete der Kurpfalz* (Stuttgart and Aalen: Konrad Theiss Verlag, 1983); *Auswanderungen aus Baden und dem Breisgau*; *Auswanderungen aus dem früheren Hochstift Speyer nach Südosteuropa und Übersee im XVIII. Jahrhundert*, Schriften zur Wanderungsgeschichte der Pfälzer, vol. 28 (Kaiserslautern: Heimatstelle Pfalz, 1969); "Auswanderer aus dem Territorium der Reichsstadt Ulm, vor allem im ausgehenden 17. und im 18. Jahrhundert," *Ulm und Oberschwaben: Zeitschrift für Geschichte und Kunst*, 42/43 (1978), 161–257.

Appendix 3. Statistics for the Fifty-three Parishes Making Up the Northern Kraichgau Cohort of Emigrants to Pennsylvania, 1717–1775

(A) PARISH	(B) POP. IN 1809	(C) AREA IN HECTARES	(D) PERSONS PER HECTARE (B ÷ C)	(E) PERSONS EMI-GRATING	(F) INDEX (D × E)
1. Adelshofen	481	688	0.7	41	28.7
2. Adersbach	422	739	0.6	30	18.0
3. Asbach	498	673	0.7	12	8.4
4. Bad Rappenau	669	1387	0.5	13	6.5
5. Bammental	679	1216	0.6	17	10.2
6. Bargen	681	824	0.8	4	3.2
7. Bonfeld*	1059	1154	0.9	73	65.7
8. Berwangen	850	844	1.0	43	43.0
9. Daisbach	405	729	0.6	16	9.6
10. Daudenzell	200	501	0.4	4	1.6
11. Diedesheim	200†	250†	0.8	3	2.4
12. Dühren	665	718	0.9	79	71.1
13. Ehrstädt	488	771	0.6	21	12.6
14. Eichtersheim	868	618	1.4	19	26.6
15. Elsenz	766	1153	0.7	12	8.4
16. Epfenbach	868	1400	0.6	29	17.4
17. Eppingen	2320	3296	0.7	66	42.2
18. Eschelbach	775	738	1.1	26	28.6
19. Eschelbronn	691	826	0.8	6	4.8
20. Fürfeld*	695	820	0.8	2	1.6

Continued

(A)	(B)	(C)	(D)	(E)	(F)
			PERSONS		
	POP.	AREA	PER	PERSONS	
	IN	IN	HECTARE	EMI-	INDEX
PARISH	1809	HECTARES	(B ÷ C)	GRATING	(D × E)
21. Gauangelloch	388	657	0.6	15	9.0
22. Grombach	636	720	0.9	13	11.7
23. Hasselbach	144	254	0.6	2	1.2
24. Helmstadt	851	1774	0.5	26	13.0
25. Hilsbach	1022	1236	0.8	13.5	10.8
26. Hoffenheim	1194	1317	0.9	102	91.8
27. Ittlingen	1047	1411	0.7	152	106.4
28. Kirchardt	710	1091	0.7	35	24.5
29. Massenbach *	752	848	0.9	64	57.6
30. Mauer	601	630	1.0	19	19.0
31. Meckesheim	879	1171	0.8	39	31.2
32. Michelfeld	823	1147	0.7	80	56.0
33. Mönchzell	446	463	1.0	6	6.0
34. Neckarbischofsheim	1429	2411	0.6	51	30.6
35. Neckargemünd	1800	1068	1.7	23	39.1
36. Neidenstein	551	648	0.9	12	10.8
37. Obergimpern	720	1269	0.6	12	7.2
38. Reichertshausen	541	938	0.6	2	1.2
39. Reihen	791	1090	0.7	53	37.1
40. Rohrbach	649	790	0.8	18	14.4
41. Schatthausen	445	569	0.8	11	8.8
42. Schluchtern	781	664	1.2	12	14.4
43. Schwaigern	1762	2205	0.8	305	244.0
44. Sinsheim	1746	2192	0.8	72	57.6
45. Stebbach	606	795	0.8	14	11.2
46. Steinsfurt	1085	1208	0.9	48	43.2
47. Tairnbach	390	207	1.9	12	22.8
48. Treschklingen *	305	502	0.6	11	6.6
49. Untergimpern	353	230	1.5	7	10.5
50. Waldangelloch	610	603	1.0	66	66.0
51. Weiler	712	1046	0.7	77.5	54.3
52. Wiesloch	1802	1732	1.0	14	14.0
53. Zuzenhausen	846	1166	0.7	55	38.5
Total	41,697	53,397	0.8	1,948	28.7

*no figures available for legal emigration
†estimated

Note: One hectare equals an area 100 meters long and 100 meters wide, or about 2.47 acres.

Schwaigern, Sinsheim, Wiesloch, Eppingen, Hilsbach, and Neckargemünd were market towns. The other 47 communities were villages (*Dörfer*).

Column (f) provides a relative measure of emigration between parishes that includes the factors of population and the size of each parish in hectares.

Sources: For population figures, von Eichrodt, *Das Großherzogthum Baden* and *Königlich Württembergisches Hof- und Staats- Handbuch*. For the area of each parish see *Das Land Baden-Württemberg*. Figures for emigration were calculated from Burgert, *The Northern Kraichgau*; Hacker, *Kurpfälzische Auswanderer vom Unteren Neckar*; and, for Schwaigern, from Wagenplast Notes.

Appendix 4. European Origins of German-Speaking, Radical Pietist Immigrants in Colonial America

Moravians

The origins of the 830 Moravian immigrants are based on the political state, or sometimes a geographic region, in which they were born. Almost all Moravian emigrants left Europe from one of their settlements in Herrnhut (Saxony), Wetteravia, the Netherlands, or London.

GERMAN-SPEAKING LANDS	N
Moravia *	83
Silesia	68
Saxony	67
Württemberg	61
Brandenburg-Prussia	27
Switzerland	19
Holstein	15
Wetteravia	14
Bavaria	13
Thuringia	11
Alsace	10
Bohemia *	10
Other	65
"Germany"	218
Total	681

* From German-speaking minority in Bohemia and Moravia

NON–GERMAN-SPEAKING EUROPE	N	
England	59	
Denmark	25	
Norway	12	
Livonia	9	
Sweden	7	
Other	19	
Total	131	

NON-EUROPEAN LANDS	N	
Carribean	8	
Ceylon	1	
Guinea	1	
Total	10	

TOTALS	N	%
German-speaking lands	681	82
Non–German-speaking Europe	131	16
Non-European lands	10	1
Unknown	8	1
Grand total	830	100%

Schwenkfelders

All 206 Schwenkfelder immigrants came from either Silesia or Saxony, and many from Silesia moved to Saxony shortly before going to Pennsylvania. The tables show origins from Silesia, Saxony, and the last residence (either in Silesia or Saxony) before emigrating to Pennsylvania.

1. From Silesia

TOWN	N	%
Harpersdorf	133	84
Armenruh	12	8
Hockenau	8	5

1. From Silesia (Continued)

TOWN	N	%
Langneundorf	5	3
Unknown	33	—
NA	15	—
Total	206	100%

2. From Saxony

TOWN	N	%
Berthelsdorf	89	79
Herrnhut	13	12
Görlitz	10	9
Unknown	81	—
NA	13	—
Total	206	100%

3. Last Residence in Europe

TOWN	N	%
Berthelsdorf	90	72
Herrnhut	13	11
Görlitz	9	7
Harpersdorf	8	6
Armenruh	4	3
Langneundorf	1	1
Unknown	81	—
Total	206	100%

Amish

The Amish originated in Switzerland, but in the early eighteenth century they spread northward into Germany. Place of origin here refers to the birthplace of the immigrants.

SWITZERLAND	N
Canton Bern	20
Canton Basel	7
Canton Vaud	1
Zehlingen	1
Other	31
Total	60

GERMANY (INCLUDING ALSACE)	N
Alsace	8
Montpeliard/Alsace	4
Palatinate	7
Württemberg	1
Hesse	1
Altenkirch/Helmeroth	1
Other	4
Total	26

TOTALS	N	%
Switzerland	60	23
Germany	26	10
Unknown	179	67
Grand total	265	100%

Waldensians

All known Waldensian immigrants came from three parishes in Württemberg. They were descended from French-speaking Waldensians who had migrated to Württemberg early in the eighteenth century.

PARISH	N	%
Dürrmenz	47	43
Grossvillars	33	30
Pinache	30	27
Total	110	100%

Dunkers

Officially known in English as the Church of the Brethren, but also called the Brethren, Dompelaars, and Tunkers. The movement began in Schwarzenau in the early eighteenth century. It spread up and down the middle Rhine region and as far north as Altona, a part of Hamburg.

PLACE OF ORIGIN	N	%	% OF KNOWN ORIGIN
Krefeld	35	13	43
Schwarzenau	29	11	35
Friesland	11	4	14
Hamburg-Altona	3	1	4
Umstadt	2	1	2
Westervain	1	0	1
Marienborn	1	0	1
Unknown	184	70	—
Total	266	100%	100%

Appendix 5. German-Speaking Immigrants Eligible for Naturalization

At least 9,448 German-speaking immigrants were naturalized in the thirteen colonies by all methods during the colonial period (see Table 5.1), and there were about 84,500 immigrants total (see Table I.1).

The median time from arrival to naturalization was thirteen years (see Chapter 3, note 28). Thus only immigrants arriving before 1763 would have been there long enough to become naturalized under normal conditions. Their total numbers are 64,500 (calculated from the same sources used in Table I.1).

With only a handful of exceptions, women were not naturalized in colonial America. Based on a very rough estimate that two-thirds of all adults and one-half of all children were male, approximately 40,000 male immigrants arrived before 1763.

At least 15 percent of the total northern Kraichgau cohort died within thirteen years of arrival. Also, I estimate that another 5 percent were children who died before reaching their majority. If one assumes this to be typical, then only 32,000 male immigrants (80 percent) lived long enough to become eligible for naturalization under normal conditions.

Thus there were 9,448 naturalizations for about 32,000 eligible immigrants (30 percent). Because many naturalization records are probably missing, especially for Virginia and South Carolina, and because general naturalization laws were in effect for Georgia and in New York for groups arriving after 1709, this should be regarded as a low estimate. A more accurate estimate might be 35 percent.

Notes

Introduction

1. For colonial population statistics see U.S. Bureau of the Census, *Historical Statistics of the United States, Colonial Times to 1970* (Washington, D.C., 1975), vol. 2, Series Z2–17, 1,168. On the numerical decline of the native population see Gary B. Nash, *Red, White, and Black: The Peoples of Early North America*, 3rd ed. (Englewood Cliffs, N.J.: Prentice Hall, 1992), 17, and James Axtell, *Beyond 1492: Encounters in Colonial North America* (New York: Oxford University Press, 1992), 235. Peter H. Wood presents a summary of population estimates for Africans, Europeans, and Native Americans during the colonial period in "The Changing Population of the Colonial South: An Overview by Race and Region, 1685–1790," in Peter H. Wood, Gregory A. Waselkov, and M. Thomas Hatley, eds., *Powhatan's Mantle: Indians in the Colonial Southeast* (Lincoln: University of Nebraska Press, 1989), 35–103, especially 38–39 and 90.

Concerning the ethnic makeup of the 1700 population, there had been some Dutch, Swedish, and French Huguenot immigration during the seventeenth century, and New Netherland (later New York) was an extremely diverse, but lightly populated settlement from the beginning (see Randall H. Balmer, *A Perfect Babel of Confusion: Dutch Religion and English Culture in the Middle Colonies* [New York: Oxford University Press, 1989] and Jon Butler, *The Huguenots in America: A Refugee People in a New World Society* [Cambridge, Mass.: Harvard University Press, 1983]). But these movements of Continental peoples to North America were dwarfed by the large English migration. Also, in 1680, only about 5 percent of the population in the colonies was black, yet by 1775, blacks made up 21 percent of the non–Native American inhabitants of the thirteen colonies (see *Historical Statistics*).

On the ethnically diverse immigration and its cultural ramifications for the pre-Revolution population, see Bernard Bailyn and Barbara DeWolfe, *Voyagers to the West: A Passage in the Peopling of America on the Eve of the Revolution* (New York: Alfred A. Knopf, 1986), and Bernard Bailyn and Philip D. Morgan, eds., *Strangers within the Realm: Cultural Margins of the First British Empire* (Chapel Hill: University of North Carolina Press, 1991).

2. The immigration estimates in Table I.1 are based on a methodology described in an earlier article of mine and the data available at that time. (See Aaron S. Fogleman, "Migrations to the Thirteen British North American Colonies, 1700–1775: New Estimates," *Journal of Interdisciplinary History*, 22 (1992): 691–709.) Henry Gemery has aptly described recent scholarship estimating immigration into early America as "transitory," and, indeed, an important "new" estimate for Afri-

cans has appeared since publication of my article. Robert Fogel now estimates that 328,000 African slaves were imported between 1700 and 1780, a figure significantly higher than mine, and his decadal distribution differs in some respects. (See Robert W. Fogel, Ralph A. Galatine, and Richard L. Manning, eds., *Without Consent or Contract: The Rise and Fall of American Slavery: Evidence and Methods* [New York: W.W. Norton & Co., 1992], 53–58, especially Table 4.2.) Because Fogel uses a residual method based upon estimates of crude birth and death rates, I have chosen not to use his results in Table I.1, which is based upon the estimates from ethnic-group historians (dependent largely on data from ship departures and arrivals), the same historians' discussions of the more qualitative aspects of migration, and an improved surname analysis of the 1790 Federal Census.

This method is not entirely satisfactory, as the large number of "less accurate" and "least accurate" designations suggest, but the estimates for Africans are reasonably close to Fogel's, and the estimates for Europeans fall within the range established by Henry Gemery (278,400 to 485,300 whites), who also used a residual method. (See Henry A. Gemery, "European Immigration to North America, 1700–1820: Numbers and Quasi-Numbers," *Perspectives in American History*, n.s. 1 [1984], 283–342.) Recently, Gemery reminded us again of the difficulties in measuring early immigration (see "Disarray in the Historical Record: Estimates of Immigration to the United States, 1700–1860," in Susan E. Klepp, ed., *The Demographic History of the Philadelphia Region, 1680–1860*, Proceedings of the American Philosophical Society, vol. 133, n. 2 [June 1989], 123–127).

See Appendix 1 for computations of immigrants as a proportion of the total population in various eras of American history.

3. It is not possible to calculate extremely accurate population growth rates —with or without the immigrants—in the eighteenth century due to the lack of good data for all ethnic groups and time periods. However, there is enough data to make some crude estimates that tell us something about the overall importance of immigration to eighteenth-century population growth. The methods and sources used here are explained in detail in Appendix 1.

It is self-evident that Continental immigrants did not speak English upon arrival, but many do not realize that most Scottish and perhaps many northern and southern Irish did not speak English. While English was rapidly spreading in the Lowlands of Scotland during the eighteenth century (see Eric Richards, "Scotland and the Uses of the Atlantic Empire," in Bailyn and Morgan, eds., *Strangers within the Realm*, 67–114), many of the immigrants came from the Highlands. Not surprisingly then, Duane Meyer found that most members of the large community of Scot Highlanders in North Carolina continued to speak Gaelic until the early nineteenth century (see *The Highland Scots of North Carolina, 1732–1776*, Durham, N.C.: Duke University Press, 1961). Also, the Ulster Scots, or Scots-Irish, "stood apart linguistically" from inhabitants of the rest of the British Isles, although relatively little is known about the way they actually spoke (see Maldwyn A. Jones, "The Scotch-Irish in British America," in Bailyn and Morgan, eds., *Strangers within the Realm*, 284–313). Both older and recent linguistic studies of Ireland—some possibly influenced by nationalism—indicate that only a few elites and government officials, as well as the English immigrant population, spoke English in the eighteenth century: The Irish spoke Irish. English did not become the language of the masses until the nineteenth century. See Jeremiah J. Hogan, *The English Language in Ireland* (Dublin: The Educational Company of Ireland, 1927), 52–61; Alan Bliss, *Spoken English in Ireland, 1600–1740* (Dublin: The Dolman Press, 1979), 325; and several essays in Diarmaid, O' Muirithe, ed., *The English Language in Ireland* (Dublin and Cork: The Mercier Press, 1977), especially P. L. Henry, "Anglo-Irish and its Irish Background," 20–36, G. B. Adams, "The Dialects of Ulster," 56–69, and Seán de Fréine, "The Dominance of the English Language in the Nineteenth Century," 71–87. Maldwyn Jones (see above) also supports this view. Kerby A. Miller argues, however, that even though most Irish did not speak English in the seventeenth and eighteenth centuries, those who emigrated to North America did. See *Emigrants and Exiles: Ireland and the Irish Exodus to North America* (New York: Oxford University Press, 1985), 137–168.

4. See, for example, Muhlenberg's letters of March 14 and 16, June 18, and September 7, 1754, and November 24, 1755, in Kurt Aland, ed., *Die Korrespondenz Heinrich Melchior Mühlenbergs aus der Anfangszeit des deutschen Luthertums in Nordamerika*, vol. 2 (Berlin and New York: Walter de Gruyter, 1987); two letters from Christopher Saur to Governor Robert Hunter Morris, March 15 and May 12, 1755, reprinted in *Historical Magazine*, 4 (1860), 100–104; and numerous references in Gottlieb Mittelberger, *Journey to Pennsylvania*, translated and edited by Oscar Handlin and John Clive (Cambridge, Mass.: Harvard University Press, 1960).

5. Whether Germans were the largest European immigrant group during the period 1700–1775 depends very much on the numbers assigned to English immigrants (one of the weakest estimates in Table I.1) and the degree to which the various British groups represented in the table should be counted separately. In some ways the aggregated figure for German-speakers, which includes immigrants anywhere from Switzerland to Holstein, or from Alsace to Prussia, reflects a variety of cultures and peoples similar to that of the disaggregated figures for "British" immigrants in the table. Yet the vast majority of German-speakers came from the southwest or Switzerland, and even many of the Swiss came lastly from the upper Rhine region and its tributaries. While regional identity among the German-speakers remained strong, even among immigrants in the colonies, these differences were much less distinguishable within the American population than those between English, Scots, Welsh, and Irish.

Further, my estimate for Germans in Table I.1 is subject to question, although it is lower than most others. Marianne Wokeck, who has analyzed the volume and flow of German immigration into Philadelphia, as well as the shipping trade that brought immigrants over, estimates 100,000 Germans arriving in all colonies from 1683 to 1776, but she has not yet given details for her estimates of those who did not come through Philadelphia. See Wokeck, "German Immigration to Colonial America: Prototype of a Transatlantic Mass Migration," in Frank Trommler and Joseph McVeigh, eds., *America and the Germans: An Assessment of a Three-Hundred-Year History*, 2 vols. (Philadelphia: University of Pennsylvania Press, 1985), vol. 2, 3–13. See also Wokeck, "The Flow and the Composition of German Immigration to Philadelphia, 1727–1775," *Pennsylvania Magazine of History and Biography*, 105 (1981), 249–278, and "A Tide of Alien Tongues: The Flow and Ebb of German Immigration to Pennsylvania, 1683–1776," (Ph.D. diss., Temple University, 1983). A. G. Roeber writes that 120,000 immigrants from the Holy Roman Empire settled in British North America between 1683 and 1783, but he provides no basis for this estimate, which is surely too high. See *Palatines, Liberty, and Property: German Lutherans in Colonial British North America* (Baltimore: Johns Hopkins University Press, 1933), ix. Georg Fertig found shipping records in Rotterdam to supplement those Wokeck and I used. He used them in conjunction with Thomas L. Purvis's surname analysis of the 1790 Federal Census ("The European Ancestry of the United States Population, 1790," *William & Mary Quarterly*, 41 [1984], 85–101) and other sources to estimate roughly 100,000 emigrants in all the colonies for the period 1683–1800, a figure close to mine after subtracting the 1775–1800 arrivals. See Fertig, "Migration from the German-Speaking Parts of Central Europe, 1600–1800: Estimates and Explanations," Working Paper No. 38, John F. Kennedy-Institut für Nordamerikastudien (Berlin, 1991), 9–11.

6. My periodization of German-speaking immigration is based upon the causes and nature of the emigration from the European point of view. This point is important because it allows us to understand that the type of immigrants arriving in the colonies varied according to time of arrival. Others periodize the immigration differently because they use different criteria to distinguish phases of immigration. Marianne Wokeck, for example, divides colonial German immigration into three periods: 1683–1726, 1727–1754, and 1755–1776. She bases her divisions upon the changing nature of the volume of arrivals, that is, on a chart of the immigration curve. She does not base them upon the causes of the emigration ("A Tide of Alien Tongues," 110). A group of Lutheran ministers who played critical roles in organizing the church in Pennsylvania devised a scheme of migration epochs while trying to understand and explain the changing nature of German-American society. Writing in 1754, during the peak period of arrivals, they divided German immigration into five periods: (1) 1680–1708; (2) 1708–1720; (3) ca. 1720–1730; (4) ca. 1730–1742; (5) 1742–1754. They based this periodization upon the activities of the immigrants after arrival, however, and not upon the conditions of their leaving Europe (see Muhlenberg, Brunnholtz, and Handschuh to Ziegenhagen, Francke, and Fresenius, Philadelphia, July 9, 1754, in Aland, *Die Korrespondenz Heinrich Melchior Mühlenbergs*, vol. 2, 170–195).

7. Although there were numerous, scattered incidents of German-speakers arriving before 1683, they did not establish any lasting communities or settlements until that date. See Klaus Wust, *The Virginia Germans* (Charlottesville: University Press of Virginia, 1969), 3–14. On the religious migrations to Pennsylvania beginning in 1683 see Klaus Deppermann, "Pennsylvanien als Asyl des frühen deutschen Pietismus," *Pietismus und Neuzeit*, 10 (1982), 190–212, and Elizabeth W. Fisher, " 'Prophesies and Revelations': German Cabbalists in Early Pennsylvania," *Pennsylvania Magazine of History and Biography*, 109 (1985), 299–333. The German-speaking radical pietist immigrations will be discussed in Chapter 4.

8. Joshua Kocherthaler, *Außführlich- und umständlicher Bericht Von der berühmten Landschafft Carolina/ In dem Engelländischen America gelegen* (Frankfurt: Georg Heinrich Oehrling, 1706 and 4th ed., 1709). Although it is not certain that Kocherthaler's book and the "Golden Book" are one in the same, Vincent H. Todd

makes a persuasive argument that this is likely (see *Christoph von Graffenried's Account of the Founding of New Bern* [Raleigh: Edwards & Broughton Printing Co., 1920, 13–14]).

9. Walter A. Knittle, *Early Eighteenth Century Palatine Emigration: A British Government Redemptioner Project to Manufacture Naval Stores* (Philadelphia: Dorrance and Co., 1937); Otto F. Raum, "Die Hintergründe der Pfälzer Auswanderung im Jahre 1709," *Deutsches Archiv für Landes- und Volksforschung*, 3 (1939), 551–567; Hans Fenske, "International Migration: Germany in the Eighteenth Century," *Central European History*, 13 (1980), 332–347.

10. Obviously, if "long-term" conditions of overpopulation did not cause the 1709–1714 emigration from the Palatinate and thereabouts, then they could not have led to much emigration from there as early as 1717 and shortly thereafter. Thus relatively few emigrated from the southwest in the late 1710s and 20s (see Table I.1). But overpopulation, scarcity, and recruitment were the most important factors for those who did leave during this period, and many came from other areas (for example, Switzerland and the Kraichgau). Switzerland did not experience depopulation during the seventeenth century wars the way southwest Germany did, hence many of its regions were "crowded" by the early eighteenth century. Further, the rapidity with which many areas in the southwest recovered was astounding, due primarily to the decline in mortality (the end of devastating wars and the plague) and the large in-migration of Swiss and others in the late seventeenth and early eighteenth centuries. These issues will be discussed at length in Chapter 1.

11. I have determined approximate locations for Germans in all the colonies using naturalization records (M. S. Giuseppi, *Naturalizations of Foreign Protestants in the American and West Indian Colonies*, Publications of the Huguenot Society of London, vol. 24 [Manchester: Sheratt & Hughes, 1921]), Thomas L. Purvis's work on their locations in 1790 ("The Pennsylvania Dutch and the German-American Diaspora in 1790," *Journal of Cultural Geography*, 6 (1986), 81–99), and secondary studies on Germans in the various colonies. For New York, see Knittle, *Early Eighteenth Century Palatine Emigration*, and Roeber, *Palatines, Liberty, and Property*, 1–24. For New Jersey, see Thomas L. Purvis ("The European Origins of New Jersey's Eighteenth-Century Population," *New Jersey History*, 100 (1982), 15–31), and Peter O. Wacker, *Land and People: A Cultural Geography of Preindustrial New Jersey: Origins and Settlement Patterns* (New Brunswick, N.J.: Rutgers University Press, 1975), 213. Information on ship arrivals in Nova Scotia and New England comes from Andreas Brinck, *Die deutsche Auswanderungswelle in die britischen Nordamerikakolonien um die Mitte des 18. Jahrhunderts* (Stuttgart: Franz Steiner Verlag, 1993), 260–266.

12. Nearly 80 percent of German-speaking immigrants who arrived 1700–1775 came through Philadelphia. See Fogleman, "Migrations to the Thirteen British North American Colonies," 700–704. See also Andreas Brinck's tabulations of ships arriving by port 1748–1754—the peak period of German immigration. Brinck found that 181 ships carrying German immigrants arrived in North American ports during these years, of which 121 (67 percent) landed in Philadelphia. When one subtracts the twelve that landed in Nova Scotia and the seven Moravian ships that landed in New York but whose occupants proceeded immediately to Pennsylvania,

then it follows that immigrants from 76 percent of the ships bound for the thirteen colonies went to Pennsylvania. See Brinck, *Die deutsche Auswanderungswelle*, 260–266.

On "Greater Pennsylvania" see Carl Bridenbaugh, *Myths & Realities: Societies of the Colonial South* (Baton Rouge: Louisiana State University Press, 1952; reprint New York: Atheneum, 1963), 127ff; Parke Rouse, *The Great Wagon Road from Philadelphia to the South* (New York: McGraw-Hill Book Co., 1973); and Bailyn and DeWolfe, *Voyagers to the West*, 14–17. See Chapter 4 for a discussion of overland migration routes east of the Blue Ridge. Klaus Wust discovered that colonists in the Shenandoah Valley used Pennsylvania currency in the mid-eighteenth century (*The Virginia Germans*, 36).

13. Purvis, "The German-American Diaspora," 94; Jeffrey A. Wyand and Florence L. Wyand, *Colonial Maryland Naturalizations* (Baltimore, Md.: Genealogical Publishing Co., 1975); Dieter Cunz, *The Maryland Germans: A History* (Princeton, N.J.: Princeton University Press, 1948); Elizabeth A. Kessel, "Germans on the Maryland Frontier: A Social History of Frederick County, Maryland, 1730–1800," (Ph.D. diss., Rice University, 1981), 1–71.

14. The best general overview of the location of German settlements in Virginia is Wust, *The Virginia Germans*. Robert D. Mitchell, *Commercialism and Frontier: Perspectives on the Early Shenandoah Valley* (Charlottesville: University Press of Virginia, 1977), provides an important analysis of German and other settlements in the Valley during the colonial period. Roeber (*Palatines, Liberty, and Property*) discusses the Piedmont Germans in some depth (see 101–108 and 135–158).

15. The settlement at New Bern (1710), established during the second phase of German immigration, had failed by mid-century (see Vincent H. Todd, *Christoph von Graffenried's Account of the Founding of New Bern* [Raleigh, N.C.: Edwards & Broughton Printing Co., 1920], on the early period). Its inhabitants scattered throughout Virginia and North Carolina. For a general overview of the Piedmont settlements see Harry Roy Merrens, *Colonial North Carolina in the Eighteenth Century: A Study in Historical Geography* (Chapel Hill: University of North Carolina Press, 1964). For more detailed studies of German settlements see Susanne M. Rolland, "From the Rhine to the Catawba: A Study of Eighteenth Century Germanic Migration and Adaptation," (Ph.D. diss., Emory University, 1991); Daniel B. Thorp, *The Moravian Community in Colonial North Carolina: Pluralism on the Southern Frontier* (Knoxville: University of Tennessee Press, 1989); Robert W. Ramsey, *Carolina Cradle: Settlement of the Northwest Carolina Frontier, 1747–1762* (Chapel Hill: University of North Carolina Press, 1964); William H. Gehrke, "The Beginnings of the Pennsylvania-German Element in Rowan and Cabarrus Counties, North Carolina," *Pennsylvania Magazine of History and Biography*, 58 (1934), 342–369; Carl Hammer, Jr., *Rhinelanders on the Yadkin: The Story of the Pennsylvania Germans in Rowan and Cabarrus* (Salisbury, N.C.: Rowan Printing Co., 1943); G. William Welker, "Early German Reformed Settlements in North Carolina," in William L. Saunders, ed., *The Colonial Records of North Carolina*, 10 vols. (Raleigh, N.C.: P.M. Hale State Printer, 1886–1890), vol. 8, 727–757; and G. D. Bernheim, *History of the German Settlements and of the Lutheran Church in North and South Carolina* (Philadelphia: The Lutheran Book Store, 1872).

16. Roeber, *Palatines, Liberty, and Property* (206–240) and Bernheim, *History of the German Settlements*.

17. George F. Jones, *The Georgia Dutch: From the Rhine and Danube to the Savannah, 1733–1783* (Athens: University of Georgia Press, 1992), and Purvis, "The German-American Diaspora."

Chapter 1

1. Population figures for Baden-Durlach in the eighteenth century are inexact, but the following estimates may suggest the nature of growth rate: 1746—82,000; 1767—93,000; 1771—99,000; 1785—109,000 (adjustments were made for territorial boundary changes). See Karl Stiefel, *Baden, 1648–1952*, 2 vols. (Karlsruhe: Badische Neuste Nachrichten GmbH, 1977), vol. 1, 427.

2. The discussion of Carl Friedrich and his policy is largely based upon the following sources: Franz Laubenberger, "Zur Aufhebung der Leibeigenschaft in den badischen Landen 1783 unter Markgraf Carl Friedrich," *Zeitschrift des Breisgau-Geschichtsvereins*, 103 (1984), 71–92; Alfred Straub, *Das badische Oberland im 18. Jahrhundert: Die Transformation einer bäuerlichen Gesellschaft vor der Industrielisierung*, Historische Studien, vol. 429 (Husum: Matthiesen Verlag, 1977); Albrecht Strobel, *Agrarverfassung im Übergang: Studien zur Agrargeschichte des badischen Breisgaus vom Beginn des 16. bis zum Ausgang des 18. Jahrhunderts*, Forschungen zur oberrheinischen Landesgeschichte, vol. 23 (Freiburg: Verlag Karl Alber, 1972); Werner Hacker, *Auswanderungen aus Baden und dem Breisgau: Obere und mittlere rechtseitige Oberrheinlande im 18. Jahrhundert archivalisch dokumentiert* (Stuttgart: Konrad Theiss Verlag, 1980; Aaron Fogleman, "Die Auswanderung aus Südbaden im 18. Jahrhundert," *Zeitschrift des Breisgau-Geschichtsvereins*, 106 (1987), 95–162.

3. Older literature has placed too much emphasis on seventeenth-century warfare as a direct "cause" of eighteenth-century emigration. Yet wars in the previous century were actually more important as an indirect cause, in that they led to enormous change and redefinition of eighteenth-century society, of which emigration was a part. See Günther Franz's classic statement on the effects of the Thirty Years' War on Germany, *Der Dreißigjährige Krieg und das deutsche Volk*, Quellen und Forschungen zur Agrargeschichte, vol. 7, Günther Franz and Wilhelm Abel, eds. (Stuttgart: Gustav Fischer Verlag, 1979), 62–77.

4. David W. Sabean traces the effects of these developments on village life and identity throughout the early modern period in Württemberg. See *Power in the Blood: Popular Culture and Village Discourse in Early Modern Germany* (Cambridge: Cambridge University Press, 1984).

5. For a brief discussion of Becher see Fenske, "International Migration," 334. For a more extensive discussion see Herbert Hassinger, *Johann Joachim Becher, 1635–1682: Ein Beitrag zur Geschichte des Merkantilismus* (Vienna: A. Holzhausens Nfg., 1951).

6. Schlettwein published his ideas later in *Neues Archiv für den Menschen und Bürger in allen Verhältnissen*, 5 vols. (Leipzig: Weingandische Buchhandlung, 1784–1787), see especially vol. 2, 76–79.

7. While free emigration was allowed in Baden by the end of the eighteenth century, the government of Württemberg did not adopt such a policy until 1817, and in the Palatinate (after 1816 ruled by Bavaria) it did not come until 1859. See Wolfgang von Hippel, *Auswanderung aus Südwestdeutschland: Studien zur württembergischen Auswanderung und Auswanderungspolitik im 18. und 19. Jahrhundert*, Industrielle Welt, vol. 36, Werner Conze, ed. (Stuttgart: Klett-Cotta, 1984), 134, and Joachim Heinz, *"Bleibe im Lande, und nähre dich redlich!": Zur Geschichte der pfälzischen Auswanderung vom Ende des 17. bis zum Ausgang des 19. Jahrhunderts*, Beiträge zur pfälzischen Geschichte und Volkskunde, vol. 1 (Kaiserslautern: Institut für pfälzische Geschichte und Volkskunde, 1989), 234.

8. Werner Hacker has published several large volumes containing the records of tens of thousands of families who emigrated legally from southwest Germany in the eighteenth century and paid the appropriate taxes. Four of his works cover the areas in which large numbers emigrated to North America (see Graph 1.1). For an extended discussion of Hacker's treatment of these sources see Aaron S. Fogleman, "Progress and Possibilities in Migration Studies: The Contributions of Werner Hacker to the Study of Early German Migration to Pennsylvania," *Pennsylvania History*, 56 (1989), 318–329.

9. Joachim Heinz found that a large majority of inhabitants of the Palatinate were serfs (see *"Bleibe im Lande"*, 60). There were exceptions, but generally, the inhabitants of cities (*Städte*) were free, while those peasants living in villages (*Dörfer*) were serfs. In the eighteenth century, the vast majority of the population in any given territory lived in the villages. The 1809 census of Baden, which designates the status of each locality, demonstrates this point. See Johann Friedrich von Eichrodt, ed., *Das Großherzogthum Baden nach seinen zehen Kreisen und Amtsbezirken topographisch skizziert* (Karlsruhe: C.F. Müller'schen Verlagshandlung, 1810).

10. An important exception to this was the collection of the traditional heriot (*Todfall*), a form of inheritance duty. In Baden-Durlach serfs were required to pay the heriot, manumission fees (for the purpose of emigration), and what amounted to export taxes on the goods they took with them (Laubenberger, "Zur Aufhebung der Leibeigenschaft in den badischen Landen," 78). In the Palatinate rulers collected the heriot and in some areas quitrents (Heinz, *"Bleibe im Lande"*, 39–41).

11. The fees for manumission from serfdom and emigration varied from state to state, but all were high. Families with two children were required to pay roughly the following amounts:

Territory	Serfs	Free Subjects
Ulm	20% + 33 guilders	10% + 33 guilders
Palatine Electorate	20%	10%
Zweibrücken	14% + 2 guilders	6% + 2 guilders
Baden-Durlach	22% + 33 guilders (appx.)	12% + 7 guilders (appx.)

Source: Fogleman, "Progress and Possibilities in Migration Studies," 323.

12. Heinz found the illegal emigration from the Palatinate to be abnormally high because of the scattered, spatially disconnected segments of the state and the

easily available transport system of the Rhine and its tributaries (*"Bleibe im Lande"*, 83–91). On policies restricting emigration or threatening punishment of those who tried, see Heinz (109–127) and von Hippel, *Auswanderung aus Südwestdeutschland*, 94–112. Werner Hacker is the most prolific publisher of official government records on emigration. In his numerous volumes he also extensively discusses the nuts and bolts of the various bureaucracies employed by these territories to collect emigration dues and insure compliance with state policy.

13. See Strobel, *Agrarverfassung im Übergang*, 132–148; Alan Mayhew, *Rural Settlement and Farming in Germany* (New York: Harper & Row, 1973), 118–177; Hermann Aubin et al., *Geschichte des Rheinlandes von der ältesten Zeit bis zur Gegenwart* (Essen: G.D. Baedeker Verlagsbuchhandlung, 1922), 123–137; Wilhelm Abel, *Agricultural Fluctuations in Europe from the Thirteenth to the Twentieth Centuries*, 3rd ed., translated and updated by Oliver Ordish (New York: Methuen and Co., Ltd., 1980), 197–219; Volker Henn, "Die soziale und wirtschaftliche Lage der rheinischen Bauern im Zeitalter des Absolutismus," *Rheinische Vierteljahresblätter*, 42 (1978), 240–257; Straub, *Das badische Oberland im 18. Jahrhundert*, 80–134; Ekkehard Liehl, *Hinterzarten: Gesicht und Geschichte einer Schwarzwaldlandschaft* (Konstanz: Rosgarten Verlag, 2nd ed., 1974), 37. The following discussion on agricultural developments, inheritance, and proto-industry is based primarily on these works.

14. An alternative for some was employment in the new proto-industries. Carl Friedrich promoted rural industries in upper Baden-Durlach and attempted to attract Swiss entrepreneurs to promote them. (See Jürgen Tacke, "Der Merkantilismus als beherrschende Idee in der Werbeschrift zur Niederlassung gewerblicher Betriebe in der Stadt Lörrach," *Das Markgräflerland*, 20 [1958], 38–40; and Straub, *Das badische Oberland*, 80–88.) In the Rhineland, on the other hand, peasants migrated into towns and cities to work in new industries (see Jeffrey M. Diefendorf, "Soziale Mobilität im Rheinland im 18. Jahrhundert," *Scripta Mercaturae—Zeitschrift für Wirtschafts- und Sozialgeschichte*, 19 (1985), 88–112.

On the concept and theory of "proto-industry" see Peter Kriedte, Hans Medick, Jürgen Schlumbohm, *Industrialization before Industrialization: Rural Industry in the Genesis of Capitalism*, translated by Beate Schempp (Cambridge: Cambridge University Press, 1981). For a critique of the proto-industry school and a discussion of the development of light industry in the Rhineland see Diefendorf, "Soziale Mobilität im Rheinland."

15. For an excellent summation of these developments, see Deppermann, "Pennsylvanien als Asyl."

16. On immigration into the southwest after the Thirty Years' War see Albert Becker, "Zur oberrheinischen Bevölkerungsgeschichte des 17. und 18. Jahrhunderts," *Zeitschrift für die Geschichte des Oberrheins*, 95 (1943), 676–685; Karl Kollnig, *Wandlungen im Bevölkerungsbild des pfälzischen Oberrheingebiets*, vol. 2 in Fritz Ernst and Karl Kollnig, eds., *Heidelberger Veröffentlichungen zur Landesgeschichte und Landeskunde* (Heidelberg: Carl Winter Universitätsverlag, 1952), 16–24; Fenske, "International Migration," 334–336; Franz, *Der Dreißigjährige Krieg*, 73–77; Strobel, *Agrarverfassung im Übergang*, 28–31; Heinz, *"Bleibe im Lande"*, 20–23 and 93–97.

17. The discussion of the relationship between demographic cycles and socio-

economic change, including in- and out-migration from the eleventh to the eighteenth centuries is based primarily upon the following sources: Karl F. Helleiner, "The Population of Europe from the Black Death to the Eve of the Vital Revolution," in E. E. Rich and C. H. Wilson, eds., *The Cambridge Economic History of Europe*, The Economy of Expanding Europe in the Sixteenth and Seventeenth Centuries, vol. 4, (Cambridge: Cambridge University Press, 1967), 1–95; Ordish (Abel), *Agricultural Fluctuations in Europe*; Kollnig, *Wandlungen im Bevölkerungsbild*; Sabean, *Power in the Blood*; Henn, "Soziale und wirtschaftliche Lage der rheinischen Bauern; Diefendorf, "Soziale Mobilität im Rheinland"; Strobel, *Agrarverfassung im Übergang*; Straub, *Das badische Oberland*; and Eberhard Gothein, *Wirtschaftsgeschichte des Schwarzwalds und der angrenzenden Landschaften* (Strassbourg: Verlag von Karl J. Trübner, 1892), 297–303.

Estimates of European population growth in the eighteenth century vary, but the population increased roughly from about 100–120 million in 1720, to 120–140 million in 1750, and to 180–190 million in 1800. See George Rudé, *Europe in the Eighteenth Century: Aristocracy and the Bourgeois Challenge* (New York: Praeger, 1972), 12; for a short discussion of the literature on eighteenth-century population growth and its causes, see 15–19.

18. The connections between demographic cycles and social change discussed here are similar to those studied by Emmanuel Le Roy Ladurie in *The Peasants of Languedoc*, translated by John Day (Urbana: University of Illinois Press, 1974). Robert Brenner has critiqued this view of demographic trends and accompanying social change in early modern European history. For his and others' views see Trevor H. Aston and C. H. E. Philpin, eds., *The Brenner Debate: Agrarian Class Structure and Economic Development in Pre-Industrial Europe* (Cambridge: Cambridge University Press, 1985).

19. Franz estimates 10 to 30 percent losses in northern Baden and 30 to 50 percent in southern Baden (*Der Dreißigjährige Krieg*, 5–8, 59 et al.). Fenske estimates a 60 to 70 percent population decline in Württemberg and 80 to 85 percent in the Palatinate ("International Migration," 333). Joachim Heinz does not make his own estimates, but discusses those of other historians, which range from 60 to 80 percent (*"Bleibe im Lande"*, 24).

20. Von Hippel suggests that the population of Württemberg reattained pre-1620 levels in the second quarter of the eighteenth century (26). In the Palatinate, these levels were attained about 1730 in the Rhine valley, and at mid-century in the western areas of this region (Heinz, *"Bleibe im Lande"*, 21 and 24). In Baden, the district of Hochberg did not fully recover its population until about 1760 (Strobel, *Agrar verfassung im Übergang*, 28–30), and Freiburg still had not recovered its pre-1620 population level by the end of the eighteenth century (Hans Helmut von Auer, *Das Finanzwesen der Stadt Freiburg i. B. von 1648 bis 1806*, part I, 1648–1700 [Karlsruhe: G. Braunsche Hofbuchdruckerei und Verlag, 1910], 14–17; and Helmut Brandl, *Der Stadtwald von Freiburg*, Veröffentlichungen aus dem Archiv der Stadt Freiburg im Breisgau, vol. 12 [Freiburg: Wagnersche Universitätsbuchhandlung, Karl Zimmer Kommissionsverlag, 1970], 124 and 143).

21. Partible inheritance was most common in the southwest, and this is where population decline in the seventeenth century and growth in the eighteenth was

most significant. Occasionally, communities practiced partible inheritance in scattered areas where impartible inheritance predominated, for example in southern Westphalia, northern Hessen, southern parts of lower Saxony, on the North Sea coast, in Upper Silesia, and around Poznan. Other areas of central Europe, such as the north-German provinces and Bavaria, experienced neither depopulation during seventeenth-century warfare nor a population explosion in the eighteenth. Hans Fenske cites the following population densities for the eighteenth century: 73.2 persons per square kilometer in Hessen, 72.5 in the Palatinate, 72.3 in Württemberg, and 66.7 in Baden (all in the southwest), whereas in the northern provinces there were less than 30 persons per square kilometer, and in west Prussia only 22.4. The average for all of Germany was 45.8 (see "Die deutsche Auswanderung," *Mitteilungen des Historischen Vereins der Pfalz*, 76 [1978], 183–220, here 186–187). Joachim Heinz estimates that the population density of the Palatine Electorate increased from 33 to 35 persons per square kilometer in 1717 to 72 in 1776, and 83 in 1791 ("*Bleibe im Lande*", 348).

22. Strobel, *Agrarverfassung im Übergang*, 31 and 84–110. It is perhaps astounding that so many peasants, insensitive to the dangers of land parcellation and large families, continued to practice partible inheritance, even as they gave up other traditional aspects of their lives. The shift to high yield commercial crops in the eighteenth century allowed many to survive on the smaller plots, but eventually the size of inherited plots became so small that even the newer methods of agriculture could not yield enough to support their families, and many sought new ways to make a living. Often small landholders began working as day laborers or artisans as well. Conversely, many artisans trying to make a living in rural areas where farmers were having difficulties began acquiring small plots or working as day laborers. Strobel (*Agrarverfassung im Übergang*, 90) found that in Hochberg (in the upper Rhine Valley) inheriting children began sharing property without dividing it, each living on and working the land equally (*Kommunhausungen*). Also, John E. Knodel has found that many began limiting fertility at this time in these areas (*Demographic Behavior in the Past: A Study of Fourteen German Village Populations in the Eighteenth and Nineteenth Centuries* [Cambridge: Cambridge University Press, 1988], 247–349). One tradition that peasants of the southwest refused to give up until well into the nineteenth century, however, was partible inheritance.

23. See von Hippel, *Auswanderung aus Südwestdeutschland*, 37. Appendix 1 contains more data on the timing and volume of emigration from the southwest in the eighteenth century. For a lengthy discussion of this subject see Fogleman, "Auswanderung aus Südbaden."

24. For a lengthy discussion of population growth, inheritance practices, and emigration from southern Baden at the parish level in the eighteenth century see Aaron Fogleman, "Die Auswanderung aus Südbaden im 18. Jahrhundert," *Zeitschrift des Breisgau-Geschichtsvereins*, 106 (1987), 95–162. Much of the discussion on inheritance practices is based upon Strobel (*Agrarverfassung im Übergang*, 40 and 79–93); Straub (*Das badische Oberland* 18, 24, 26, 55); Jürgen Tacke, "Studien zur Agrarverfassung der oberen badischen Markgrafschaft im 16. und 17. Jahrhundert," *Das Markgräflerland*, 18 (1956), 9–118, here 32–33; Eberhard Gothein, *Wirtschaftsgeschichte des Schwarzwalds und der angrenzenden Landschaften* (Strassbourg: Verlag

von Karl J. Trübner, 1892), 288 and 297; and Mayhew, *Rural Settlement and Farming*, 130–135.

Inhabitants in north Germany, Bavaria, and in some areas of the southwest like the Black Forest usually practiced some form of impartible inheritance, or a mixture of partible and impartible inheritance. Yet noninheriting sons and daughters in such areas did not make up a large proportion of the emigration because population growth was not problematic where they lived. Demographic pressure led to emigration, and this pressure occurred primarily in areas practicing partible inheritance. For inheritance practices throughout Germany see Mayhew, *Rural Settlement*, 118–177, especially 130–135, and Knodel, *Demographic Behavior in the Past*, 23–24.

25. Tacke, "Studien zur Agrarverfassung," 33.

26. The discussion of St. Peter is based primarily upon the following sources: Hans-Otto Mühleisen, ed., *St. Peter im Schwarzwald: Kulturgeschichtliche und historische Beiträge anlässlich der 250-Jahrfeier der Einweihung der Klosterkirche* (Munich and Zurich: Verlag Schnell & Steiner, 1977); W. Stülpnagel, "St. Peter," in Administration of the Baden-Württemberg State Archives, ed., *Freiburg im Breisgau, Stadtkreis und Landkreis: Amtliche Kreisbeschreibung*, vol. 2 (Freiburg im Breisgau: Druckhaus Rombach, 1974), 897–924; Ursmar Engelmann, ed., *Das Tagebuch von Ignaz Speckle, Abt von St. Peter im Schwarzwald*, vol. 1 (Stuttgart: W. Kohlhammer Verlag, 1965); Edgar Fleig, *Handschriftliche, wirtschafts- und verfassungsgeschichtliche Studien zur Geschichte des Klosters St. Peter auf dem Schwarzwald* (Freiburg: Universitätsdruckerei H.M. Poppen & Sohn, 1908); Julius Mayer, *Geschichte der Benediktinerabtei St. Peter auf dem Schwarzwald* (Freiburg: Herder'sche Verlagshandlung, 1893); Eberhard Gothein, "Die Hofverfassung auf dem Schwarzwald dargestellt an der Geschichte des Gebiets von St. Peter," *Zeitschrift für die Geschichte des Oberrheins*, n.s. 1 (1886), 257–316.

For further elaboration on these circumstances in St. Peter, see Fogleman, "Auswanderung aus Südbaden," 131–138.

27. Other factors, such as climatic and economic catastrophes, wars, and religious persecution, are often mentioned in migration literature as causes for emigration from southwest Germany and Switzerland in the eighteenth century. While they certainly played a role for many emigrants, they can best be understood as precipitants or catalysts acting on an underlying substrata of population growth and pressure. For a lengthy discussion and critique of the literature on the causes of eighteenth-century emigration from Germany see Aaron S. Fogleman, "Hopeful Journeys: German Immigration and Settlement in Greater Pennsylvania, 1717–1775," (Ph.D. diss., University of Michigan, 1991), 84–91.

28. On recruitment by private and government-sponsored foreign agents, see Lowell C. Bennion, "Flight from the Reich: A Geographical Exposition of Southwest German Emigration, 1683–1815," (Ph.D. diss., Syracuse University, 1971). Recent literature on state settlement and recruitment of migrants in eastern Europe includes Arnold Scheuerbrandt, "Die Auswanderung aus dem heutigen Baden-Württemberg nach Preußen, in den habsburgischen Südosten, nach Rußland und Nordamerika zwischen 1683 und 1811," *Historischer Atlas von Baden-*

Württemberg, part XII.5 (Stuttgart: Kommission für geschichtliche Landeskunde in Baden-Württemberg, 1985); Karl Stumpp, *Die Auswanderung aus Deutschland nach Rußland in den Jahren 1763 bis 1862* (Tübingen: Karl Stumpp, 1974); Joseph Häßler, *Die Auswanderung aus Baden nach Rußland und Polen im 18. und 19. Jahrhundert*, vol. 1, in Albert Köbele, ed., *Beiträge zur Familien- und Heimatkunde in Baden* (Grafenhausen, 1959); Horst Glassl, *Das österreichische Einrichtungswerk in Galizien, 1772–1790*, Veröffentlichungen des Osteuropa-Instituts, vol. 41 (Wiesbaden: Osteuropa-Institut, 1975); Walter Kuhn, "Das österreichische Siedlungswerk des 18. Jahrhunderts," *Südostdeutschesarchiv*, 3 (1963), 1–26; Walter Kuhn, "Die preußische Kolonisation unter Friedrich dem Großen," *Deutsche Ostsiedlung im Mittelalter und Neuzeit* (Cologne and Vienna, 1971), 182–196; Friedrich Lotz, "Die ersten deutschen Kolonisten in der Batschka," *Südostdeutschesarchiv*, 3 (1960), 169–176; Friedrich Stahl, "Die Einwanderung in ostpreußische Städte 1740–1806," *Zeitschrift für Ostforschung*, 1 (1952), 544–553.

29. In France, population pressure did stimulate the internal migration and out-migration of many Huguenots, but other than this, the French simply did not emigrate. See Warren C. Scoville, *The Persecution of the Huguenots and French Economic Development, 1680–1720* (Berkeley and Los Angeles: University of California Press, 1960). On the very limited French migration to Canada, see Gustave Lanctot, *A History of Canada*, vol. III, *From the Treaty of Utrecht to the Treaty of Paris, 1713–1763*, translated by Margaret M. Cameron (Toronto: Clarke, Irwin, and Company, Ltd., 1965), 101–109.

30. Hungary may have been an exception to the pattern of large, government-sponsored settlements in eastern Europe. Hans Fenske estimates that at least 350,000 Germans emigrated to Hungary in the eighteenth century, but that only one in four went as a result of government recruitment and was settled with public financial aid. Most followed invitations of private landowners or relatives already living in the area, or went to royal free cities, often on their own initiative. See "International Migration," 343–345.

On religious-group migrations to British North America, see Chapter 4. Also, Bailyn and DeWolfe's *Voyagers to the West* contains several chapters that provide excellent descriptions of private, large-scale speculative enterprises involving immigrants in North America.

31. The advertisements that spell out what each government offered to immigrants who settled in their respective colonies are reprinted in Hacker, *Auswanderungen aus Baden und dem Breisgau*, 170–176, and Hacker, *Auswanderungen aus Rheinpfalz und Saarland im 18. Jahrhundert* (Stuttgart: Konrad Theiss Verlag, 1987), 177. Other examples from eastern Europe include six years' freedom from all taxes for immigrants in Hungary (1723) and five years' freedom in the Banat and Batschka (1736); three years' freedom from royal taxation and two years' freedom from seigniorial dues in Dunasceckcsö, Hungary (1753); and ten years' freedom from taxation in Galicia, Hungary, and Lodomerien (1782) (see Werner Hacker, *Auswanderungen aus dem nördlichen Bodenseeraum im 17. und 18. Jahrhundert* [Singen: Hegau-Geschichtsverein, 1975], 138–142). Three years' freedom from taxation was offered in the Banat (1723) (Hacker, *Auswanderungen aus Rheinpfalz und Saar-*

land, 177); and six years' freedom in Tokaj, Hungary (1727) (see Anton Tafferner, "Die frühe Ansiedlungszeit der Kameralherrschaft Tokaj [Tockey] an der oberen Theiß," *Südostdeutsches Archiv*, 12 [1969], 73–117.

32. Anton Tafferner's documents collection, *Quellenbuch zur donauschwäbischen Geschichte* (Munich: Verlag Hans Menschendörfer, 1974), provides details on the German-speaking group settlements in Habsburg lands. Arnold Scheuerbrandt provides excellent cartography of settlements throughout eastern Europe in "Die Auswanderung aus dem heutigen Baden-Württemberg."

33. See William Penn, *Eine Nachricht Wegen der Landschafft Pennsilvania in America* (Frankfurt am Main, 1683), which was a translation of the original printed in London by Benjamin Clark in 1675; Daniel Falkner, *Curieuse Nachricht von Pennsylvania in Nord-Amerika/ Welche/ Auf Begehren guter Freunde/ Über vorgelegte 103. Frage/ bei seiner Abreiß aus Teutschland nach obigem Lande Anno 1700* (Frankfurt: Andreas Otto Buchhändler, 1702); Gabriel Thomas, *Continuation der Beschreibung der Landschafft Pennsylvaniae An denen End-Graentzen Americae. Über vorige des Herrn Pastorii Relationes* (Frankfurt: Andreas Otto Buchhändlern, 1702); Franz Daniel Pastorius, *Umstaendige Geographische Beschreibung Der zu allerletzt erfundenen Provintz Pennsylvaniae In denen End-Graentzen Americae. In der West-Welt gelegen* (Frankfurt: Andreas Otto Buchhändlern, 1704); and especially Joshua Kocherthaler, *Außfhrlich- und umständlicher Bericht Von der berühmten Landschafft Carolina/ In dem Engelländischen America gelegen* (Frankfurt: Georg Heinrich Oehrling, 1706), which went through four editions, the most influential of which was the fourth in 1709.

South Carolina began offering bounties and other benefits to Irish immigrants as early as 1731. Georgia adopted a similar policy in 1766, but the British vetoed it the following year. Two North Carolina acts of 1771 providing special benefits and land to Scottish immigrants were also vetoed. In 1773 the British government began to take steps to restrict all colonial governors or other officers from granting land in America. See Bailyn and DeWolfe, 29–66, especially 55.

34. For descriptions of Native Americans in recruitment literature see, for example, Gabriel Thomas, *Continuation der Beschreibung der Landschafft Pennsylvaniae*, and Pastorius, *Umstaendige Geographische Beschreibung*.

35. On the published lists of legal emigrants see Aaron S. Fogleman, "Progress and Possibilities," 326.

Hans Fenske estimates that about 115,000 of the nearly 900,000 total emigrants went to the thirteen colonies or United States during the entire century, which is compatible with my estimate of 84,500 for the years 1700–1775. See his comprehensive estimates in "International Migration," 344–347. Württemberg may have been one of the few large territories in which a majority emigrated to British North America. The data on emigration from this state in the eighteenth century is not as complete as it is for the areas covered by Werner Hacker, however. Wolfgang von Hippel estimates that 60 percent may have emigrated to America from Württemberg (*Auswanderung aus Südwestdeutschland*, 43). It was not until well into the nineteenth century that most Germans began emigrating to the United States as opposed to eastern Europe.

36. Stephanie G. Wolf, *Urban Village: Population, Community, and Family Structure in Germantown, Pennsylvania, 1683–1800* (Princeton, N.J.: Princeton University Press, 1976), 329–330, and James T. Lemon, *The Best Poor Man's Country: A Geographical Study of Early Southeastern Pennsylvania* (Baltimore, Md.: Johns Hopkins University Press, 1972), xiii–xvi and 1–41, especially 1–5, 10, 13, and 41.

37. Wolfgang von Hippel and Mark Häberlein provide some data in these areas. Von Hippel (*Auswanderung aus Südwestdeutschland*, 46–58) found that 60 to 78 percent of emigrants from Württemberg to eastern Europe from 1749 to 1754 were farmers (*Bauern*), while 69 percent of the emigrants to America during the same years were craftsmen, and only 25.1 percent worked in agriculture. Still fewer (10.3 percent) were *Bauern*. But distinctions between farmers and craftsmen were blurred in the eighteenth century, both in Germany and among Germans in North America. Throughout the century many pursued both occupations. Häberlein analyzes property values of legal emigrants listed in Werner Hacker's volume, *Auswanderungen aus Baden und dem Breisgau*. Focusing on emigrants to America from twenty villages in Baden-Durlach during the years 1732–1754, he presents data suggesting that only about one in five owned substantial property, and more than one in three were poor. (See Häberlein, "German Migrants in Colonial Pennsylvania: Resources, Opportunities, and Experience," *William & Mary Quarterly*, 50 (1993), 555–574). Using the same source, I compared wealth levels of east versus west emigrants from five of these villages (Bauschlott, Berghausen, Eggenstein, Staffort, and Welsh-Neureut) and found that about one-third of the emigrants in both directions were very poor, but that the upper two-thirds of those who went to America were somewhat wealthier than those who went to eastern Europe. The extremely large percentage of missing data and other problems make it very difficult to generalize wealth data from Hacker's published emigrant lists.

38. Fogleman, "Auswanderung aus Südbaden," 144, documents a large Protestant migration from southern Baden to Hungary in the eighteenth century. On radical pietist migrations to eastern Europe in the eighteenth century see Stumpp, *Die Auswanderung aus Deutschland nach Rußland*, 166–167; Lawrence Klippenstein, "The Mennonite Migration to Russia, 1786–1988," in John Friesen, ed., *Mennonites in Russia, 1788–1988: Essays in Honour of Gerhard Lohrenz* (Winnipeg, Manitoba: Canadian Mennonite Bible College, 1989), 13–42; J. Taylor Hamilton and Kenneth G. Hamilton, *History of the Moravian Church, the Renewed Unitas Fratrum, 1722–1957* (Bethlehem, Pa.: The Moravian Church, 1967), 187–190; John A. Hostetler, *Hutterite Society* (Baltimore, Md.: Johns Hopkins University Press, 1974), 3–136.

39. Immigrant letters often reveal the dissatisfaction of subjects in Germany and Switzerland with overcrowding and land scarcity, as well as with a growing state apparatus that was increasing the tax burden on peasants. In a collection of letters from New York, Pennsylvania, and New Jersey to immigrants' home villages in Nassau-Dillenberg, for example, they emphasize abundance of land, fish, and game, and low taxes, tithes, and customs. As one immigrant wrote, "Not a person knows how big this land is" ("Es weis noch kein Mensch, wie gros das Land ist"). See Adolf Gerber, *Die Nassau-Dillenberger Auswanderung nach Amerika im 18.*

Jahrhundert: Das Verhalten der Regierungen dazu und die späteren Schicksale der Aus- *wanderer* (Flensburg: Flensburger Nachrichten, Deutscher Verlag GmbH, 1930), especially the letters, 14–45.

Letters such as these were usually intended for general reading before the family, if not the entire village, in the homeland. Knowing the increasingly difficult conditions under which many of their fellow villagers lived and the importance of letters from abroad in stimulating migrations and providing valuable information to those who did go, the writers of these letters often explicitly contrasted the scarcity and heavy taxation at home with the relative lack thereof in their new homelands.

Other examples from North America include letters from Christopher Saur to his home village (1724) in R. W. Kelsey, ed., "An Early Description of Pennsylvania: Letter of Christopher Sower, Written in 1724, Describing Conditions in Philadelphia and Vicinity, and the Sea Voyage from Europe," *Pennsylvania Magazine of History and Biography*, 45 (1921), 243–254; from Durs Thommen (1737) in Leo Schelbert, "Dokumentarbericht zur Auswanderung einer Basler Familie im Jahre 1736," *Basler Zeitschrift für Geschichte und Altertumskunde*, 75 (1975), 89–119, here 104; from Johannes Müller (1749) in Gerber, *Die Nassau-Dillenburger Auswanderung*, 14–15; from Johannes Schlessmann (1753) in Otto Langguth, *Pennsylvania German Pioneers from the County of Wertheim*, translated and edited by Don Yoder, Publications of the Pennsylvania German Folklore Society, vol. 12 (Allentown, Pa., 1947), 147–289, here 262–264.

40. "Ich hab ein Blatz genommen von 350 Jucharten samt 2 Heüßern und Scheuren und habe, mit s.v. (Verlaub), 6 Pfert, 2 Fühli, 15 Stuck Rindvieh und hab etwan 35 Seckh Haberen, auch 46 Seckh Weitzen, 25 Seckh Roggen, 23 Seckh Welsh Korn. Von dießem meinem Land darff ich für ein Jahr nichts Mehrers geben als 7 Schilling, daß ist so viel als 7 Mahl 5 Schweitzerbatzen, für Zehenden, Bodenzinß und alle Gefel (Abgaben). Gutte Freyheiten hat es in diesem Land mit allerhand Sachen." Reprinted in Schelbert, "Von der Macht des Pietismus," 104.

41. The voyage to Philadelphia proved disastrous—only forty-eight of the 156 passengers survived long enough to reach America. See "Lebenslauf des Johann Georg Jungmann in Bethlehem," *Der Deutsche Pioneer*, 1 (1869), 230–233. Jungmann became a Moravian in Pennsylvania.

42. See Gottlieb Mittelberger, *Journey to Pennsylvania*, edited and translated by Oscar Handlin and John Clive (Cambridge, Mass.: Harvard University Press, 1960). The original, *Reise nach Pennsylvanien*, was written by Gottlieb after his return to Württemberg in 1754 and published in Stuttgart in 1756.

Chapter 2

1. One of the last witch trials and burnings in central Europe occurred in Schwaigern in 1713. During the proceedings the accused witch was kept in the tower.

2. Page 59, Amtsprotocoll 1743, in volume 1, Karl Wagenplast Notes, Gemeindearchiv Schwaigern.

3. The fifty-three communities represent an arbitrary collection within this area chosen by Annette K. Burgert for inclusion in her volume, *Eighteenth Century Emigrants*, vol. 1, *The Northern Kraichgau*, Publications of the Pennsylvania German Society, vol. 16 (Breinigsville, Pa.: Pennsylvania German Society, 1983). See the bibliographic essay for a discussion of this valuable source for the study of emigration from this region to Greater Pennsylvania. On the establishment of the *Ritterschaftskanton*, see Volker Press, "Die Ritterschaft im Kraichgau zwischen Reich und Territorium 1500–1623," *Zeitschrift für die Geschichte des Oberrheins*, 122 (1974), 35–98. Arnold Scheuerbrandt has recently published an excellent overview of the general conditions of emigration from the Kraichgau and the relevant literature on the subject (see "Die Amerikaauswanderung aus dem Kraichgau und seinen Randbereichen im 18. Jahrhundert," *Kraichgau: Beiträge zur Landschafts- und Heimatforschung*, 9 [1985], 65–97).

4. See Appendix 2 for a summary of these and other important statistics on the northern Kraichgau and its emigrants. The area of the parishes was calculated from information in the regional geographical lexicon edited by the Landesarchivdirektion Baden-Württemberg, *Das Land Baden-Württemberg, Amtliche Beschreibung nach Kreisen und Gemeinden*, vol. 4, *Regierungsbezirk Stuttgart, Regionalverbände Franken und Ostwürttemberg* (Stuttgart: Verlag W. Kohlhammer, 1980). On population figures for 1809 see Eichrodt, *Das Großherzogthum Baden*, and *Königlich Württembergisches Hof- und Staats- Handbuch auf die Jahre 1809 und 1810* (Stuttgart: Joh. Frid. Steinkopf, 1810).

5. On Swiss immigration into the Kraichgau during this period, see Karl Diefenbacher, Hans Ulrich Pfister, and Kurt H. Hotz, eds., *Schweizer Einwanderer in den Kraichgau nach dem Dreißigjährigen Krieg* (Sinsheim: Heimatsverein Kraichgau e.V., 1983).

6. For a thorough discussion of the lower nobility's struggle against the territorial states in this region, including the Kraichgau, see Volker Press, *Kaiser Karl V., König Ferdinand und die Entstehung der Reichsritterschaft*, vol. 60 in *Institut für europäische Geschichte Mainz, Vorträge*, 2nd ed. (Wiesbaden: Franz Steiner Verlag GmbH, 1980) and Press, "Die Ritterschaft im Kraichgau."

7. Heinz-Theo Krahl, "Adelshofen von den ersten Siedlungsanfängen bis zur Bauernbefreiung im 19. Jahrhundert," in Wilhelm Wolfmüller et al., eds., *700 Jahre Adelshofen, 1287–1987*, Eppinger stadtgeschichtliche Veröffentlichungen, vol. 1 (Eppingen: Stadt Eppingen, 1987), 18–114; Gustav Neuwirth, *Geschichte der Gemeinde Ittlingen* (Ittlingen: Gemeinde Ittlingen, 1981), 73; *Das Land Baden-Württemberg*, vols. IV–V; D. Heinrich Neu, *Aus der Vergangenheit von Hoffenheim* (Hoffenheim: Verlag der Evangelischen Kirchengemeinde Hoffenheim, 1953), 55.

8. My interpretation of the struggles between the local nobility and peasants during the rebuilding years of the early eighteenth century is based upon the local histories and sources cited throughout this section. It is a critical aspect of community development and conflict that has been overlooked by many Anglo-American historians. Even the German authors of these community studies have

failed to make connections between developments in the various parishes. They offer no larger interpretation of events during this period.

9. B 187 Sinsheimer Briefschaften, 1617–1725, vol. I, Nr. 114, Stadtarchiv Sinsheim and Neu, *Aus der Vergangenheit von Hoffenheim*, 10–11 and 79–87.

10. The actual complaints were as follows: (1) There are not enough visitations (by the pastor) in the parish. (2) [Illegible] (3) To stop those who are allowing their livestock to ruin the village's common forest. (4) That they be allowed to bring the required duty in wood to one place all at once, and not to several different places. (5) That the hunters not be allowed to sell wood from the common forest before the village has cut its share and distributed it among its members. (6) That the village commons be better marked. (7) That the annual duty (to the *Herrschaft*) on corn and oats (300 liters each) be part of a general duty, and not given separately. (8) A complaint against tolls collected for roads, bridges, and paths. (9) That the Jews are letting their horned cattle run all over the parish, tearing things up. (There were six Jewish families in Hoffenheim in 1720; see Neu, *Aus der Vergangenheit*, 134.) (10) That the use of outside carpenters be better regulated. Nr. 127, B 187 Sinsheimer Briefschaften, 1617–1725, vol. I, Stadtarchiv Sinsheim.

11. Neu, *Aus der Vergangenheit*, 12.

12. "Der Waldt nimbt ab, Ehrliche leüthe, kennen vor solchen gesindel weder zu dorff noch zu feld, das Ihrige nicht sicher erhalten, in Summa die ehrliche alte ein gesessene Bürger undt Bürgerkindter werden dadurch gekräncket, und mit dießen liederlichen bey der Nachbarschafft verdächteig angesehen." Nr. 50, Sinsheimer Briefschaften, Stadtarchiv Sinsheim.

13. Nr. 41, Sinsheimer Briefschaften.

14. A 100, Bitte der Einwohner an die kurfürstliche Regierung der Pfalz um Hilfeleistung gegen die Gewalt, die die Herren von Venningen gegen sie ausüben, 1717, and A 101, Nov. 28, 1717, Antwort des Georg Friedrich von Venningen an den kurfürsten von der Pfalz auf Klage von Einwohnern von Weiler, Fuhrdienste, Botengänge usw. betreffend, Stadtteil Weiler, Stadtarchiv Sinsheim.

15. Krahl, "Adelshofen von den ersten Siedlungsanfängen," 55–90.

16. Neuwirth, *Geschichte der Gemeinde Ittlingen*, 81–128.

17. Ibid. The following twelve complaints were lodged against: (1) a wine tax; (2) the inheritance duty (*Drittpfennigabgabe*) on houses; (3) the misuse of the mandatory work requirements for the lord (*Frondienste*); (4) infringements upon the villagers' rights to take lumber and firewood from the Herrschaft's forests; (5) excessive punishment for minor infractions of village ordinances; (6) the sale of a salt monopoly to a Jewish merchant; (7) the use of hounds for hunting (by the nobility); (8) confiscation of the village's cellar (under the town hall) for use as a jail; (9) confiscation of the village property assessment books by the Herrschaft; (10) the sale of the village bakery by the Herrschaft; (11) the ban by the Herrschaft on meetings of the village assembly in the town hall; (12) inappropriate assessments of the inheritance tax against particular individuals (Neuwirth, *Geschichte der Gemeinde Ittlingen*, 91–92).

18. Although the Lutheran Church selected pastors at the consistory, rather than the local or congregational level, new pastors were sent to congregations for a trial sermon, in which parishioners could register their disapproval with the consis-

tory, if necessary, and request a new appointment. Given the previous arbitrary actions of the von Gemmingens and von Kochendorfs and their interests at the time, it is very likely (though not certain), that the new preacher did not hold the trial sermon and that the Ittlingers had no input on his appointment (see Neuwirth, 105).

19. Neuwirth, *Geschichte der Gemeinde Ittlingen*, 95–108.

20. For designations of villages (*Dörfer*) and market towns see Eichrodt, *Das Großherzogthum Baden*, and *Königlich Württemberg Hof- und Staats- Handbuch auf die Jahre 1809 und 1810* (Stuttgart: Joh. Frid. Steinkopf, 1810). The market towns were Schwaigern, Eppingen, Hilsbach, Neckargemünd, Sinsheim, and Wiesloch.

21. Neuwirth, *Geschichte der Gemeinde Ittlingen*, 95–105.

22. On types of village forms throughout Germany see Mayhew, *Rural Settlement and Farming in Germany*. For the Kraichgau, I have studied detailed geological survey maps that show the outlines of all villages and the locations of their buildings and houses. From these maps it is not difficult to discern the location of eighteenth-century village boundaries. This and personal inspection of the actual villages confirm that all fifty-three communities in the cohort were and are nuclear settlements. Some are slightly less so than others, but none are long, drawn-out one-street villages. In fact, the overwhelming preponderance of nuclear villages is a prominent feature of rural landscapes throughout southwest Germany.

23. See Appendix 3 for statistics on population, area, and emigration for each parish.

24. There are scattered references to the dispute regarding Bonfeld in B 578 Schatzungswesen zu Bonfeld, 1619–1762, Kanton Craichgauer Archiv, Ludwigsburger Schloßarchiv, Ludwigsburg. For disputes involving Hoffenheim and Ittlingen see Neu (20) and Neuwirth (*Geschichte der Gemeinde Ittlingen*, 177–184) respectively.

25. Neu, *Aus der Vergangenheit*, 38 and 72–73.

26. "In diesem Land ist's grad als wann in der Alten Burg ein Hauß wäre und im Hinden Berg und eines in dem Weisenberg, so ist das Land beschaffen, so stehen die Häuser im Wald." Johann Michael Wagner to his family in Schwaigern, 1744/45, 73, Karl Wagenplast Notes, Gemeindearchiv Schwaigern.

27. Burgert, *The Northern Kraichgau*, 271–272. Johannes Neu settled in Lancaster.

28. Heinz Schuchmann, "Der Eschelbronner Pfarrer Josua "Kocherthaler" und die pfälzische Massenauswanderung nach Nordamerika 1708/09," *Kraichgau-Heimatsforschung im Landkreis Sinsheim*, 2 (1970), 154–159; Scheuerbrandt, "Die Amerikaauswanderung aus dem Kraichgau," 76–81. There is little published information on Anna Maria Heinrich, wife of the town locksmith, who was tried and executed as a witch in Schwaigern in 1713 (see Königlicher Statistisch-topographischer Bureau, eds., *Beschreibung des Oberamts Brackenheim* [Stuttgart: H. Lindemann, 1873], 416). Three years later Hans Heinrich Heinrich and Hans Michel Heinrich emigrated to Pennsylvania. They were very likely related to Anna Maria, and were perhaps her children.

29. For example, of the nineteen emigrants from Ehrstädt whose place of settlement in Pennsylvania is known, ten went to New Hanover. Twenty-seven of the eighty-five Hoffenheimers went to New Hanover as well, while twelve went to

Philadelphia and ten to Lancaster. Twenty-eight of the ninety-six Ittlingers went to Lancaster and eleven to New Hanover. Twenty-eight of sixty-five Sinsheimers went to Lancaster; ten of the thirty-nine from Waldangelloch settled in Upper Tulpehocken; and all eight from Gauangelloch went to New Holland. Settlement patterns in Pennsylvania will be discussed more fully in Chapter 3.

30. In his letter home to Schwaigern from Pennsylvania, Johann Michael Wagner (one of the revelers) mentions the fate of several other Schwaigerners who traveled on the same ship with him (Wagner to friends in Schwaigern, 1744/45, 73, Wagenplast Notes).

Chapter 3

1. Wagner to Family in Schwaigern, vol. I, Wagenplast Notes, 73, 1744–1745.
2. Kelsey, "An Early Description of Pennsylvania."
3. Mittelberger, *Journey to Pennsylvania*, 16.
4. Two important analyses of the immigrants shipping business and labor contracting are Wokeck, "A Tide of Alien Tongues," and Farley Grubb, "German Immigrants to Pennsylvania, 1709–1820," *Journal of Interdisciplinary History*, 20 (1990), 417–436.
5. I would like to thank Jon Gjerde for his comments on an earlier version of this chapter presented at the annual meeting of the American Historical Association in San Francisco. Professor Gjerde suggested using the term "collective strategy" to describe the behavior of German immigrants settling in the colonies.
6. Letters home from immigrants had a powerful influence on other villagers, who read tales of three or four families in America owning as much land as an entire village in Germany (see Leo Schelbert, ed., "Von der Macht des Pietismus: Dokumentarbericht Zur Auswanderung einer Basler Familie im Jahre 1736," *Basler Zeitschrift für Geschichte und Alterstumkunde*, 75 (1975), 89–119, here 104; "Lebenslauf des Johann Georg Jungmann in Bethlehem"; Johann Michael Wagner to his family in Schwaigern, 1744/45, 73, Karl Wagenplast Notes, Gemeindearchiv Schwaigern). For contemporary accounts by older German immigrants on the increasing difficulties of getting land in mid-eighteenth-century Pennsylvania, see the entry for March 1747 in Theodore G. Tappert and John W. Doberstein, eds., *The Journals of Henry Melchior Muhlenberg*, vol. I (Philadelphia: Evangelical Lutheran Ministerium of Pennsylvania and the Muhlenberg Press, 1942), as well as Aland, *Die Korrespondenz Heinrich Melchior Mühlenbergs*, vol. I, June 15, 1751, and vol. II, March 14, 16, and July 9, 1754, November 24, 1755, and August 14, 1761. See also Christopher Saur's newspaper, *Pennsylvanische Berichte* (printed in Germantown), September 1, 1755, October 2, 1756, and March 5, 1757.
7. "Wer wil ziehen in die neue Welt, Der muß haben einen Säckel Gelt; Und dazu einen guten Magen, daß er kan die Schiffs-Kost ertragen." Anonymous letter from 1753, reprinted in Leo Schelbert and Hedwig Rappolt, eds., *"Alles ist ganz anders hier": Auswandereschicksale in Briefen aus Zwei Jahrhunderten* (Olten and Freiburg: Walter-Verlag, 1977), 130–131.

8. "Es ist nicht so gut in diesem Land wie man es sagen tut, aber wer brav Geld herein bringen thut, wer [*sic*] hat es gut. Wer Geld rein bringen thut, daß er ein Stück Land kaufen kann, hat's gut." Wagner to family members in Schwaigern, 1744/45, 73, Karl Wagenplast Notes, Gemeindearchiv Schwaigern. On Güldin, see "Diary of the Rev. Samuel Guldin, relating to his Journey to Pennsylvania, June to September, 1710," *Journal of the Presbyterian Historical Society*, 14 (1930), 28–41 and 64–73, especially 70.

9. See Häberlein, "German Migrants in Colonial Pennsylvania," especially 567.

10. Schelbert, "Von der Macht des Pietismus," especially 104–105.

11. This is a witty pun that cannot be translated without losing the joke. Literally, it means "I live every day as well as Wuchere." One of the richest families in Schwaigern was named Wuchere, and *Wucherer* is the German word for money lender, or usurer. See Lohrmann's letter home to Schwaigern, 1739, A 1246, Gemeindearchiv Schwaigern.

12. The average wealth of families emigrating from Schwaigern to Pennsylvania before 1776 was 322 guilders (n = 51). But because a few families, such as the Lohrmanns, were extremely wealthy, the average represents a skewed picture of what was typical. The median wealth of Schwaigern emigrant families was 155 guilders. This better reflects the norm. All data on the wealth of Schwaigerners was calculated from Wagenplast Notes, Gemeindearchiv Schwaigern.

13. See the anonymous letter reprinted in Schelbert and Rappolt, eds., "*Alles ist ganz anders hier*," 128–130, and Rüdel's letter to his family in Schwaigern, written in 1750 (Wagenplast Notes, 53–55). Farley Grubb estimates that about one-half of German immigrants arriving in Philadelphia were redemptioners, or indentured servants ("German Immigration to Pennsylvania," 436).

14. Analysis of the number of townships in which immigrants from each parish settled reveals a significant amount of "clustering" in the colonies. For example, thirty-two of fifty-two from Weiler (62 percent) settled in just three townships, while fifty-eight of 129 from Hoffenheim (45 percent) settled in three townships (not necessarily the same three as those from Weiler). When the "clusterers" for all fifty-three parishes are tabulated, they constitute a significant proportion of the total northern Kraichgau cohort: 534 of 1,830 (for whom data is available), or 29 percent, settled in one township, while 784 (43 percent) settled in two, and 972 (53 percent) settled in three.

15. On the *Charming Nancy* see the ship lists in Ralph B. Strassburger and William J. Hinke, *Pennsylvania German Pioneers: A Publication of the Original Lists of Arrivals in the Port of Philadelphia from 1727–1808*, 3 vols. (Norristown, Pa.: Pennsylvania German Society, 1934), vol. 1, 188–194. The Amish who sailed on the same ship as the Lohrmanns made up one of the largest, most important migrations of that group to colonial America (see "A Review of the Founding of The Lancaster County Church Settlement, Based on the Alms Book and the Ministry," *The Diary*, December, 1983, 17–22).

16. Peter and Margaretha Lohrmann (from Germantown) to [unknown] in Schwaigern, 1739, A 1246 Gemeindearchiv Schwaigern. On the Heinrichs, see Wagenplast Notes, p. 124. Peter Lohrmann died in 1749, but apparently as late

as 1750, Schwaigerners still went to Germantown to receive assistance, perhaps from Margaretha Lohrmann or others. In that year, Johann Georg Rüdel arrived in Philadelphia with a group from Schwaigern. On their sixth day they made it to Germantown, where they received lodging for four days. During that time, Rüdel purchased 200 *Morgen* (about 178 acres) of uncleared land deep in the backcountry, then moved on (see Rüdel's letter to Schwaigern, September 15, 1750, Wagenplast Notes, 53–55).

17. See Rolland, "From the Rhine to the Catawba," especially chapters 3, 4, and 5.

18. Antoni Müller (Philadelphia) to Lettweiler, August 1, 1759, reprinted in Hacker, *Auswanderungen aus Rheinpfalz und Saarland*, 773; Scherer Sr. (Dörnigheim) to Johann Conrad Scherer (Pikeland Twp.), May 15, 1754, reprinted in "Documents Relating to Early German Settlers in America," *German American Annals*, n.s. 4 (1906), 252–261, here 254–256; Durs Thommen (Quitopahilla, or Lebanon) to the city government of Basel, October 3, 1737, reprinted in Schelbert, "Von der Macht des Pietismus," 104–105; Barbara Börlin (Conestoga Twp.) to Johannes Voegely (Bennweyl), November 1, 1740, and Börlin (Lebanon Twp.) to Hans Senn (Bennweyl), October 20, 1748, reprinted in Schelbert and Hedwig, "*Alles ist ganz anders hier*", 134–136; Gerster wrote at least three letters from 1737 to 1740, two of which have been reprinted in Schelbert and Hedwig, 119–125.

19. Maria Barbara Kober (in Philadelphia) to Johann Adam Kober (in Schwaigern), November 2, 1767, 29–31, Wagenplast Notes. In 1771 Kober was still trying to recover her inheritance. That year she wrote home again and sent another messenger with a power of attorney to Schwaigern requesting her inheritance (Kober to [unknown], 1771, 78, Wagenplast Notes). During her struggle to prove her existence, Kober sent a sealed affidavit dated June 1, 1770, from the Lutheran pastor, Henry Melchior Muhlenberg, and another from the mayor of Philadelphia, which stated that Kober was alive and that she attended Zion Lutheran Church in Philadelphia. Kober's brother had maintained that she was dead and that nothing should be sent to the imposter in Philadelphia (see A 1247, Sammlung einzelner Unterlagen zu Familie Kober durch Karl Wagenplast, Gemeindearchiv Schwaigern). Some biographical data on Kober can be found in Burgert, *Eighteenth Century Emigrants*, 54 and Strassburger and Hinke, *Pennsylvania German Pioneers*, vol. I, 243–245.

20. Sehner was granted 70 guilders by the authorities in Schwaigern (see Wagenplast Notes, 130). When Antoni Müller wrote home to Lettweiler in 1759, he was trying to recover an inheritance. He appointed a professional to act as his power of attorney (Hacker, 773). Müller had no luck because he had emigrated illegally, but many others, sometimes even illegal emigrants, were successful. In 1752, two brothers and two sisters of the Junt family from Benken in Canton Basel emigrated illegally and settled in the Shenandoah Valley of Virginia. In 1756, the two brothers returned and successfully collected their property, worth 14,585 Basler pounds. (See Schelbert and Hedwig, "*Alles ist ganz anders hier*," 136–137.) For a thorough discussion of German-speaking immigrants and their connections with their home villages regarding matters of property and inheritance see A. G. Roeber, "Origins and Transfer of German-American Concepts of Property and Inheritance," *Perspectives in American History*, n.s. 3 (1986), 115–171.

21. In her study of first-generation land owners in Frederick County, Maryland (some born in Europe, some in Pennsylvania), Elizabeth Kessel also came to this conclusion (see "Germans on the Maryland Frontier"), as did Rolland in her study of Germans from Pennsylvania settling beyond the Catawba, in North Carolina ("From the Rhine to the Catawba"). This suggests that Henretta, rather than Lemon, may have come closer to describing the *mentalité* of colonial German immigrants. See James A. Henretta, "Family and Farms: *Mentalité* in Pre-Industrial America," *William & Mary Quarterly*, 35 (1978), 3–32, and Lemon, *"The Best Poor Man's Country."*

22. The meaning and importance of ethnicity is a much-debated issue. I have found Harry S. Stout's ideas on the topic persuasive. See "Ethnicity: The Vital Center of Religion in America," *Ethnicity*, 2 (1975), 204–224.

23. There are exceptions to this trend, but it appears to be generally true. The term "Dutch," often considered a corruption of *"Deutsch,"* which means German, was actually not a corruption at all. It was a legitimate, well-known term used by the English in the early modern period to describe the people who lived along the Rhine. The "Low Dutch" came from the area of the present Netherlands, while the "High Dutch" came from the area of the middle and upper Rhine. See Don Yoder, "Palatine, Hessian, Dutchman: Three Images of the German in America," 107–129, in Albert F. Buffington, ed., *Ebbes fer Alle—Ebbes fer Dich: Something for Everyone—Something for You*, Publications of the Pennsylvania German Society, vol. 14 (Breinigsville, Pa.: The Pennsylvania German Society, 1980). The entry for "Dutch" in the *Oxford English Dictionary* supports this view.

24. See Thomas L. Purvis, "Patterns of Ethnic Settlement in Late Eighteenth-Century Pennsylvania," *Western Pennsylvania Historical Magazine*, 70 (1987), 107–122.

25. Data for computing the Index of Dissimilarity is available through the recent contributions of Thomas L. Purvis. Purvis has developed the best technique to date for handling the old, familiar problem of identifying nationality by surname when names were frequently changed, often beyond recognition, after arrival in America. His impressive, excruciatingly difficult analyses, used in other ways by Purvis himself to demonstrate the importance of ethnicity in the early American population, make it possible to provide a rough measure of ethnic segregation in settlement patterns by county in 1790 in some states. Purvis has published several articles in which he revises the long-accepted estimates of ethnic distribution by state in 1790 by Howard F. Barker and Marcus L. Hansen (American Council of Learned Societies, "Report of Committee on Linguistic and National Stocks in the Population of the United States," American Historical Association, *Annual Report for the Year 1931*, I [Washington, D.C., 1932], 107–441), and the recent work of Forrest McDonald and Ellen Shapiro McDonald ("The Ethnic Origins of the American People, 1790," *William & Mary Quarterly*, 3d Ser., 37 [1980], 179–199). See "The European Ancestry of the United States Population," 85–101. In this and other articles he explains his new, more accurate technique for surname analysis. He has done analyses by county for New Jersey, New York, Maryland (for 1800), and Pennsylvania, and he has examined Germans in all states. See "The European Origins of New Jersey's Eighteenth-Century Population," *New Jersey History*, 100 (1982), 15–31; "The National Origin of New Yorkers in 1790," *New York History*, 67

(1986), 133–153; "Patterns of Ethnic Settlement in Late Eighteenth-Century Pennsylvania"; "The Pennsylvania Dutch and the German-American Diaspora in 1790," *Journal of Cultural Geography*, 6 (1986), 81–99. I wish to thank Dr. Purvis for providing me with the results of his work, including an unpublished manuscript on Maryland.

26. In 1790 the white population of Frederick County, Maryland, was 57 percent German; that of adjacent Carroll County was 50 percent German. In the Shenandoah Valley, Harrison County was 42 percent German; Shenandoah County was 57 percent German. And in the North Carolina piedmont, Stokes County was 34 percent German; Lincoln County was 26 percent German. See Purvis, "Pennsylvania Dutch and the German-American Diaspora," 94. On settlement in western Maryland, see Kessel, "Germans on the Maryland Frontier," 110–190, especially 111–112. On Virginia see Wust, *Virginia Germans*, 17–42, especially 23.

27. The population model of backcountry settlement in Greater Pennsylvania has a long developmental history, beginning with Frederick Jackson Turner, whose well-known safety-valve thesis on frontier settlement need not be repeated here (see *The Frontier in American History* [New York: Henry Holt and Co., 1920]). Following up on Turner's ideas, Ray Allen Billington describes settlement of the "Old West" (1700–1763) in terms of population pressure driving the gradual expansion of the frontier in all colonies and regions. He briefly discusses the movement of Scots-Irish, Germans, and others from Pennsylvania southward into the Shenandoah Valley and the Carolina piedmont (see *Westward Expansion: A History of the American Frontier* [New York: The MacMillan Company, 1949], 80–102). It was Carl Bridenbaugh, however, who first fully developed the theme of gradual expansion from Pennsylvania southward, along the Great Wagon Road, through the valley, and into the Carolina backcountry (see *Myths & Realities*, 122–126). His work influenced many later historians.

Lemon, in *Best Poor Man's Country*, stresses that those who did not settle near Philadelphia chose to be near markets and county courts (64–65). John J. McCusker and Russell R. Menard, in *The Economy of British America, 1607–1789* (Chapel Hill: University of North Carolina Press, 1985), stress that demographic and market forces worked together to shape settlement patterns in Pennsylvania (207–208).

28. Analysis of first and last residences of the northern Kraichgau immigrants suggests that they followed a similar pattern.

I have used a letter-cluster sampling method to match immigrants in the ship lists (Strassburger and Hinke, *Pennsylvania German Pioneers*) with those in the naturalization lists for the years 1761 through 1765, when 69 percent of the total naturalizations under the 1740 Act of Parliament occurred. For all immigrants whose last names began with the letter "L" (one of only two or three letters in both the German and English alphabets that could not be easily misinterpreted by colonial officials), the mean time from arrival in Philadelphia to naturalization was fifteen years and the median thirteen years (n = 47). Letter-cluster sampling works best when linking records of only one ethnic group, as I have done. See Michael D. Ornstein and A. Gordon Darroch, "National Mobility Studies in Past Time: A Sampling Strategy," *Historical Methods*, 11 (1978), 152–161, and John A. Phillips, "Achieving a Critical Mass While Avoiding an Explosion: Letter-Cluster Sampling and Nominal Record Linkage," *Journal of Interdisciplinary History*, 9 (1979), 493–508. For the most comprehensive edition of colonial naturalizations under the 1740 Act of Parliament see Giuseppi, *Naturalizations of Foreign Protestants*.

The 4,443 adult men who were naturalized from 1761 to 1765 may represent 30 to 40 percent of all Germans eligible from the peak period of immigration (1749–1754). Women were not naturalized, and many men either left the colony or died before becoming eligible. The naturalization data may be biased toward representing property holders, if developments described in Chapter 5 are reasonably accurate. For dates of township settlement, see JoAnne Hottenstein and Sibl Welch, eds., *Incorporation Dates for Pennsylvania Municipalities* (Harrisburg: Department of Internal Affairs, 1965).

29. Mitchell, *Commercialism and Frontier*, 15–58; the Moravian itinerant preachers and missionaries Leonard Schnell and Vitus Handrup reached Patterson's Creek in 1747, where a man told them another Moravian minister had been five years before (William J. Hinke and Charles E. Kemper, eds., "Moravian Diaries of Travels through Virginia," *Virginia Magazine of History and Biography*, 12, n. 1, [July 1904], 55–82); Louis De Vorsey, Jr., "The Colonial Georgia Backcountry," in Edward J. Cashin, ed., *Colonial Augusta: "Key of the Indian Countrey"* (Macon, Ga.: Mercer University Press, 1986), 3–26, as quoted in Albert H. Tillson, Jr., "The Southern Backcountry: A Survey of Current Research," *Virginia Magazine of History and Biography*, 98 (1990), 387–422.

30. Kessel came to a similar conclusion for Germans in Frederick County, Maryland: When choosing where to settle, they tried to get the best buy for land, but they also tried to settle with other Germans ("Germans on the Maryland Frontier," 111–112).

31. Henry Melchior Muhlenberg recorded the incident in his journal in January 1747. See *The Journals of Henry Melchior Muhlenberg*, vol. I, 138.

32. On religious developments and conflicts in the German churches, see Dietmar Rothermund, *The Layman's Progress: Religious and Political Experience in Colonial Pennsylvania, 1740–1770* (Philadelphia: University of Pennsylvania Press, 1961); Roeber, *Palatines, Liberty, and Property*; Charles H. Glatfelter, *Pastors and People*, vol. 2, *The History*, vol. 15 in *Publications of the Pennsylvania German Society* (Breinigsville, Pa., 1981); John B. Frantz, "The Awakening of Religion among the German Settlers in the Middle Colonies," *William & Mary Quarterly*, 33 (1976), 266–288; Martin E. Lodge, "The Crisis of the Churches in the Middle Colonies, 1720–1750," *Pennsylvania Magazine of History and Biography*, 95 (1971), 195–220.

33. For examples of Reformed and Lutheran pastors helping new immigrants get started, see Johannes Brunner to Michael Schlatter, September 11, 1748, Michael Schlatter's Correspondence, Zacharias Collection, Evangelical and Reformed Historical Society of the United Church of Christ, Lancaster, Pennsylvania; and Henry Melchior Muhlenberg to Theophilius Krome, November 24, 1755, in *Die Korrespondenz Heinrich Melchior Mühlenbergs*, vol. II, 252–266, especially 256–257.

34. I calculated the number of ministers from information in Frederick L. Weis, *The Colonial Clergy of Virginia, North Carolina and South Carolina* (Baltimore, Md.: Genealogical Publishing Co., 1976); Bernheim, *History of the German Settle-*

ments; and Welker, "Early German Reformed Settlements". I calculated the number of communities from the above sources and from church records in the North Carolina State Archives, Raleigh, N.C., the Charles L. Coon Records, Duke University Library, Durham, N.C., and the Archives of the North Carolina Lutheran Synod, Salisbury, N.C.

35. For New England, Kenneth A. Lockridge clearly develops the themes of community, lack of geographic mobility, and growing socioeconomic tensions in "Land, Population and the Evolution of New England Society 1630–1790," *Past & Present: A Journal of Historical Studies*, 39 (1968), 62–80. Jackson Turner Main (*Social Structure of Revolutionary America* [Princeton, N.J.: Princeton University Press, 1965]) and James Lemon (*Best Poor Man's Country*) emphasize extreme geographic mobility in the eighteenth century. Lemon's work has heavily influenced views of mobility and individualism in the middle colonies. Allan Tully, *William Penn's Legacy: Politics and Social Structure in Provincial Pennsylvania, 1726–1755* (Baltimore, Md.: Johns Hopkins University Press, 1977), emphasizes high geographic mobility in Pennsylvania, but does not believe that it significantly disrupted communities and community structure (64–65).

36. Virginia DeJohn Anderson, *New England's Generation: The Great Migration and the Formation of Society and Culture in the Seventeenth-Century* (Cambridge: Cambridge University Press, 1991), especially 114; James Horn, *Adapting to a New World: English Society in the Seventeenth-Century Chesapeake* (Chapel Hill: University of North Carolina Press, 1994), especially 181–186.

Other recent studies on geographic mobility in the colonial period include Douglas L. Jones, *Village and Seaport: Migration and Society in Eighteenth-Century Massachusetts*, (Hanover, N.H.: University Press of New England, 1981); Georgia C. Villaflor and Kenneth L. Sokoloff, "Migration in Colonial America: Evidence from Militia Muster Rolls," *Social Science History*, 6 (1982), 539–570; Daniel Scott Smith, "Migration of American Colonial Militiamen: A Comparative Note," *Social Science History*, 7 (1983), 475–479; Richard Beeman, *The Evolution of the Southern Backcountry: A Case Study of Lunenburg County, Virginia, 1746–1832* (Philadelphia: University of Pennsylvania Press, 1984); John W. Shy, "Migration and Persistence in Revolutionary America," in Elise Marienstras and Barbara Karsky, eds., *Autre Temps, Autre Espace: Etudes sur l'Amérique pré-industrielle* (Nancy: Presses universitaires de Nancy, 1986), 215–227; Lorena S. Walsh, "Staying Put or Getting Out: Findings for Charles County, Maryland, 1650–1720," *William & Mary Quarterly*, 44 (1987), 89–103.

37. Main and Lemon's argument for extreme geographic mobility is still accepted for Pennsylvania, with some modifications. See Stephanie Wolf, *Urban Village*; Alan Tully, *William Penn's Legacy*; Laura Becker, "The American Revolution as a Community Experience: A Case Study of Reading, Pennsylvania" (Ph.D. diss., University of Pennsylvania, 1978); McCusker and Menard, *The Economy of British North America*. Sharon Salinger suggests that mobility among former servants (often immigrants) was limited, and thus an exception to the above trend. See *"To Serve Well and Faithfully": Labor and Indentured Servitude in Pennsylvania, 1682–1800*, (Cambridge: Cambridge University Press, 1987).

Carl Bridenbaugh wrote that Germans in the South stayed put more than the

Scots-Irish (see *Myths & Realities*, 133), a proposition that John Shy recently found to hold true in Orangeburg, South Carolina (see "Migration and Persistence," 223–226).

38. Sources for Table 3.4: Secular: from Burgert, *Eighteenth-Century Emigrants from German-Speaking Lands to North America*. Moravians: from the Moravian burial records at the Moravian Archives in Bethlehem, Pennsylvania, and Winston-Salem, North Carolina. Amish: from Hugh F. Gingerich and Rachel W. Kreider, *Amish and Amish Mennonite Genealogies* (Gordonville, Pa.: Pequea Publishers, 1986); Richard K. MacMaster, *Land, Piety, and Peoplehood: The Establishment of Mennonite Communities in America, 1683–1790*, The Mennonite Experience in America, vol. 1 (Scottsdale, Pa. and Kitchener, Ont.: Herald Press, 1985); Joseph F. Beiler, "Our Fatherland in America," *The Diary* (1972), 98–100, 120, and (1976), 69 and 72; John M. Slabaugh (cartographer), "Early Amish Landowners, Berks Co., Pa. Survey Map (Gordonville, Pa.: Abner Beiler, 1986). New England: Richard Archer, "New England Mosaic: A Demographic Analysis for the Seventeenth Century," *William & Mary Quarterly*, 47 (1990), 477–502, 485.

I have counted the initial settlement outside Philadelphia as the first move for the secular immigrants because virtually all of them began in Philadelphia, and Philadelphia was a viable alternative where they could live permanently, as the 14 percent who did so suggests. The large majority of Moravians entered through New York, though many entered through Philadelphia or Charleston. With few exceptions they proceeded immediately upon arrival to their northern headquarters communities in Nazareth and especially Bethlehem (both in Pennsylvania), or to their colony in Wachovia, North Carolina, if they entered through Charleston. Because the port of arrival was never really an alternative for settlement for almost all of these well-planned, group migrations, I have counted the "first move" as the first move from Bethlehem, Nazareth, or the first town of settlement in Wachovia, North Carolina. When measuring mobility of New England migrants in the seventeenth century, Archer counted the first move after initial settlement as the "first move" (see "New England Mosaic"). His data, too, are biased toward stability, as he explains.

39. A bias exists for the Amish and Moravian data, however, because it does not include those who may have left the fold. It is not possible to estimate the number of Amish who left their religious community, but well under 20 percent of the Moravians did so. Of the 830 Moravian immigrants (including non-Germans), only thirteen were reported in the records I used as having left the church. However, there are no data on the deaths of a total of 141 (17 percent), many of whom probably left the church. Some of these, however, returned to Germany without leaving the church, and others could not be located, even though they remained in the church. Thus 17 percent should be considered a maximum figure.

40. Schlessmann's two letters can be found in Langguth, *Pennsylvania German Pioneers from the County of Wertheim*, 262–266.

41. My analysis of data in Rolland, "From the Rhine to the Catawba," Appendix A, which includes information on the movement of fifty-nine individuals and families from Pennsylvania to the area beyond the Catawba in North Carolina (some of these migrants were second-generation Europeans), also suggests relative

stability. Counting the initial move from Pennsylvania, 74 percent moved no more than twice, and 98 percent moved no more than three times.

42. I am indebted to Rosalind Beiler for pointing out the *Neukommer-Einwohner* dialogues to me. See Christopher Saur's almanacs beginning with the year 1751, *Der Hoch-Deutsch Americanische Calender, Auf das Jahr Nach der Gnaden-reichen Geburt unsers Herrn und Heylandes Jesu Christi 1751* (Germantown, 1750). Each almanac contains one long "feature article," which, along with shorter articles on planting, religion, and other aspects of life in Pennsylvania, was designed to give advice to Germans living in the colonies. Saur begins the *Neukommer-Einwohner* dialogue, "Ein Gespräch Zwischen einem Neukommer und einem Einwohner in Pensylvanien" ("A Dialogue between a Newcomer and a Settler in Pennsylvania"), with the issue for 1751 and concludes it with the 1757 issue. (After seven years, he states in the 1758 issue, some people were starting to get tired of it). He may have taken the idea from another German almanac publisher, Gotthard Armbrüster, whose *Neu-eingerichteter Americanischer Geschichts-Calender* contains an article in the 1750 issue (one year prior to the beginning of Saur's dialogue) entitled "Ein Gespräch zwischen einem ehrlichen Neuländer aus Pennsylvania, und einem Teutschen Bauer, von dem Natur- und Kirchen Reich in America überhaupt, und besonders in Pennsylvania" ("A Dialogue between an Honest Newlander from Pennsylvania and a German Farmer, on the Flora and Fauna and the Nature of Religion in America in General, and Especially Pennsylvania"). Armbrüster's almanac was printed in Philadelphia in 1750 by Benjamin Franklin and Johann Böhm. The concept of using published dialogues between migrants and established colonists may also have come from Europe. A pamphlet containing questions and answers between an Englishman and a German about conditions in the Palatinate at the beginning of the large emigration to New York and North Carolina employs this idea. See "The Palatine Catechism, or a True Description of Their Compact: In a Pleasant Dialogue between an English Tradesman and a High-Dutchman" (London: Blackheath and Camberwell, 1709).

43. "Man hat in meinem Land von der Neuen Welt geredet; Und es ist mir wohl eine *Neue Welt*; Dann es ist hier schier alles gantz anderst als wo ich gewohnt habe." *Nekommer-Einwohner* dialogue, *Hoch-Deutsch Americanische Calender*, for 1751. The almanacs have no pagination.

44. "Wan ich dran gedencke was man in der Pfaltz alle vor vielerley Geld geben muß, nur daß die Herrschafft und die Bedienten ihren grosen Staat führen und debuschieren können, und daß die alte Einwohner hier im Lande leben wie Edel-Leuth, ja besser als manche Edel-Leuth in Teutschland, dan mancher der 10-20,000 Gulden Reich ist, gibt kaum 5 biß 10 Gulden des Jahrs und manches Jahr gar nichts: Und wan ein solcher etwa ein Gulden oder ein Paar zum Armen-Tax gibt, so ists nur deßwegen daß die Armen versorgt werden und einem kein Bettler vor die Thür kommen darff." Ibid.

45. "Und ich habe den harten Zug über die See gethan, daß ich meine Sache verbessern möge, und mir ein geruhiger Leben schaffen, als ich eines gehabt habe: Und darum bin ich so im Land herum gezogen den besten Platz auszusuchen den ich finden kan, nach meinem Vermögen; damit, weil ich noch arbeiten kan, ich meine Sache in einen solchen Standt setzen möge, daß ich im Alter etwas im Vor-

rath habe, und wan ich nicht mehr so hart arbeiten kan, ich es auch nicht nöthig habe, und hernach GOTT dienen könne, damit ich auch seelig sterben möge." Ibid.

Chapter 4

1. The Moravians implemented the "choir" system only in their closed communities. Its principle purpose was to provide mutual support and exchange in spiritual and secular matters for members, who met regularly in choir groups. The Moravians established choirs for younger boys, younger girls, older boys, older girls, single brothers, single sisters, married couples, widows, and widowers.

2. A copy of Salome Meurer's journal lies in the Moravian Archives in Bethlehem. See "Diarium der Reiße Geselschaft von Geschwister Uttlis, Schwester Schrobbin, 4. Ledige Schwestern, und 12. Mädgen von Bethlehem bis nach Bethabara in der Wachau vom 2ten Octob., bis 31. Octob. 1766," JF II 1b. It has recently been published in both German and English. See Aaron S. Fogleman, "Herrnhuter Frauen auf dem Weg von Pennsylvania nach North Carolina: Das Reisejournal der Salome Meurer, 1766," *Pietismus und Neuzeit*, 19 (1993), 97–116, and Fogleman, "Women on the Trail in Colonial America: A Travel Journal of German Moravians Migrating from Pennsylvania to North Carolina in 1766," *Pennsylvania History*, 61 (1994), 206–234.

3. October 31, 1766, Diarium von Bethabara u. Bethanien, and Meurer's journal. As with the boys and men in the previous migration, the community soon put this group of new arrivals to work, except for a few of the girls who first had to recover from a fever. The day after their arrival, the Elders' Conference (*Ältesten Conferenz*) opened a letter of instruction from Bethlehem, which indicated that Anna Maria Schrobbin should join the Elders' Conference. Richard Utley, the English minister, was to begin preaching in both English and German. Anna Maria Kraussin became the chief supervisor of the older girls' choir and entered the Elders' Conference. On November 2, Anna Maria Brendelin announced her engagement to Jacob Bonn, a surgeon who had been living in Wachovia since 1758. (They married on November 25.) On November 3, they spent the day visiting in Bethania. On November 4, the Ministers' Conference (*Helfer-Conferenz*) met and decided what kind of work each would do — milking, washing, tending to the cattle, etc. (Schrobb to [unknown], November 20, 1766, Official Correspondence, Box 5, Folder 1, Document 7; Diarium von Bethabara u. Bethanien, November 2–4, 1766; Minutes of the Ältesten Conferenz, November 1, 1766, Moravian Archives, Winston-Salem).

4. For the number of German congregations in 1776, see Lester J. Cappon, ed., *Atlas of Early American History: The Revolutionary Era, 1760–1790* (Princeton, N.J.: Princeton University Press, 1976), 38, whose total numbers are probably too low.

5. On Mittelberger, see "Journey to Pennsylvania," 48. Leo Schelbert provides a useful overview of many elements of radical pietism in "Pietism Rejected: A Reinterpretation of Amish Origins," in Trommler and McVeigh, eds., *America and the Germans*, vol. 1, 118–127. See also John Joseph Stoudt, "Pennsylvania and

the Oecumenical Ideal," *Bulletin of the Theological Seminary of the Reformed Church in the United States*, 12 (1941), 171–197.

6. See sources for Table 4.1 and, additionally, Donald F. Durnbaugh et al., eds., *The Brethren Encyclopedia*, III, *Lists-Maps* (Philadelphia and Oak Brook, Ill.: The Brethren Encyclopedia, Inc., 1984); Lee C. Hopple, "The Geography of Schwenkfelderism," in Peter C. Erb, ed., *Schwenkfelders in America* (Pennsburg, Pa.: Schwenkfelder Library, 1987), 21–26, here 24.

7. Sources for Table 4.1: Mennonites: C. Henry Smith, *The Mennonite Immigration to Pennsylvania in the Eighteenth Century* (Norristown, Pa.: Pennsylvania German Society, 1929), 220–221, lists a minimum number. The higher figure comes from Harold S. Bender in Harold S. Bender et al., eds., *The Mennonite Encyclopedia* (Scottsdale, Pa.: Mennonite Publishing House, 1959), 777. Moravians: A total of 830 Moravian immigrants came to the thirteen colonies, but only 700 of them were from German-speaking lands. Moravian burial registers (Moravian Archives, Bethlehem, Pa., and Winston-Salem, N.C.); John W. Jordan, "Moravian Immigration to Pennsylvania, 1734–1765," *Pennsylvania Magazine of History and Biography*, 3 (1909), 228–248. Amish: Gingerich and Kreider, *Amish and Amish Mennonite Genealogies*; MacMaster, *Land, Piety, Peoplehood*, 50–78; Beiler, "Our Fatherland in America," 69 and 72; "Review of the Founding of the Lancaster County Church Settlement"; Slabaugh, "Early Amish Landowners." Church of the Brethren (Dunkers): Martin G. Brumbaugh, *A History of the German Baptist Brethren in Europe and America* (Mt. Morris, Ill.: Brethren Publishing House, 1899), 54–70. Schwenkfelders: Samuel K. Brecht, *The Genealogical Record of the Schwenkfelder Families* (New York and Chicago: Rand McNally & Co., 1923). Waldensians: Don Yoder, ed., *Pennsylvania German Immigrants, 1709–1786* (Baltimore, Md.: Genealogical Publishing Co., 1980). Other German-speaking religious groups were Catholics (231 are so enumerated in the Philadelphia ship lists [Strassburger and Hinke, *Pennsylvania German Pioneers*]) and Jews, for which four heads of family appear in the ship lists and seventeen others appear in the naturalization lists for Pennsylvania and New York (Giuseppi, *Naturalizations*).

8. On early, radical pietist migrations to Pennsylvania, see Julius F. Sachse, *German Pietists of Provincial Pennsylvania* (Philadelphia: Julius F. Sachse, 1895). Deppermann, "Pennsylvanien als Asyl," and Fisher, "Prophesies and Revelations." On later migrations and ships see the sources listed in Table 4.1, together with the ship lists in Strassburger and Hinke, *Pennsylvania German Pioneers*.

9. Townships containing two radical pietist congregations included Philadelphia, Providence, Worcester, Towamencin, Frederick, and Lower Salford in Philadelphia County; Oley and Hereford in Berks County; Lebanon, Derry, Donegal, Conestoga, Elizabeth, and Bethel in Lancaster County; Coventry in Chester County; and Codorus and Hellam in York County.

10. For a brief summary of the history of the Moravian church up to the beginning of their emigration to North America in the 1730s, see Thorp, *The Moravian Community in Colonial North Carolina*, 11–34. On the fifteenth-century origins of the Moravians, their relationship to the Hussite movement, and their later development, see Ferdinand Seibt, "Die Zeit der Luxemberger und der hussitischen Revolution," in Karl Bosl, ed., *Handbuch der Geschichte der böhmischen*

Länder (Stuttgart: Anton Hiersmann, 1967), 351–568; Howard Kaminsky, *A History of the Hussite Revolution* (Berkeley and Los Angeles: University of California Press, 1967); Frantisek M. Dobiàs, "Das Prinzip der Autorität in der Taboriten-Konfession," *Evangelische Theologie*, 32 (1972), 251–267; Frederick G. Heymann, "The Hussite Revolution and Reformation and its Impact on Germany," in *Festschrift für Hermann Heimpel*, vol. 2 (Göttingen: Vandenkoek und Ruprecht, 1972), 610–626; F. G. Heymann, "The Hussite-Utraquist Church in the Fifteenth and Sixteenth Centuries," *Archiv für Reformationsgeschichte*, 52 (1962), 1–15; F. G. Heymann, "John Rokycana—Church Reformer between Hus and Luther," *Church History*, 8 (1959), 240–280; Siegfried Hoyer, "Häresien zwischen Hus und Luther: Ein Beitrag zur ideologischen Vorbereitung der frühbürgerlichen Revolution in Deutschland," (Habilitation thesis, Leipzig, 1966).

   For an excellent bibliography on the Hussite movement in general, see Jarold K. Zeman, *The Hussite Movement and the Reformation in Bohemia, Moravia, and Slovakia (1350–1650): A Bibliographical Study Guide* (Ann Arbor: University of Michigan Slavic Publications, 1977). On early Hussite theology, see Jan Hus, *De ecclesia: The Church*, translated by David S. Schaff (Westport, Conn.: Greenwood Press, 1976). On Zinzendorf and his theology, see Lew Aalen, "Die Theologie des Grafen von Zinzendorf: Ein Beitrag zur 'Dogmengeschichte des Protestantismus,'" in Martin Greschat, ed., *Zur Neueren Pietismusforschung* (Darmstadt: Wissenschaftliche Buchgesellschaft, 1977), 319–353; Dietrich Mayer, "Nikolaus Ludwig Graf von Zinzendorf (1700–1760)," in Heinrich Fries and Georg Kreitschmer, eds., *Klassiker der Theologie*, 2 vols. (Munich: Verlag C. H. Beck, 1983), vol. 1, 22–38, Erich Beyreuther, *Der Junge Zinzendorf* (Marburg an der Lahn: Verlag der Francke-Buchhandlung GmbH, 1957); E. Beyreuther, *Zinzendorf und die Christenheit* (Marburg: Francke, 1961). On Bethlehem, the headquarters community in North America, see Joseph M. Levering, *A History of Bethlehem, Pennsylvania, 1741–1892, With Some Account of Its Founders and their Early Activity in America* (Bethlehem, Pa.: Times Publishing Co., 1903); Gillian L. Gollin, *Moravians in Two Worlds: A Study of Changing Communities* (New York: Columbia University Press, 1967); Beverly P. Smaby, *The Transformation of Moravian Bethlehem: From Communal Mission to Family Economy* (Philadelphia: University of Pennsylvania Press, 1988). For a good denominational history of the renewed *Unitas Fratrum*, see Hamilton and Hamilton, *History of the Moravian Church*.

   11. On the concept of "separating to unite," see John Joseph Stoudt's excellent discussion, "Pennsylvania and the Oecumenical Ideal."

   12. For a brief discussion of their ecumenical activities in Pennsylvania in 1742, see John J. Stoudt, "Count Zinzendorf and the Pennsylvania Congregation of God in the Spirit: The First American Oecumenical Movement," *Church History*, 9 (1940), 366–380.

   13. On the definition of sectarianism, see Winthrop S. Hudson, *Religion in America* (New York: MacMillan Publishing Company, 1987), 80. For Zinzendorf's metaphysics of gender, see Aalen, "Theologie des Grafen von Zinzendorf," especially 331–332. On the cloister at Ephrata, see E. G. Alderfer, *The Ephrata Commune: An Early American Counterculture* (Pittsburgh, Pa.: University of Pittsburgh Press, 1985).

14. Sources for the number and occupation of Moravian immigrants include Jordan, "Moravian Immigration to Pennsylvania, 1734–1765;" idem., "Moravian Immigration to America, 1734–1800" (Am 705, Historical Society of Pennsylvania, Philadelphia); George Neisser, *A History of the Beginnings of Moravian Work in America*, translated and edited by William N. Schwarze and Samuel H. Gapp, Moravian Archives Publications, vol. 1 (Bethlehem: Archives of the Moravian Church, 1955); Edmund de Schweinitz, "The Financial History of the Province and its Sustentation Fund," unpublished typescript in the Moravian Archives, Bethlehem, 1877. I also looked at the published and unpublished burial registers for every Moravian community in North America and many in Germany to find those immigrants overlooked in the above sources. The burial records are in the Moravian Archives in Bethlehem, Pennsylvania and Winston-Salem, North Carolina.

For Lutheran and Reformed ministers, see Glatfelter, *Pastors and People*, vol. 2, 189–205. The number quoted represents those working in New York, Pennsylvania, New Jersey, Maryland, and Virginia only. To these should be added a small number who worked in the Carolinas and Georgia and New England.

15. Gillian Gollin, *Moravians in Two Worlds* (25–49), contrasts the heavy influence of nobility on the community at Herrnhut with the lack of such influence in Bethlehem; but the large number of noble families living in North America, their high rank in the Moravian hierarchy, and the residence built for Zinzendorf indicate that aristocratic influence on Moravian society in America may have been greater than Gollin realized.

16. On the planning and design of Zinzendorf's residence, called the Manor House, see Gemein-Rath gehalten in Bethlehem, November 21, 1754, Gemein-rat Protocoll 1754–1756, Bethlehem Conferenzen, Moravian Archives, Bethlehem; and Albert F. Jordan, "The Chronicle of Peter Boehler," *Transactions of the Moravian Historical Society*, 22 (1971), 158–159. William C. Reichel, "Historical Sketch of Nazareth Hall," *Transactions of the Moravian Historical Society*, 1 (1876), 1–27; William C. Reichel, "Red Rose of the Olden Time and Old Inn, Nazareth," *Transactions of the Moravian Historical Society*, 2 (1877–1886), 270–332; Reichel, *Historical Sketch of Nazareth Hall, from 1755 to 1869* (Philadelphia: Lippincott & Co., 1869), 11–28; and H. H. Hacker, *Nazareth Hall: An Historical Sketch and Roster of Principals, Teachers and Pupils* (Bethlehem, Pa.: Times Publishing Co., 1910), 11–21; Robert P. L. Frick, "Moravian Architecture" (bound typescript, Reeves Memorial Library, Moravian College, Bethlehem, Pa.), appendices A and B. The old manor house, "Nazareth Hall," still stands and is owned by the Moravian Church. I would like to thank the director of the Moravian Historical Society, Susan M. Dreydoppel, for providing me with information on the Manor House.

17. The twenty-four Moravians who left Bethlehem, Pennsylvania, for Bethabara, North Carolina, in two groups on September 18 and October 2, 1755, were selected on September 11 and 12, 1755. See "Diary of the Little Pilgrim Congregation that on Oct. 2, 1755 left Bethlehem for the Wachau in North Carolina," written by Johann Michael Sauter, in Adelaide L. Fries, ed., *Records of the Moravians in North Carolina*, vol. I (Raleigh, N.C.: Edwards & Broughton Printing Co., 1922), 140–147. On October 2, 1766, another group of eighteen women and older girls, and two men left Bethlehem for Bethabara. Church officials did not make known

which of the older girls would make the journey until September 14. See Des Bethlehemischen Ledig-Schwester Chor-Diarii, vol. II (1757–1766), Moravian Archives, Bethlehem. Johann Heinrich Müller, who later became the famous printer (Henry Miller), used the Lot himself to decide whether he would volunteer to emigrate to America (see Donald J. Lineback, "An Annotated Edition of the Diary of Johann Heinrich Müller [1702–1782], Pietist and Printer of the American Revolution" [Ph.D. diss., University of North Carolina, 1975], 4–5). On the screening of potential emigrants to the settlement in Wachovia, North Carolina, and the use of the Lot, see Thorp, 35–57 and 86–87.

18. Meurer's story is told in two sources, both written by himself and now located in the Moravian Archives in Bethlehem. The first is his diary—377 pages in length ("Johann Philipp Meurer von Ingweyler aus dem Elsaß, Anno 1742, Diarium von 1708," JC IV 1). The second is a translation of a letter to his aunt and uncle in Germany, which he wrote on board the *Catherine* while anchored in Long Island Sound, and later updated in Philadelphia ("Br. Jn. Philipp Meurer's Journal to Pennsylvania from Febr. 25–June 15th, A. 1742," JC IV 2a). A brief synopsis of part of the diary appeared in English in [editor unknown] "From London to Philadelphia, 1742," *Pennsylvania Magazine of History and Biography*, 37 (1913), 94–106.

19. For passenger lists of the Moravians emigrating to Georgia, see George Neisser, *A History of the Beginnings of Moravian Work in America*, translated and edited by William N. Schwarze and Samuel H. Gapp, Moravian Archives Publications, vol. 1 (Bethlehem, Pa.: The Moravian Church, 1955), 6–9. For passenger lists of the Salzburgers, see I. Daniel Rupp, *A Collection of Upwards of Thirty Thousand Names of German, Swiss, Dutch, French, and Other Immigrants in Pennsylvania from 1727 to 1776*, 2nd rev. ed. (Philadelphia: Leary Stuart, 1898), 449–451.

20. On the different kinds of Lutheran pietism present in the colonies, including that practiced by the Halle pietists, see Roeber, *Palatines, Liberty, and Property*. Roeber does not discuss the Moravians, however.

21. "Die wahre Kirche Jesu Christi seit der Apostel Zeit keine schädlicheren Gefährlichere und Verschmitzere Feinde gehabt als die Zinzendorffische Secte." Muhlenberg to Johann Philipp Frensenius, 15 November 1751, in Aland, *Die Korrespondenz Heinrich Melchior Mühlenbergs*, vol. I, 443–454, here 443.

22. Other Moravian missionaries returned to Patterson's Creek in 1747 and twice in 1748, each time preaching to large numbers of German, Dutch, and English settlers in one of the most isolated outposts of white settlement in the thirteen colonies. In 1748 Matthias Gottlieb Gottschalk wrote a report on which communities in Pennsylvania, Maryland, and Virginia presented potential for further Moravian activities and which did not. William J. Hinke and Charles E. Kemper translated and edited excerpts of some of these diaries for the *Virginia Magazine of History and Biography*. See "Moravian Diaries of Travels through Virginia," v. 11, n. 2 (October 1903), 113–131, v. 11, n. 3 (January 1904), 225–242 and 370–393, vol. 12, n. 1 (July 1904), 55–82, v. 12, n. 2 (October 1904), 134–153, v. 12, n. 3 (January 1905), 271–284. There are many other journals of these itinerant preachers and scouts that have not yet been edited or translated. In addition to the above, I have looked at JB I 5a and JB I 5d, Moravian Archives, Bethlehem.

23. "Extracts from the Diary of Leonhard Schnell and Robert Hussey, of

their Journey to Georgia, November 6, 1743–April 10, 1744," Hinke and Kemper, eds., *Virginia Magazine of History and Biography*, v. 11 (January 1904), 370–393; "Diary of the Journey of Rev. L. Schnell and V. Handrup to Maryland and Virginia, May 29th to August 4, 1747," Hinke and Kemper, v. 12, n. 1 (July 1904), 55–61; "Extracts from the Diary of Bro. Gottschalk's Journey through Maryland and Virginia, March 5–April 20, 1748," Hinke and Kemper, v. 12, n. 1 (1904), 62–76; "Extracts from the Diary of Leonhard Schnell and John Brandmüller of their Journey to Virginia, October 12–December 12, 1749," Hinke and Kemper, v. 11, n. 2 (October 1903), 113–131.

24. Hamilton and Hamilton, *History of the Moravian Church*, 105–106.

25. The following discussion on the nature of Moravian overland migrations and the settlement of Wachovia is based primarily upon their translated and published travel journals, and other handwritten journals still not translated or published at the Moravian Archives in Bethlehem and Winston-Salem. See "Diary of the Journey of the First Colony of Single Brethren to North Carolina, October 8–November 17, 1753," in Hinke and Kemper, v. 12, n. 2 (October 1904), 134–153 and v. 12, n. 3 (January 1905), 271–284; "Diary of the Little Pilgrim Congregation that on Oct. 2, 1755 left Bethlehem for the Wachau in North Carolina," in Fries, *Moravian Records*, I, 140–147; Adelaide Fries, ed., "Travel Diary of Bishop and Mrs. Reichel and Their Company from Lititz to Salem in the Wachau (Wachovia) from May 22, to June 15, 1780" and "Extract from the Travel Diary of the Beloved Br. and Sr. Reichel and the Single Br. Christ. Heckewelder from Salem to Lititz" in Newton D. Mereness, ed., *Travels in the American Colonies* (New York: Macmillan Co., 1916), 586–599 and 603–613; "Br. Sauters Nachricht von seiner Reise nach North-Carolina mit dem Br. Keiter u. dem kl. Joseph Müller, u. mit Br. Keiter wieder heraus, vom 3then Jul. bis 29then Aug. als ein Brief an Br. Joseph" (1755), S743:5 Moravian Archives, Winston-Salem, North Carolina; "Diarium der Reise Geselschaft von Geschwister Uttlis, Schwester Schrobbin, 4. ledige Schwestern, und 12. Mägden von Bethlehem bis nach Wachau vom 2then October, bis 31. Octob. 1766," JF II 1b; "Kurze Nachricht von der Reise der Geschw. Schweinizens, Tierschens, der bru. Schaub, Ranke, Stöhrs, Göpferts, der Schw. Anna Leinbachin, u. der 6. grossen Mägden . . . von Bethlehem, d. 30. May bis zu ihrer Ankunft in Bethabara, d. 28. Jun. 1771," JE S II 3, Moravian Archives, Bethlehem.

26. On this famous immigrant trail see Bridenbaugh, *Myths and Realities*, 129–130; Bailyn and DeWolfe, *Voyagers to the West*, 14–17; and especially Rouse.

27. See the travel journal of one of these colonists, probably Bernhard Adam Grube, in Hinke and Kemper, "Diary of the Journey of the First Colony of Single Brethren to North Carolina."

28. Although the first colony of 1753 went up the Shenandoah Valley using the Great Wagon Road, all subsequent migrants avoided this route and traversed Virginia *east* of the Blue Ridge Mountains. Moravians crossed the Potomac near Leesburg, Virginia, and then traveled through the Piedmont, traversing the Rappahannock, Rapidan, North Anna, James, and Appomattox rivers. They entered North Carolina at the point where the Roanoke River intersects the border—more than 100 miles east of the Great Wagon Road. Here they reentered the Moravian support network, as Wachovians journeyed northward to meet them, give direc-

tions, and supply provisions. From the Roanoke they traveled westward through Hillsborough and on to Wachovia.

29. For Herrnhut's instructions to the emigrants and Bethabara, and Ettwein's arrangements concerning this migration, see Unity *Vorsteher Collegium* to Elders' Conference, August 1, 1765, Official Correspondence, Box 5, Folder 1, Document 1; Unity Directory to Elders' Conference, August 3, and September 11, 1765, Document 2; Unity Directory to Immigrants, August 20 and September 11, 1765, Document 3; Ettwein to Marschall, autumn 1765, Box 4, Folder 28, Moravian Archives, Winston-Salem.

30. Ettwein read the instructions the January arrivals brought with them from Europe, which included financial arrangements for their trip, and wrote back that they would comply (see Ettwein to *Vorsteher Collegium*, February 1766, Official Correspondence, Box 4, Folder 30, Moravian Archives, Winston-Salem). See also Elders' Conference to Provincial Synod, April 14, 1766, Folder 31, Moravian Archives, Winston-Salem.

31. Marschall to Elders' Conference, June 24, 1766, Folder 33, Moravian Archives, Winston-Salem. In the end only twelve older girls made the trip (see Meurer's journal).

32. Matthaeus Schrobb to [unknown], November 20, 1766, Official Correspondence, Box 5, Folder 1, Document 7, and October 11–20, 1766, Diarium von Bethabara u. Bethanien in der Wachau auf das Jahr 1766, Moravian Archives, Winston-Salem.

33. "Nun ist in Bethabara eine Complete Gemeine nach allen Chören." October 31, 1766, Diarium von Bethabara u. Bethanien.

34. Thorp, *Moravian Community*, 107–147.

35. *Moravian Records*, vol. 1, 323.

36. Thorp, *Moravian Community*, 33.

37. MacMaster, *Land, Piety, Peoplehood*, 50–78.

38. On the voyages of the Moravian ships and the passengers they brought to North America, see Jordan, "Moravian Immigration to Pennsylvania." As the title implies, these passengers lists do not constitute a comprehensive register of Moravian immigrants during the colonial period. They must be supplemented with Jordan's bound manuscript, "Moravian Immigration to America, 1734–1800," and the Moravian church records in Bethlehem and Winston-Salem. Jordan did not include more than a hundred of the immigrants, including a few who arrived in the northern colonies and virtually all who immigrated via Charleston, South Carolina, or the West Indies.

Of the 1,608 measurable immigrants in the northern Kraichgau cohort, twenty-six died "at sea" (1.6 percent). Farley Grubb found that overall passage mortality of German immigrants arriving in Philadelphia from 1727 to 1805 (based on 1,566 observations) was 3.8 percent. Though much lower than the average passage mortality rate of slaves in the eighteenth century (9 to 15 percent), it was still very high, the equivalent of 184 per 1,000 as an annual crude death rate (see Grubb, "Morbidity and Mortality on the North Atlantic Passage: Eighteenth-Century German Immigration," *Journal of Interdisciplinary History*, 17 [1987], 565–585. Grubb also provides a good summary of the literature on mortality and health conditions of eighteenth-century immigrants, especially Germans. For contemporary comments on Moravian health conditions, see Johann Philipp Meurer's journal, JC IV 2a, Moravian Archives, Bethlehem.

Chapter 5

1. The most comprehensive edition of colonial naturalizations after 1740 is Giuseppi, *Naturalizations of Foreign Protestants*. On the remarks of the Supreme Court clerk, see Edward Burd to James Burd, November 26, 1765, vol. VI, 135, and James Burd to Edward Burd, December 11, 1765, #595 C (outgoing correspondence), Shippen Family Papers, Historical Society of Pennsylvania, Philadelphia (henceforth HSP).

2. The community diaries of the Moravians reveal that they had been going through this routine since 1750, shortly after they were first eligible to be naturalized under the new law passed by Parliament, which required seven years' residency in the colonies. On this particular trip and the "naturalization kit," see Bethlehem community diary, September 23 and 30, 1765, and Publica: Documents on the Oath, Moravian Archives, Bethlehem, Pa.

3. Samuel Purviance, Jr. to [unknown], September 20, 1765, Shippen Family Papers, HSP. Both documents also appear in Richard K. MacMaster, Samuel L. Horst, and Robert F. Ulle, eds., *Conscience in Crisis: Mennonites and Other Peace Churches in America, 1739–1789. Interpretations and Documents* (Scottsdale, Pa., and Kitchener, Ontario: Herald Press, 1979), Studies in Anabaptist and Mennonite History, vol. 20, 204–207. On Penn's people bribing Germans to become naturalized so that they could legally vote for the Proprietary ticket, see Sally Schwartz, *"A Mixed Multitude": The Struggle for Toleration in Colonial Pennsylvania* (New York: New York University Press, 1987), 236.

4. There is a great deal of literature on the elections and political issues of the mid-1760s. See, for example, Theodore Thayer, *Pennsylvania Politics and the Growth of Democracy, 1740–1776* (Harrisburg: Pennsylvania Historical and Museum Commission, 1953); James H. Hutson, *Pennsylvania Politics, 1746–1770: The Movement for Royal Government and its Consequences* (Princeton, N.J.: Princeton University Press, 1972); and Schwartz, *"A Mixed Multitude"*. On rumors concerning Franklin, see the many cartoons that appeared in the Pennsylvania press concerning him in 1764 and 1765, for example, "The March of the Paxton Men," anonymous, in the collection at the Library Company of Philadelphia. These cartoons have been reproduced in Charles C. Sellers, *Benjamin Franklin in Portraiture* (New Haven, Conn.: Yale University Press, 1962). For an extended discussion of Franklin's activities see, for example, William S. Hanna, *Benjamin Franklin and Pennsylvania Politics* (Stanford, Calif.: Stanford University Press, 1964), 154–187.

5. Muhlenberg's journal from late June to late October 1765 is filled with references to all these activities (see vol. II, 244–277). On Penn's motives for approving the charter at St. Michael's, see Thayer, *The Growth of Democracy*, 119–120. For a lengthy discussion of developments at St. Michael's, see Roeber, *Palatines, Liberty, and Property*, 243–282.

6. Muhlenberg, *Journals*, II, September 22–23, October 1, 21, 23, and 24, 1765, et al.

7. Ibid., October 5, 1765.

8. For examples of literature deemphasizing German involvement in colonial politics, see Richard Hofstadter, *America at 1750: A Social Portrait* (New York: Alfred A. Knopf, 1971), 18; Dieter Cunz, *The Maryland Germans: A History* (Princeton, N.J.: Princeton University Press, 1948); Wust, *The Virginia Germans*; Tully, *William Penn's Legacy*; Laura Becker, "American Revolution as a Community Experience: A Case Study of Reading, Pennsylvania" (Ph.D. diss., University of Pennsylvania, 1978); Jerome H. Wood, *Conestoga Crossroads: Lancaster, Pennsylvania, 1730–1790* (Harrisburg: Pennsylvania Historical and Museum Commission, 1979).

9. See, for example, Patricia U. Bonomi, *Under the Cope of Heaven: Religion, Society, and Politics in Colonial America* (New York: Oxford University Press, 1986); Schwartz, *A Mixed Multitude*; MacMaster, *Land, Piety, and Peoplehood*; Hutson, *Pennsylvania Politics*; Gary B. Nash, *Urban Crucible: The Northern Seaport and the Origins of the American Revolution* (Cambridge, Mass.: Harvard University Press, 1986); Thayer, *The Growth of Democracy*.

Two exceptions to this trend are Rothermund, *The Layman's Progress*, who emphasizes secularization in Pennsylvania German society during the late colonial period and links this to political developments in the 1760s, in which Germans played an important role; and Elizabeth Kessel, who argues that German political participation in Maryland was significant in the late colonial period ("Germans on the Maryland Frontier," 283–323).

10. See Wayne L. Bockelman and Owen S. Ireland, "The Internal Revolution in Pennsylvania: An Ethnic-Religious Interpretation," *Pennsylvania History*, 41 (1974), 125–159, and Kenneth W. Keller, *Rural Politics and the Collapse of Pennsylvania Federalism*, Transactions of the American Philosophical Society, vol. 72, part 6 (Philadelphia, 1982).

11. MacMaster, *Land, Piety, Peoplehood*.

12. See the following works by Roeber: *Palatines, Liberty, and Property*, "Origins and Transfer of German-American Concepts," and "'The Origin of Whatever Is Not English among Us': The Dutch-Speaking and the German-Speaking Peoples of Colonial British America," in Bailyn and Morgan, eds., *Strangers within the Realm*, 220–283.

13. For descriptions of the signing-in ceremony, see Mittelberger, *Journey to Pennsylvania*, 32; Strassburger and Hinke, *Pennsylvania German Pioneers*, vol. I, xxii–xxix and xxxviii; Br. Jn. Philipp Meurer's Journal to Pennsylvania from Febr. 25–June 15th, A. 1742, JC IV 2a, Moravian Archives, Bethlehem, Pennsylvania. The texts of the oaths are printed by Strassburger and Hinke, *Pennsylvania German Pioneers*, I, 3–6. For Saur's comments, see his two letters to Governor Robert Hunter Morris, written March 15 and May 12, 1755, both reprinted in *Historical Magazine*, 4 (1860), 100–104. On the German societies, see Günther Moltmann, "Die deutsche Amerikawanderung in der Kolonialzeit und das Redemptioner-System," *Zeitschrift für Kulturaustausch*, 32 (1982), 318–323. For a thorough analysis of the immigrant trade and all these issues see Wokeck, "A Tide of Alien Tongues."

14. See Appendix 5 for the method used in calculating the number of Germans eligible for naturalization.

15. The sharp decline in naturalizations after 1765 corresponds to the equally sharp decline in immigration after 1754 (see Graph 5.1). Immigration did not resume until 1763, and given the propensity of Germans to wait about thirteen years before applying for naturalization (see the discussion of Map 3.2), the newest arrivals could not have followed this trend before the outbreak of the Revolution. See Fogleman, "Hopeful Journeys," (305–313), for a discussion of the historiography on naturalization and what happened in 1765.

16. William R. Sheperd, *History of the Proprietary Government in Pennsylvania*, Studies in History, Economics and Public Law, vol. 6 (New York: Columbia University Press, 1896), 26–53, especially 27 and 34.

17. Richard Peters to the Proprietors, August 30, 1740, vol. 1, Letterbooks, Richard Peters Papers, HSP. On rent offensives in northern Ireland and Scotland, see Wayland F. Dunaway, *The Scotch-Irish of Colonial Pennsylvania* (Chapel Hill: University of North Carolina Press, 1944), 28–32; R. J. Dickson, *Ulster Emigration to Colonial America, 1718–1775*, (London: Routledge and Kegan Paul, 1966), 1–18; Ian C. C. Graham, *Colonists from Scotland: Emigration to North America, 1707–1783*, (Ithaca, N.Y.: Cornell University Press, 1956), 1–22.

18. There is a great deal of literature on how Quaker pacifist principles influenced politics in war and peace during this period. See, for example, MacMaster, *Land, Piety, Peoplehood*; Schwartz, *A Mixed Multitude*; Hutson, *Pennsylvania Politics, 1746–1770*; and Thayer, *The Growth of Democracy*. For Boehm's comments, see Boehm to the Classis of Amsterdam, July 25, 1741, in Hinke, *Life and Letters of the Rev. John Philip Boehm*, 318–347.

19. Boehm, *Life and Letters*, 334–335 and 346–347.

20. Peters to the Proprietors, October 20, 1741, Letterbook, vol. 1, Richard Peters Papers.

21. Conrad Weiser, "Serious Advice to our Countrymen the Germans, Worthy Countreymen in pensilvania" (Philadelphia, September 20, 1741), Conrad Weiser Papers, vol. 1, 8; "Answer to Conrad Weiser's Printed Letter to the Germans" (September 29, 1741), Official Correspondence, vol. 3, Penn Papers; Peters to Thomas Penn, October 8, 1741, Letter Book, vol. 1, Peters Papers—all in the Historical Society of Pennsylvania, Philadelphia. For election returns, see the above letter by Peters for sheriff, and Tully, *William Penn's Legacy*, 93, for the Assembly.

22. Peters to the Proprietors, October 20, November 14, December 12, 1741; to Thomas Penn, January 21; to John Penn, March 1; and to the Proprietors, June 3, 1742, Peters Papers. Governor Thomas to the Proprietors, June 4, 1742, vol. 3, Official Correspondence, Penn Papers. Alan Tully discusses Kinsey's relationship to the proprietors and his tendency as attorney general to usurp the authority of the county courts (see 97–98 and numerous other places).

23. Peters to the Proprietors, October 20, 1741. On the operations of the General Loan Office, see Mary M. Schweitzer, *Custom and Contract: Household, Government, and the Economy in Colonial Pennsylvania* (New York: Columbia University Press, 1987), especially chapters 4 and 5.

24. Peters to the Proprietors, October 17 and November 17, 1742, January 15 and 30, March 14, June 4, October/November, 1743, Peters Papers. George Thomas to the Penns, June 4, 1742. Richard Hockley to Thomas Penn, November 1, 1742,

Official Correspondence (incoming), Penn Manuscripts, in HSP. For pamphlets dealing with land policy and the elections, see "To the Free-holders of the Province of Pennsylvania" (Philadelphia, 1742), and "The Case of the Inhabitants of Pennsylvania," (Philadelphia, 1742), both anonymous and in HSP. There are many analyses of the election riot of 1742. Peters explains it in the above letter of November 17, 1742, as does Richard Hockley in his letter of November 1, 1742. See also Norman S. Cohen, "The Philadelphia Election Riot of 1742," *Pennsylvania Magazine of History and Biography*, 92 (1968), 306–319; William T. Parson, "The Bloody Election of 1742," *Pennsylvania History*, 36 (1969), 290–306; Nash, *Urban Crucible*, 145; Schwartz, *"Mixed Multitude"*, 174–176; and Tully, *William Penn's Legacy*, 33–34.

25. Germans were well aware of their special problems as alien immigrants. See the dialogue in Gotthard Armbrüster's almanac, "Ein Gespräch zwischen einem ehrlichen Neuländer aus Pennsylvania, und einem Teutschen Bauer, von dem Natur- und Kirchen Reich in America Überhaupt, und besonders in Pennsylvania," *Neu-eingerichteter Americanischer Geschichts-Calender*, Philadelphia, 1749 (for the year 1750). See also David Henderson, *Des Landmanns Advocat* (Philadelphia: Henry Miller, 1761), which contains a chapter on naturalization and its importance, and the article on naturalization in Henry Miller's almanac, *Der Neuste, Verbessert- und Zuverläßige Americanische Calender*, Philadelphia, 1762 (for the year 1763).

26. Minutes of the Provincial Council of Pennsylvania, Colonial Records, vol. 6, 1754–1756, *Pennsylvania Archives* (Harrisburg, 1851), 729; Gov. Morris to Thomas Penn, November 22, 1755, ibid., 738–742; Schwartz, *"Mixed Multitude,"* 212.

27. The quote comes from Schwartz, *"Mixed Multitude,"* 205.

28. The newspaper report is from Benjamin Franklin and Anton Armbrüster's *Philadelphische Zeitung*, November 27, 1755. See also Schwartz, *"Mixed Multitude,"* 214.

29. *Pennsylvanische Berichte*, March 16, April 1, July 1, September 1, 1755.

30. *Pennsylvanische Berichte*, September 1, 1755.

31. See also Saur's *Hoch-Deutsch Americanischer Calender*, 1754 (for the year 1755), *Pennsylvanische Berichte*, September 1 and 16, 1755 and October 2, 1756, March 5, 1757, and July 20, 1759. Franklin and Armbrüster made some of the same points in their newspaper, *Pennsylvanische Zeitung*, September 6 and November 27, 1755. See also an anonymous broadside published in 1751, "The Case of the Inhabitants of Pennsylvania in relation to Paper Currency," in the Library Company of Philadelphia (henceforth LCP).

32. *Pennsylvanische Berichte*, July 20 and August 31, 1759, and *Neu-eingerichteter Americanischer Geschichts-Calender*, printed by Peter Miller and Ludwig Weiss, Philadelphia, 1759 (for the year 1760). On the King's repeal of the bill, see the debate in *Journal of the Commissioner for Trade and Plantations from January 1759 to December 1763* (London: His Majesty's Stationery Office, 1935), 108–111, 120, and James Munro, ed., *Acts of the Privy Council of England. Colonial Series*, vol. IV (London: His Majesty's Stationery Office, 1911), 439–440, and the final result in Mitchell and Flanders, *Statutes at Large*, vol. V, 443–445.

33. Schwartz, *"Mixed Multitude"*, 225–229.

34. For pamphlets on these issues in the 1764 election, see "Eine Anrede an die

Deutschen Freyhalter der Stadt und County Philadelphia," printed by Anton Armbrüster, 1764; "Eine Neue Anrede an die Deutschen in Philadelphia County, u.,"
(Philadelphia, 1764) and "Der Lockvögel Warnungsgesang Vor den Stoßvögeln:
Oder, Nöthige Beantwortung der sogenannten Getreuen Warnung gegen die Lockvögel, u." (September 29, 1764), both printed by Henry Miller and now in LCP.
Also, there is an entire series of cartoons in the Library Company of Philadelphia for the years 1764 and 1765 (reproduced in Sellars, *Franklin in Portraiture*),
almost all of which deal with these issues. For broadsides, see the following, all in
LCP: "Explanatory Remarks on the Assembly's Resolves, published in the *Pennsylvania Gazette*, No. 1840" (Benjamin Franklin, 1764); "To the Freeholders and
other Electors for the City and County of Philadelphia, and Counties of Chester
and Bucks," anonymous, 1764; "To the Freeholders and Electors of the City and
County of Philadelphia," anonymous (October 1, 1764). Similar rhetoric can be
found in broadsides (also located in LCP) published during the 1765 campaign:
"An die Deutschen, vornehmlich die zum Wählen berechtigten, in Philadelphia—
Bucks—und Berks County," David Deschler and Johannes and Daniel Wister (circa
September 25, 1765); "To the Freeholders and other Electors of Assembly-Men, for
Pennsylvania," anonymous (October 1, 1765).

On Franklin and Wharton's opinions, see Benjamin Franklin to Richard Jackson, October 11, 1764, and Thomas Wharton to Franklin, August 14, 1765, in *The
Papers of Benjamin Franklin*, vols. 11, 397, and 12, 239–241; Schwartz, *"Mixed Multitude"*, 229–234.

35. Roeber thoroughly explores these issues and their meaning in *Palatines,
Liberty, and Property*, especially chapters 6 and 8, and in "Germans, Property, and
the First Great Awakening" and "The Origins and Transfer of German-American
Concepts of Property and Inheritance." As Roeber points out (*Palatines, Liberty,
and Property*, 191), Christopher Saur began discussing security of property, including the importance of naturalization, in his almanacs and newspapers in 1751 because he was concerned that successful immigrants did not know how to secure
their property. David Henderson's legal handbook, *Des Landmanns Advocat* (1761),
contains a chapter on naturalization, explaining the requirements and procedure
and emphasizing its importance in protecting German property from the proprietor's right to escheat.

36. William Allen to Thomas Penn, March 13, 1765, Penn Manuscripts, Official Correspondence (incoming).

37. On developments in the Survey Office, see Office of the Surveyor General
Letterbook, 1762–1764, RG-17 Records of the Bureau of Land Records, Pennsylvania State Archives, Harrisburg.

38. See *Der Wochentliche Philadelphische Staatsbote*, printed by Henry Miller,
July 1, 22, and 29, 1765, and the *Pennsylvania Gazette*, June 20, 1765. For a copy of
the handbill issued by the Land Office, see Copied Survey, vol. D-113-240, Land
Records, Pennsylvania State Archives. For brief discussions of the new land policy,
see Thomas Sergeant, *View of the Land Laws of Pennsylvania, with Notices of its Early
History and Legislation* (Philadelphia and Pittsburgh: James Kay, Jr., and John I.
Kay, Co., 1838), 55–60.

39. Sheperd, *History of Proprietary Government*, 30–31; William Allen to

Thomas Penn, March 13, 1765; John Penn to Thomas Penn, May 20, 1765; James Tilghman to John Penn, October 8, 1765; John Penn to Thomas Penn, October 14, 1765; Richard Hockley to Thomas Penn, December 15, 1765; John Penn to Thomas Penn, December 15, 1765. Penn Manuscripts, Official Correspondence, vol. X, HSP.

40. Rowland Berthoff and John M. Murrin, "Feudalism, Communalism, and the Yeoman Freeholder: The American Revolution Considered as a Social Accident," in Stephen G. Kurtz and James H. Hutson, eds., *Essays on the American Revolution* (Chapel Hill: University of North Carolina Press, 1973), 256–288, here 267–272.

41. This "aristocratic offensive" was part of a larger scheme of dependence, tenancy, and even aristocratic paternalism developing in many colonies during the generation before the Revolution (see Wood, *The Radicalism of the American Revolution*, 55–56). On the aristocratic offensive in France, see Barrington Moore, Jr., *Social Origins of Dictatorship and Democracy: Lord and Peasant in the Making of the Modern World* (Boston: Beacon Press, 1966), 63–69.

Chapter 6

1. In 1790, Pennsylvania was ethnically segregated, as outlined in Chapter 3. Also, 57 percent of the white population of Washington County, Maryland, was German, as was 50 percent of adjacent Frederick County. Yet Montgomery County, on the southeastern border of Frederick, and Fairfax and Loudoun counties, just across the Potomac in Virginia, were less than 5 percent German. Most counties in the northern Shenandoah Valley of Virginia were over 20 percent German, and one, Dunmore County, was 57 percent German. But Culpeper (13 percent) was the only county along the eastern boundary of the Valley (just across the Blue Ridge) with at least a 5 percent German population. In North Carolina, Stokes County was 34 percent German, while the adjacent counties of Rockingham and Surry were less than 5 percent German. In Tennessee, Sullivan County was 30 percent German, but no other county in the state was 5 percent or more. See Purvis, "The Pennsylvania Dutch and the German-American Diaspora in 1790."

On the German churches, see Glatfelter, *Pastors and People*, vol. 2, who traces the growth of congregations, ministers, and other church institutions for the Lutherans and Reformed (see especially 189–237 for their changing relationship with Europe during the Revolutionary Era).

For Pennsylvania German marriage patterns, see M. Walter Dunmore, "A Population Study of the Pennsylvania Germans in Berks and Neighboring Counties," *Historical Review of Berks County*, 28 (1963), 113–116. Dunmore's data reveal that 72 percent of German marriages in Berks, Lancaster, and Lehigh Counties (all in Pennsylvania) from 1752 to 1910 were between "Germans" and other Germans or Swiss, and that most of the marriages to other ethnic groups occurred in the nineteenth and early twentieth centuries. In North Carolina, marriages between Germans and non-Germans were rare well into the nineteenth century (see David Isaiah Offman and Paul G. Kinney, eds., "Genealogical Records of Early German and Other Families that Settled in the Area of North Carolina of Ala-

mance, Chatham, Guilford, Randolph, Rowan Cos.," which is available on micro-
film through the Church of Jesus Christ of Latter-Day Saints). Also, an impression-
istic survey of the northern Kraichgau cohort of immigrants and their descendants
in Pennsylvania shows that marriage to non-Germans was extremely rare throughout the eighteenth century.

2. Wood, *Radicalism of the American Revolution*, 245 and 260–261; Keller,
Rural Politics and the Collapse of Pennsylvania Federalism.

Appendix 1

1. This "immigration index" is a measure I developed to make comparisons
of the relative effects of immigration on overall population growth between different eras in American immigrant history.

2. This is not to suggest that the figures in column (D) reflect an exact proportion of all living immigrants in the total population. Some died before the end
of the decade, and a few even left the colonies. Also, many new arrivals survived for
many decades; while still "immigrants," they are not reflected in the proportions
of immigration in later decades. However, the table does suggest in which decades
the immigration as a proportion of total population may have been highest.

3. Grubb, "Morbidity and Mortality on the North Atlantic Passage," 579.
See Chapter 2 for an explanation of the northern Kraichgau immigrant cohort.

Bibliography

Two important sources that made this study possible are the published migrant lists by Annette K. Burgert (*Eighteenth Century Emigrants*, vol. 1, *The Northern Kraichgau*) and Werner Hacker (*Kurpfälzische Auswanderer vom Unteren Neckar*). They are based on two different kinds of sources and yield different kinds of results, but taken together, give a fairly complete picture of the number of emigrants to Pennsylvania from the northern Kraichgau and their movements within Pennsylvania following their arrival in Philadelphia.

Both Burgert, an American, and Hacker, a German, have years of experience compiling and publishing lists of German-speaking migrants in the eighteenth century. In his volume, Hacker studied the region of the lower Neckar, which includes the northern Kraichgau region studied by Burgert. Hacker published information on all legal emigrants from this region, listing the year the request to emigrate was made (usually the actual year of emigration), destinations (the large majority went to eastern Europe), the status of the migrants as serfs or free subjects, and some information on their wealth.

On the other hand, Burgert only studied the emigrants who went to North America, more specifically, Pennsylvania. The value of her work is that she used several kinds of sources, both German and American, and linked these records for individual migrants, thus giving a fairly complete picture of how they moved *within* Pennsylvania after their arrival.

Hacker primarily used official government documents kept for emigrants who left their territory legally: they had first asked permission, and then payed the enormous taxes and fees required. Most of Burgert's emigrants had left illegally and so could not be found by Hacker. She used primarily German and Pennsylvania German church records, but also ship lists, wills, naturalization records, and other sources to trace migrants.

Burgert studied fifty-three parishes in the northern Kraichgau, forty-eight of which were also covered by Hacker. Another, Schwaigern, was studied by Karl Wagenplast, whose notes in the city archives of Schwaigern I used. Wagenplast studied the legal emigration in a manner similar to Hacker's. A combined total of 1,950 different migrants to Pennsylvania are on all three lists (Burgert's, Hacker's, and Wagenplast's). Because they represent most if not all of the emigrants from these fifty-three parishes, I have analyzed their movements as a cohort.

The following is a list of all sources used in this study.

I. Primary Sources

A. MANUSCRIPTS

Bethlehem, Pa., Moravian Archives
    Burial registers
    J series; journals
    Miscellaneous church records
    Single Sisters Diary
Harrisburg, Pa., Pennsylvania State Archives
    D-113-240 land records
    RG-17 records of the Bureau of Land Records
Ludwigsburg, Ludwigsburger Schloßarchiv, Kanton Craichgauer Archiv.
    Schatzungswesen zu Bonfeld, 1619–1762
Philadelphia, Historical Society of Pennsylvania
    Am 705, Moravian Immigration to America, 1734–1800
    Conrad Weiser Papers
    Newspapers:
        Pennsylvanische Berichte, Germantown, Christopher Saur
    Penn Papers:
        Penn Manuscripts; official correspondence
        Pennsylvania Cash Accounts (Edmund Physick)
    Political pamphlets collection
    Richard Peters Papers
    Shippen Family Papers
Philadelphia, Library Company of Philadelphia
    Broadsides
    Political cartoons, 1764–1765
    Political pamphlets collection
    Almanacs:
        Neu-eingerichteter Americanischer Geschichts-Calender, Philadelphia,
            Gotthard Armbrüster, Peter Miller, and Ludwig Weiss
        Der Neuste, Verbessert- und Zuverläßige Americanische Calender,
            Philadelphia, Henry Miller
        Der Hoch-Deutsch Americanische Calender, Germantown, Christopher
            Saur
    Newspapers:
        Philadelphische Zeitung, Philadelphia, Benjamin Franklin and Anton
            Armbrüster

Der Wochentliche Philadelphische Staatsbote, Philadelphia, Henry Miller
Schwaigern, Gemeindearchiv
   A series; Akten vermischten Inhalts
   Karl Wagenplast Notes
Sinsheim, Stadtarchiv Sinsheim, Sinsheimer Briefschaften, 1617–1725
Winston-Salem, N.C., Moravian Archives
   Burial records
   Community diaries
   Journals
   Minutes of the Ältesten Conferenz
   Official correspondence

B. EIGHTEENTH-CENTURY PUBLISHED MATERIALS

Eichrodt, Johann Friedrich von, ed. *Das Großherzogthum Baden nach seinen zehen Kreisen und Amtsbezirken topographisch skizziert*. Karlsruhe: C. F. Müller'schen Verlagshandlung, 1810.
Falkner, Daniel. *Curieuse Nachricht von Pennsylvania in Nord-Amerika/ Welche/ Auf Begehren guter Freunde/ Über vorgelegte 103. Frage/ bei seiner Abreiß aus Teutschland nach obigem Lande Anno 1700*. Frankfurt and Leipzig: Andreas Otto Buchhändler, 1702.
Henderson, David. *Des Landmanns Advocat*. Philadelphia: Henry Miller, 1761.
Kocherthaler, Joshua. *Ausßführlich- und umständlicher Bericht Von der berühmten Landschafft Carolina/ In dem Engelländischen America gelegen*. Frankfurt: Georg Heinrich Oehrling, 1706, and 4th rev. ed., 1709.
Königliche Württembergisches Hof- und Staats- Handbuch auf die Jahre 1809 und 1810. Stuttgart: Joh. Frid. Steinkopf, 1810.
"The Palatine Catechism, or a True Description of Their Compact: In a Pleasant Dialogue between an English Tradesman and a High-Dutchman." London: Blackheath and Camberwell, 1709.
Pastorius, Franz Daniel. *Umstaendige Geographische Beschreibung Der zu allerletzt erfundenen Provintz Pennsylvaniae In denen End-Graentzen Americae. In der West-Welt gelegen*. Frankfurt and Leipzig: Andreas Otto Buchhändler, 1702.
Penn, William. *Eine Nachricht Wegen der Landschafft Pennsilvania in America*. Translation of 1675 original. Frankfurt, 1683.
Schlettwein, Johann August. *Neues Archiv für den Menschen und Bürger in allen Verhältnissen*. Leipzig: Weingandische Buchhandlung, 1784–1787.
Thomas, Gabriel. *Continuation der Beschreibung der Landschafft Pennsylvaniae An denen End-Graentzen Americae. Über vorige des Herrn Pastorii Relationes*. Frankfurt and Leipzig: Andreas Otto Buchhändler, 1702.
Zeiller, Martin. *Topographia Palatinatus Rheni et Vicinarum Regionum*. Frankfurt: Matthäus Merian, 1645.

C. MODERN PUBLISHED MATERIALS

Aland, Kurt, ed. *Die Korrespondenz Heinrich Melchior Mühlenbergs aus der Anfangszeit des deutschen Luthertums in Nordamerika*, vols. 1 and 2. Berlin and New York: Walter de Gruyter, 1986 and 1987.

Brecht, Samuel K. *Genealogical Record of the Schwenkfelder Families*. New York and Chicago: Rand McNally & Co., 1923.

Burgert, Annette K. *Eighteenth Century Emigrants from German-Speaking Lands to North America*, vol. 1, *The Northern Kraichgau*. Publications of the Pennsylvania German Society, vol. 16. Breinigsville, Pa.: The Pennsylvania German Society, 1983.

"Diary of the Rev. Samuel Guldin, Relating to His Journey to Pennsylvania, June to September, 1710." *Journal of the Presbyterian Historical Society* 14 (1930), 28–41, 64–73.

Diefenbacher, Karl, Hans Ulrich Pfister, and Kurt H. Holz, eds. *Schweizer Einwanderer in den Kraichgau nach dem Dreißigjährigen Krieg*. Sinsheim et al.: Heimatverein Kraichgau e.V., 1983.

"Documents Relating to Early German Settlers in America." *German American Annals* n.s. 4 (1906), 252–261.

Durnbaugh, Donald F. "Two Early Letters from Germantown." *Pennsylvania Magazine of History and Biography* 84 (1960), 219–233.

Engelmann, Ursmar, ed. *Das Tagebuch von Ignaz Speckle, Abt von St. Peter im Schwarzwald*, vol. 1. Stuttgart: W. Kohlhammer Verlag, 1965.

Fries, Adelaide L., ed. *Records of the Moravians in North Carolina*, vol. 1. Raleigh: Edwards & Broughton Printing Co., 1922.

———, ed. "Travel Diary of Bishop and Mrs. Reichel and Their Company from Lititz to Salem in the Wachau (Wachovia) from May 22, to June 15, 1780" and "Extract from the Travel Diary of the Beloved Br. and Sr. Reichel and the Single Br. Christ. Heckenwelder from Salem to Lititz." In *Travels in the American Colonies*, edited by Newton D. Mereness. New York: Macmillan Co., 1916, 586–599, 603–613.

Gingerich, Hugh F., and Rachel W. Kreider. *Amish and Amish Mennonite Genealogies*. Gordonville, Pa.: Pequea Publishers, 1986.

Giuseppi, M. S. *Naturalizations of Foreign Protestants in the American and West Indian Colonies*. Publications of the Huguenot Society of London, vol. 24. Manchester: Sheratt & Hughes, 1921.

Hacker, Werner. "Auswanderer aus dem Territorium der Reichsstadt Ulm, vor allem im ausgehenden 17. und im 18. Jahrhundert." *Ulm und Oberschwaben: Zeitschrift für Geschichte und Kunst* 42/43 (1978), 161–257.

———. *Auswanderungen aus Baden und dem Breisgau: Obere und mittlere rechtsseitige Oberrheinlande im 18. Jahrhundert archivalisch dokumentiert*. Stuttgart and Aalen: Konrad Theiss Verlag, 1980.

———. *Auswanderungen aus dem früheren Hochstift Speyer nach Südosteuropa und Übersee im XVIII. Jahrhundert*. Schriften zur Wanderungsgeschichte der Pfälzer, 28. Kaiserslautern: Heimatstelle Pfalz, 1969.

———. *Auswanderungen aus dem nördlichen Bodenseeraum im 17. und 18. Jahrhundert*. Singen: Hegau-Geschichtsverein, 1975.

———. *Auswanderungen aus Rheinpfalz und Saarland im 18. Jahrhundert.* Stuttgart: Konrad Theiss Verlag, 1987.

———. *Kurpfälzische Auswanderer vom Unteren Neckar, Rechtrheinische Gebiete der Kurpfalz.* Stuttgart and Aalen: Konrad Theiss Verlag, 1983.

Hinke, William J., ed. *Life and Letters of the Rev. John Philip Boehm, Founder of the Reformed Church in Pennsylvania, 1683–1749.* Philadelphia: Sunday School Board of the Reformed Church in the United States, 1916.

Hinke, William J., and Charles E. Kemper, eds. "Moravian Diaries of Travels through Virginia." *Virginia Magazine of History and Biography* 11 (1903–1904), 113–131, 225–242, and 370–393; and 12 (1904–1905), 55–82, 134–153, 271–284.

Historical Magazine 4 (1860), 100–104. Letters from Christopher Saur.

Hus, Jan. *De ecclesia. The Church.* Translated by David S. Schaff. Westport, Conn.: Greenwood Press, 1976.

Jones, Henry Z. *The Palatine Families of New York: A Study of the German Immigrants Who Arrived in Colonial New York in 1710.* Universal City, Calif.: Henry Z. Jones, 1985.

Journal of the Commissioner for Trade and Plantations from January 1759 to December 1763. London: His Majesty's Stationery Office, 1935.

Kelsey, R. W., ed. and trans. "An Early Description of Pennsylvania: Letter of Christopher Sower. Written in 1724, Describing Conditions in Philadelphia and Vicinity, and the Sea Voyage from Europe. *Pennsylvania Magazine of History and Biography* 45 (1921), 243–254.

Labaree, Leonard W., ed. *The Papers of Benjamin Franklin,* vols. 4, 11, and 12. New Haven, Conn.: Yale University Press, 1961, 1967, and 1968.

Landesarchivdirektion Baden-Württemberg, ed. *Das Land Baden-Württemberg, Amtliche Beschreibung nach Kreisen und Gemeinden,* vol. 4, *Regierungsbezirk Stuttgart, Regionalverbände Franken und Ostwürttemberg.* Stuttgart: Verlag W. Kohlhammer, 1980.

"Lebenslauf des Johann Georg Jungmann." *Der deutsche Pioneer* 1 (1869), 230–233.

Lineback, Donald J. "An Annotated Edition of the Diary of Johann Heinrich Müller (1702–1782), Pietist and Printer of the American Revolution." Ph.D. diss., University of North Carolina, 1975.

MacMaster, Richard K., Samuel L. Horst, and Robert F. Ulle, eds. *Conscience in Crisis: Mennonites and Other Peace Churches in America, 1739–1789. Interpretations and Documents.* Studies in Anabaptist and Mennonite History, vol. 20. Scottsdale, Pa., and Kitchener, Ont.: Herald Press, 1979.

Meurer, Johann Philipp. "From London to Philadelphia, 1742." *Pennsylvania Magazine of History and Biography* 37 (1913), 94–106.

Minutes of the Provincial Council. *Colonial Records of Pennsylvania,* vol. 6. Philadelphia: Jo. Severns & Co., 1851.

Mitchell, James T., and Henry Flanders, eds. *The Statutes at Large of Pennsylvania from 1682 to 1801.* Harrisburg: Clarence M. Bush, 1896–1902.

Mittelberger, Gottlieb. *Gottlieb Mittelberger's Journey to Pennsylvania in the Year 1750 and Return to Germany in the Year 1754.* Translated and edited by Oscar Handlin and John Clive. Cambridge, Mass.: Harvard University Press, 1960.

Munro, James, ed. *Acts of the Privy Council of England. Colonial Series,* vol. 4. London: His Majesty's Stationery Office, 1911.

Offman, David I., and Paul G. Kinney. "Genealogical Records of Early German and Other Families that Settled in the Area of North Carolina of Alamance, Chatham, Guilford, Randolph, Rowan Cos." Microfilmed in 1973.

Reincke, Abraham. "A Register of Members of the Moravian Church between 1727–1754." *Transactions of the Moravian Historical Society* 1 (1873), 283–426.

Rupp, I. Daniel. *A Collection of Upwards of Thirty Thousand Names of German, Swiss, Dutch, French and Other Immigrants in Pennsylvania from 1727 to 1776*, 2nd rev. ed. Philadelphia: Leary Stuart, 1898.

Schelbert, Leo, ed. "Von der Macht des Pietismus: Dokumentarbericht zur Auswanderung einer Basler Familie im Jahre 1736." *Basler Zeitschrift für Geschichte und Altertumskunde* 75 (1975), 89–119.

Schelbert, Leo, and Hedwig Rappolt. *"Alles ist ganz anders hier": Auswandererschicksale in Briefen aus zwei Jahrhunderten*. Olten and Freiburg: Walter-Verlag, 1977.

Slabaugh, John M. (cartographer). "Early Amish Landowners, Berks Co., Pa. Survey Map." Gordonville, Pa.: Abner Beiler, 1986.

Strassburger, Ralph B., and William J. Hinke, eds. *Pennsylvania German Pioneers: A Publication of the Original Lists of Arrivals in the Port of Philadelphia from 1727–1808*. Norristown, Pa.: Pennsylvania German Society, 1934.

Tafferner, Anton. *Quellenbuch zur donauschwäbischen Geschichte*. Munich: Verlag Hans Menschendörfer, 1974.

Tappert, Theodore G., and John W. Doberstein, eds. and trans. *The Journals of Henry Melchior Muhlenberg*, 3 vols. Philadelphia: Muhlenberg Press, 1942–1958.

U.S. Bureau of the Census. *Historical Statistics of the United States, Colonial Times to 1970*. Washington, D.C., 1975.

———. *Statistical Abstract of the United States, 1992*. Washington, D.C., 1992.

Wolfe, Richard J. "The Colonial Naturalization Act of 1740, with a List of Persons Naturalized in New York Colony, 1740–1769." *The New York Genealogical and Biographical Record* 94 (1965), 132–147.

Wyand, Jeffrey A., and Florence L. Wyand. *Colonial Maryland Naturalizations*. Baltimore: Genealogical Publishing Co., 1975.

Yoder, Don, ed. *Pennsylvania German Immigrants, 1709–1786*. Baltimore: Genealogical Publishing Co., 1980.

II. Secondary Sources

A. ON EUROPE

Aalen, Lew. "Die Theologie des Grafen von Zinzendorf: Ein Beitrag zur 'Dogmengeschichte des Protestantismus.'" In *Zur Neueren Pietismusforschung*, edited by Martin Greschat, 319–353. Darmstadt: Wissenschaftliche Buchgesellschaft, 1977.

Abel, Wilhelm. *Agricultural Fluctuations in Europe from the Thirteenth to the Twentieth Centuries*, 3rd ed. Translated and updated by Oliver Ordish. New York: Methuen and Co., Ltd., 1980.

Aston, Trevor H., and C. H. E. Philpin, eds. *The Brenner Debate: Agrarian Class Structure and Economic Development in Pre-Industrial Europe*. Cambridge: Cambridge University Press, 1985.

Aubin, Hermann et al. *Geschichte des Rheinlandes von der ältesten Zeit bis zur Gegenwart*. Essen: G.D. Baedeker Verlagsbuchhandlung, 1922.

Auer, Hans Helmut von. *Das Finanzwesen der Stadt Freiburg i. B. von 1648 bis 1806*. Karlsruhe: G. Braunsche Hofbuchdruckerei und Verlag, 1910.

Becker, Albert. "Zur oberrheinischen Bevölkerungsgeschichte des 17. und 18. Jahrhunderts." *Zeitschrift für die Geschichte des Oberrheins* 95 (1943), 676–685.

Bennion, Lowell C. "Flight from the Reich: A Geographical Exposition of Southwest German Emigration, 1683–1815." Ph.D. diss., Syracuse University, 1971.

Beyreuther, Erich. *Der Junge Zinzendorf*. Marburg an der Lahn: Verlag der Francke-Buchhandlung GmbH, 1957.

———. *Zinzendorf und die Christenheit*. Marburg an der Lahn: Verlag der Francke-Buchhandlung GmbH, 1961.

Bliss, Alan. *Spoken English in Ireland, 1600–1740*. Dublin: The Dolman Press, 1979.

Brandl, Helmut. *Der Stadtwald von Freiburg*. Veröffentlichungen aus dem Archiv der Stadt Freiburg im Breisgau, vol. 12. Freiburg: Wagnersche Universitätsbuchhandlung, Karl Zimmer Kommissionsverlag, 1970.

Brinck, Andreas. *Die deutsche Auswanderungswelle in die britischen Nordamerikakolonien um die Mitte des 18. Jahrhunderts*. Stuttgart: Franz Steiner Verlag, 1993.

Diefendorf, Jeffrey M. "Soziale Mobilität im Rheinland im 18. Jahrhundert." *Scripturae Mercaturae—Zeitschrift für Wirtschafts- und Sozialgeschichte* 19 (1985), 88–112.

Dobiás, Frantisek M. "Das Prinzip der Autorität in der Taboriten-Konfession." *Evangelische Theologie* 32 (1972), 251–267.

Fenske, Hans. "Die deutsche Auswanderung." *Mitteilungen des Historischen Vereins der Pfalz* 76 (1978), 183–220.

———. "International Migration: Germany in the Eighteenth Century." *Central European History* 13 (1980), 332–347.

Fertig, Georg. "Migrations from the German-Speaking Parts of Central Europe, 1600–1800: Estimates and Explanations." Working Paper No. 38, John F. Kennedy-Institut für Nordamerikastudien. Berlin, 1991.

Fleig, Edgar. *Handschriftliche, wirtschafts- und verfassungs- geschichtliche Studien zur Geschichte des Klosters St. Peter auf dem Schwarzwald*. Freiburg im Breisgau: Universitätsdruckerei H. M. Poppen & Sohn, 1908.

Fogleman, Aaron. "Die Auswanderung aus Südbaden im 18. Jahrhundert." *Zeitschrift des Breisgau-Geschichtsvereins* 106 (1987), 95–162.

Franz, Günther. *Der Dreißigjährige Krieg und das deutsche Volk*. Quellen und Forschungen zur Agrargeschichte, edited by Günther Franz and Wilhelm Abel, vol. 7. Stuttgart and New York: Gustav Fischer Verlag, 1979.

Gerber, Adolf. *Die Nassau-Dillenberger Auswanderung nach Amerika im 18. Jahrhundert: Das Verhalten der Regierungen dazu und die späteren Schicksale der Auswanderer*. Flensburg: Flensburger Nachrichten, Deutscher Verlag GmbH, 1930.

Glassl, Horst. *Das österreichische Einrichtungswerk in Galizien 1772–1790*. Veröffentlichungen des Osteuropa-Instituts, vol. 41. Wiesbaden: Osteuropa-Institut, 1975.

Gothein, Eberhard. "Die Hofverfassung auf dem Schwarzwald dargestellt an der Geschichte des Gebiets von St. Peter." *Zeitschrift für die Geschichte des Oberrheins*, n.s. 1 (1886), 257–316.

———. *Wirtschaftsgeschichte des Schwarzwalds und der angrenzenden Landschaften.* Strassbourg: Verlag von Karl J. Trübner, 1892.

Häßler, Joseph. *Die Auswanderung aus Baden nach Rußland und Polen im 18. und 19. Jahrhundert.* Beiträge zur Familien- und Heimatkunde in Baden, vol. 1, edited by Albert Köbele. Grafenhausen, 1959.

Hamilton, J. Taylor, and Kenneth G. Hamilton. *History of the Moravian Church, the Renewed Unitas Fratrum, 1722–1957.* Bethlehem, Pa.: The Moravian Church, 1967.

Hassinger, Herbert. *Johann Joachim Becher 1635–1682: Ein Beitrag zur Geschichte des Merkantilismus.* Vienna: A. Holzhausens Nfg., 1951.

Heinz, Joachim. *"Bleibe im Lande, und nähre dich redlich!": Zur Geschichte der pfälzischen Auswanderung vom Ende des 17. bis zum Ausgang des 19. Jahrhunderts.* Beiträge zur pfälzischen Geschichte und Volkskunde, vol. 1. Kaiserslautern: Institut für pfälzische Geschichte und Volkskunde, 1989.

Helleiner, Karl F. "The Population of Europe from the Black Death to the Eve of the Vital Revolution." In *The Cambridge Economic History of Europe*, vol. 4, *The Economy of Expanding Europe in the Sixteenth and Seventeenth Centuries*, edited by E. E. Rich and C. H. Wilson, 1–95. Cambridge: Cambridge University Press, 1967.

Henn, Volker. "Die soziale und wirtschaftliche Lage der rheinischen Bauern im Zeitalter des Absolutismus." *Rheinische Vierteljahresblätter* 42 (1978), 240–257.

Heymann, Frederick G. "The Hussite Revolution and Reformation and its Impact on Germany." In *Festschrift für Hermann Heimpel*, vol. 2, 610–626. Göttingen: Vandenkoek und Ruprecht, 1972.

———. "The Hussite-Utraquist Church in the Fifteenth and Sixteenth Centuries." *Archiv für Reformationsgeschichte* 52 (1962), 1–15.

———. "John Rokycana—Church Reformer between Hus and Luther." *Church History* 8 (1959), 240–280.

Hippel, Wolfgang von. *Auswanderung aus Südwestdeutschland: Studien zur württembergischen Auswanderung und Auswanderungspolitik im 18. und 19. Jahrhundert.* Industrielle Welt, edited by Werner Conze, vol. 36. Stuttgart: Klett-Cotta, 1984.

Hogan, Jeremiah J. *The English Language in Ireland.* Dublin: The Educational Company of Ireland, 1927.

Hoyer, Siegfried. "Häresien zwischen Hus und Luther: Ein Beitrag zur ideologischen Vorbereitung der frühbürgerlichen Revolution in Deutschland." Habilitation thesis, Karl Marx University, Leipzig, 1966.

Kaminsky, Howard. *A History of the Hussite Revolution.* Berkeley and Los Angeles: University of California Press, 1967.

Klippenstein, Lawrence. "The Mennonite Migration to Russia, 1786–1988." In *Mennonites in Russia, 1788–1988: Essays in Honour of Gerhard Lohrenz*, edited by John Friesen. Winnipeg, Manitoba: Canadian Mennonite Bible College, 1989.

Knodel, John E. *Demographic Behavior in the Past: A Study of Fourteen German Village Populations in the Eighteenth and Nineteenth Centuries.* Cambridge: Cambridge University Press, 1988.

Königlicher Statistisch-topographischer Bureau, ed. *Beschreibung des Oberamts Brackenheim.* Stuttgart: H. Lindemann, 1873.

Kollnig, Karl. *Wandlungen im Bevölkerungsbild des pfälzischen Oberrheingebiets.* Heidelberger Veröffentlichungen zur Landesgeschichte und Landeskunde, vol. 2, edited by Fritz Ernst and Karl Kollnig. Heidelberg: Carl Winter Universitätsverlag, 1952.

Krahl, Heinz-Theo. "Adelshofen von den ersten Siedlungsanfängen bis zur Bauernbefreiung im 19. Jahrhundert." In *700 Jahre Adelshofen, 1287–1987,* edited by Wilhelm Wolfmüller et al., 18–114. Eppinger stadtgeschichtliche Veröffentlichungen, vol. 1. Eppingen: Stadt Eppingen, 1987.

Kriedte, Peter, Hans Medick, and Jürgen Schlumbohm. *Industrialization before Industrialization: Rural Industry in the Genesis of Capitalism.* Translated by Beate Schempp. Cambridge: Cambridge University Press, 1981.

Kuhn, Walter. "Das österreichische Siedlungswerk des 18. Jahrhunderts." *Südostdeutsches Archiv* 3 (1963), 1–26.

———. "Die preußische Kolonisation unter Friedrich dem Großen." In *Deutsche Ostsiedlung im Mittelalter und Neuzeit.* Cologne and Vienna, 1971.

Ladurie, Emmanuel Le Roy. *The Peasants of Languedoc.* Translated by John Day. Urbana: University of Illinois Press, 1974.

Langguth, Otto. *Pennsylvania German Pioneers from the County of Wertheim.* Translated and edited by Don Yoder. Publications of the Pennsylvania German Folklore Society, vol. 12. Allentown, Pa., 1947.

Laubenberger, Franz. "Zur Aufhebung der Leibeigenschaft in den badischen Landen 1783 unter Markgraf Carl Friedrich." *Zeitschrift des Breisgau-Geschichtsvereins* 103 (1984), 71–92.

Liehl, Ekkehard. *Hinterzarten: Gesicht und Geschichte einer Schwarzwaldlandschaft,* 2nd ed. Konstanz: Rosgarten Verlag, 1974.

Lotz, Friedrich. "Die ersten deutschen Kolonisten in der Batschka." *Südostdeutschesarchiv* 3 (1960), 169–176.

Mayer, Julius. *Geschichte der Benediktinerabtei St. Peter auf dem Schwarzwald.* Freiburg im Breisgau: Herder'sche Verlagshandlung, 1893.

Mayhew, Alan. *Rural Settlement and Farming in Germany.* New York: Harper & Row, 1973.

Meyer, Dietrich. "Nikolaus Ludwig Graf von Zinzendorf (1700–1760)." In *Klassiker der Theologie,* vol. 1, edited by Heinrich Fries and Georg Kreitschmer, 22–38. Munich: Verlag C. H. Beck, 1983.

Moore, Barrington, Jr. *Social Origins of Dictatorship and Democracy: Lord and Peasant in the Making of the Modern World.* Boston: Beacon Press, 1966.

Mühleisen, Hans-Otto, ed. *St. Peter im Schwarzwald: Kulturgeschichtliche und historische Beiträge anlässlich der 250- Jahrfeier der Einweihung der Klosterkirche.* Munich and Zurich: Verlag Schnell & Steiner, 1977.

Neu, D. Heinrich. *Aus der Vergangenheit von Hoffenheim*. Hoffenheim: Verlag der Evangelischen Kirchengemeinde Hoffenheim, 1953.

Neuwirth, Gustav. *Geschichte der Gemeinde Ittlingen*. Ittlingen: Gemeinde Ittlingen, 1981.

O'Muirithe, Diarmaid, ed. *The English Language in Ireland*. Dublin and Cork: The Mercier Press, 1977.

Press, Volker. *Kaiser Karl V., König Ferdinand und die Entstehung der Reichsritterschaft*. Institut für europäische Geschichte Mainz, Vorträge, vol. 60, 2nd ed. Wiesbaden: Franz Steiner Verlag GmbH, 1980.

———. "Die Ritterschaft im Kraichgau zwischen Reich und Territorium 1500–1623." *Zeitschrift für die Geschichte des Oberrheins* 122 (1974), 35–98.

Raum, Otto F. "Die Hintergründe der Pfälzer Auswanderung im Jahre 1709." *Deutsches Archiv für Landes- und Volksforschung* 3 (1939), 551–567.

Röhm, Helmut. *Die Vererbung des landwirtschaftlichen Grundeigentums in Baden-Württemberg*. Remagen: Selbstverlag der Bundesanstalt für Landeskunde, 1957.

Rudé, George. *Europe in the Eighteenth Century: Aristocracy and the Bourgeois Challenge*. New York: Praeger, 1972.

Sabean, David. *Power in the Blood: Popular Culture and Village Discourse in Early Modern Germany*. Cambridge: Cambridge University Press, 1984.

Scheuerbrandt, Arnold. "Die Amerikaauswanderung aus dem Kraichgau und seinen Randbereichen im 18. Jahrhundert." *Kraichgau: Beiträge zur Landschafts- und Heimatsforschung* 9 (1985), 65–97.

———. "Die Auswanderung aus dem heutigen Baden-Württemberg nach Preußen, in den habsburgischen Südosten, nach Rußland und Nordamerika zwischen 1683 und 1811." *Historischer Atlas von Baden-Württemberg,* part XII.5. Stuttgart: Kommission für geschichtliche Landeskunde in Baden-Württemberg, 1985.

Schuchmann, Heinz. "Der Eschelbronner Pfarrer Josua 'Kocherthaler' und die pfälzische Massenauswanderung nach Nordamerika 1708/09." *Kraichgau-Heimatsforschung im Landkreis Sinsheim* 2 (1970), 154–159.

Scoville, Warren C. *The Persecution of the Huguenots and French Economic Development, 1680–1720*. Berkeley and Los Angeles: University of California Press, 1960.

Seibt, Ferdinand. "Die Zeit der Luxemberger und der hussitischen Revolution." In *Handbuch der Geschichte der böhmischen Länder*, 351–568. Stuttgart: Anton Hiersmann, 1967.

Stahl, Friedrich. "Die Einwanderung in ostpreußische Städte 1740–1806." *Zeitschrift für Ostforschung* 1 (1952), 544–553.

Stiefel, Karl. *Baden, 1648–1952*, 2 vols. Karlsruhe: Badische Neuste Nachrichten, GmbH, 1977.

Straub, Alfred. *Das badische Oberland im 18. Jahrhundert: Die Tranformation einer bäuerlichen Gesellschaft vor der Industrialisierung*. Historische Studien, vol. 429. Husum: Matthiesen Verlag, 1977.

Strobel, Albrecht. *Agrarverfassung im Übergang: Studien zur Agrargeschichte des badischen Breisgaus vom Beginn des 16. bis zum Ausgang des 18. Jahrhunderts*. Forschungen zur oberrheinischen Landesgeschichte, vol. 23. Freiburg and Munich: Verlag Karl Alber, 1972.

Stülpnagel, W. "St. Peter." In *Freiburg im Breisgau, Stadtkreis und Landkreis: Amtliche Kreisbeschreibung*, vol. 2, edited by the Administration of the Baden-Württemberg State Archives, 897–924. Freiburg im Breisgau: Druckhaus Rombach, 1974.

Stumpp, Karl. *Die Auswanderung aus Deutschland nach Rußland in den Jahren 1763 bis 1862.* Tübingen: Karl Stumpp, 1974.

Tacke, Jürgen. "Der Merkantilismus als beherrschende Idee in der Werbeschrift zur Niederlassung gewerblicher Betriebe in der Stadt Lörrach." *Das Markgräflerland.* 20 (1958), 38–40.

———. "Studien zur Agrarverfassung der oberen badischen Markgrafschaft im 16. und 17. Jahrhundert." *Das Markgräflerland* 18 (1956), 9–118.

Tafferner, Anton. "Die frühe Ansiedlungszeit der Kameralherrschaft Tokaj (Tockey) an der oberen Theiß." *Südostdeutsches Archiv* 12 (1969), 73–117.

Zeman, Jarold K. *The Hussite Movement and the Reformation in Bohemia, Moravia, and Slovakia (1350–1650): A Bibliographical Study Guide.* Ann Arbor: University of Michigan Slavic Publications, 1977.

B. ON NORTH AMERICA

Alderfer, E. G. *The Ephrata Commune: An Early American Counterculture.* Pittsburgh: University of Pittsburgh Press, 1985.

Anderson, Virginia DeJohn. *New England's Generation: The Great Migration and the Formation of Society and Culture in the Seventeenth Century.* Cambridge: Cambridge University Press, 1991.

Archer, Richard. "New England Mosaic: A Demographic Analysis for the Seventeenth Century." *William & Mary Quarterly* 47 (1990), 477–502.

Axtell, James. *Beyond 1492: Encounters in Colonial North America.* New York: Oxford University Press, 1992.

Bailyn, Bernard, ed. *Strangers within the Realm: Cultural Margins of the First British Empire.* Chapel Hill: University of North Carolina, 1991.

Bailyn, Bernard, and Barbara DeWolfe. *Voyagers to the West: A Passage in the Peopling of America on the Eve of the American Revolution.* New York: Alfred A. Knopf, 1986.

Balmer, Randall H. *A Perfect Babel of Confusion: Dutch Religion and English Culture in the Middle Colonies.* New York: Oxford University Press, 1989.

Barker, Howard F., and Marcus L. Hansen. "Report of the Committee on Linguistic and National Stocks in the Population of the United States." *Annual Report for the Year 1931*, I. Washington, D.C.: American Historical Association, 1932, 107–441.

Becker, Laura. "The American Revolution as a Community Experience: A Case Study of Reading, Pennsylvania." Ph.D. diss., University of Pennsylvania, 1978.

Beeman, Richard. *The Evolution of the Southern Backcountry: A Case Study of Lunen-*

burg County, Virginia, 1746–1832. Philadelphia: University of Pennsylvania Press, 1984.

Beiler, Joseph F. "Our Fatherland in America." *The Diary* (1972), 98–100, 120; (1976), 69, 72.

Beiler, Rosalind J. "Gemeinschaft or Gesellschaft? Germans in Colonial New Jersey." Unpublished typescript. University of Pennsylvania, 1989.

Bender, Harold S. et al. *The Mennonite Encyclopedia*. Scottsdale, Pa.: Mennonite Publishing House, 1959.

Bernheim, G. D. *History of the German Settlements and of the Lutheran Church in North and South Carolina*. Philadelphia: The Lutheran Bookstore, 1872.

Berthoff, Rowland, and John Murrin. "Feudalism, Communalism, and the Yeoman Freeholder: The American Revolution Considered as a Social Accident." In *Essays on the American Revolution*, edited by Stephen G. Kurtz and James H. Hutson, 256–288. Chapel Hill: University of North Carolina Press, 1973.

Billington, Ray A. *Westward Expansion: A History of the American Frontier*. New York: The MacMillan Company, 1949.

Bockelman, Wayne L., and Owen S. Ireland. "The Internal Revolution in Pennsylvania: An Ethnic-Religious Interpretation," *Pennsylvania History* 41 (1974), 125–159.

Bonomi, Patricia U. *Under the Cope of Heaven: Religion, Society, and Politics in Colonial America*. New York: Oxford University Press, 1986.

Bridenbaugh, Carl. *Myths and Realities: Societies of the Colonial South*. Baton Rouge: Louisiana State University Press, 1952.

Brumbaugh, Martin G. *A History of the German Baptist Brethren in Europe and America*. Mt. Morris, Ill.: Brethren Publishing House, 1899.

Butler, Jon. *The Huguenots in America: A Refugee People in a New World Society*. Cambridge, Mass.: Harvard University Press, 1983.

Cappon, Lester J., ed. *Atlas of Early American History: The Revolutionary Era, 1760–1790*. Princeton, N.J.: Princeton University Press, 1976.

Cohen, Norman S. "The Philadelphia Election Riot of 1742." *Pennsylvania Magazine of History and Biography* 92 (1968), 306–319.

Cunz, Dieter. *The Maryland Germans: A History*. Princeton, N.J.: Princeton University Press, 1948.

Deppermann, Klaus. "Pennsylvanien als Asyl des frühen deutschen Pietismus." *Pietismus und Neuzeit* 10 (1982), 190–212.

Dickson, R. J. *Ulster Emigration to Colonial America, 1718–1775*. London: Routledge and Kegan Paul, 1966.

Dunaway, Wayland F. *The Scotch-Irish of Colonial Pennsylvania*. Chapel Hill: University of North Carolina Press, 1944.

Dunmore, M. Walter. "A Population Study of the Pennsylvania Germans in Berks and Neighboring Counties." *Historical Review of Berks County* 28 (1963), 113–116.

Durnbaugh, Donald F. et al., eds. *The Brethren Encyclopedia*. Philadelphia and Oak Brook, Ill.: The Brethren Encyclopedia, Inc., 1984.

Eaker, Lorena S. "The Germans in North Carolina." *The Palatine Immigrant* 6 (1980), 3–34.

Fisher, Elizabeth W. "'Prophesies and Revelations': German Cabbalists in Early Pennsylvania." *Pennsylvania Magazine of History and Biography* 109 (1985), 299–333.

Fogel, Robert W., and Stanley L. Engerman. *Time on the Cross: The Economics of American Negro Slavery.* Boston and Toronto: Little, Brown and Company, 1974.

Fogel, Robert W., Ralph A. Galatine, and Richard L. Manning. *Without Consent or Contract: The Rise and Fall of American Slavery: Evidence and Methods.* New York: W. W. Norton & Co., 1992.

Fogleman, Aaron S. "Herrnhuter Frauen auf dem Weg von Pennsylvania nach North Carolina: Das Reisejournal der Salome Meurer, 1766." *Pietismus und Neuzeit* 19 (1993), 98–116.

———. "Hopeful Journeys: German Immigration and Settlement in Greater Pennsylvania, 1717–1775." Ph.D. diss., University of Michigan, 1991.

———. "Migrations to the Thirteen British North American Colonies: New Estimates." *Journal of Interdisciplinary History* 22 (1992), 691–709.

———. "Progress and Possibilities in Migration Studies: The Contributions of Werner Hacker to the Study of Early German Migration to Pennsylvania." *Pennsylvania History* 56 (1989), 318–329.

———. "Women on the Trail in Colonial America: A Travel Journal of German Moravians Migrating from Pennsylvania to North Carolina in 1766." *Pennsylvania History* 61 (1994), 206–234.

Frantz, John B. "The Awakening of Religion among the German Settlers in the Middle Colonies." *William & Mary Quarterly* 33 (1976), 266–288.

Frick, Robert P. L. "Moravian Architecture." Bound typescript. Bethlehem, Pa.: Reeves Memorial Library, Moravian College, n.d.

Galenson, David. *White Servitude in Colonial America: An Economic Analysis.* Cambridge: Cambridge University Press, 1981.

Gehrke, William H. "The Beginnings of the Pennsylvania-German Element in Rowan and Cabarrus Counties, North Carolina." *Pennsylvania Magazine of History and Biography* 58 (1934), 342–369.

Gemery, Henry. "Disarray in the Historical Record: Estimates of Immigration to the United States, 1700–1860." In *The Demographic History of the Philadelphia Region, 1600–1860,* edited by Susan E. Klepp. Proceedings of the American Philosophical Society, vol. 133, n. 2 (June 1989), 123–127.

———. "European Immigration to North America, 1700–1820: Numbers and Quasi-Numbers." *Perspectives in American History* n.s. 1 (1984), 283–342.

Glatfelter, Charles H. *Pastors and People,* vol. 1, *Pastors and Congregations,* and vol. 2, *The History.* Publications of the Pennsylvania German Society, vols. 12 and 15. Breinigsville, Pa.: The Pennsylvania German Society, 1979, 1981.

Gollin, Gillian L. *Moravians in Two Worlds: A Study of Changing Communities.* New York: Columbia University Press, 1967.

Grabbe, Hans-Jürgen. "European Immigration to the United States in the Early National Period, 1783–1820." In *The Demographic History of the Philadelphia Region, 1600–1860,* edited by Susan E. Klepp. Proceedings of the American Philosophical Society, vol. 133, n. 2 (June 1989), 190–214.

Graham, Ian C. C. *Colonists from Scotland: Emigration to North America, 1707–1783.* Ithaca, N.Y.: Cornell University Press, 1956.

Grubb, Farley. "German Immigration to Pennsylvania, 1709–1820." *Journal of Interdisciplinary History* 20 (1990), 417–436.

———. "Morbidity and Mortality on the North Atlantic Passage: Eighteenth-Century German Immigration." *Journal of Interdisciplinary History* 17 (1987), 565–585.

Häberlein, Mark. "German Migrants in Colonial Pennsylvania: Resources, Opportunities, and Experience." *William & Mary Quarterly* 50 (1993), 555–574.

Hacker, H. H. *Nazareth Hall: An Historical Sketch and Roster of Principals, Teachers and Pupils.* Bethlehem, Pa.: Times Publishing Co., 1910.

Hammer, Carl, Jr. *Rhinelanders on the Yadkin: The Story of the Pennsylvania Germans in Rowan and Cabarrus.* Salisbury, N.C.: Rowan Printing Co., 1943.

Hanna, William S. *Benjamin Franklin and Pennsylvania Politics.* Stanford, Calif.: Stanford University Press, 1964.

Hansen, Marcus L. *The Atlantic Migration, 1607–1860.* New York: Harper Torchbooks edition, 1961.

Henretta, James A. *The Evolution of American Society, 1700–1815: An Interdisciplinary Analysis.* Lexington, Mass., and Toronto: D.C. Heath and Company, 1973.

———. "Family and Farms: *Mentalité* in Pre-Industrial America." *William & Mary Quarterly* 35 (1978), 3–32.

Henretta, James A., and Nobles, Gregory H. *Evolution and Revolution: American Society, 1600–1820.* Lexington, Mass., and Toronto: D.C. Heath and Company, 1987.

Hofstadter, Richard. *America at 1750: A Social Portrait.* New York: Alfred A. Knopf, 1971.

Hopple, Lee C. "The Geography of Schwenkfelderism." In *Schwenkfelders in America*, 21–26. Pennsburg, Pa.: Schwenkfelder Library, 1987.

Horn, James. *Adapting to a New World: English Society in the Seventeenth-Century Chesapeake.* Chapel Hill: University of North Carolina Press, 1994.

Hostetler, John A. *Hutterite Society.* Baltimore, Md.: Johns Hopkins University Press, 1974.

Hottenstein, JoAnne and Sibl Welch, eds. *Incorporation Dates for Pennsylvania Municipalities.* Harrisburg: Department of Internal Affairs, 1965.

Hudson, Winthrop S. *Religion in America.* New York: MacMillan Publishing Company, 1987.

Hull, William I. *William Penn and the Dutch Quaker Migration to Pennsylvania.* Swarthmore College Monographs on Quaker History, vol. 2. Philadelphia: Patterson & White, 1935.

Hutson, James H. *Pennsylvania Politics, 1746–1770: The Movement for Royal Government and Its Consequences.* Princeton, N.J.: Princeton University Press, 1972.

Jones, Douglas L. *Village and Seaport: Migration and Society in Eighteenth-Century Massachusetts.* Hanover, N.H.: University Press of New England, 1981.

Jones, George F. *The Georgia Dutch: From the Rhine and Danube to the Savannah, 1733–1783.* Athens: University of Georgia Press, 1992.

Jordon, Albert F. "The Chronicle of Peter Boehler." *Transactions of the Moravian Historical Society* 22 (1971), 158–159.

Jordan, John W. "Moravian Immigration to Pennsylvania, 1734–1765." *Pennsylvania Magazine of History and Biography* 3 (1909), 228–248.

Keller, Kenneth W. *Rural Politics and the Collapse of Pennsylvania Federalism.* Transactions of the American Philosophical Society, vol. 72, part 6. Philadelphia, 1982.

Kessel, Elizabeth A. "Germans on the Maryland Frontier: A Social History of Frederick, Maryland, 1730–1800." Ph.D. diss., Rice University, 1981.

Kettner, James H. *The Development of American Citizenship, 1608–1870.* Chapel Hill: University of North Carolina Press, 1978.

Knittle, Walter A. *Early Eighteenth Century Palatine Emigration: A British Government Redemptioner Project to Manufacture Naval Stores.* Philadelphia: Dorrance and Co., 1937.

Kulikoff, Allan. "Uprooted Peoples: Black Migrants in the Age of the American Revolution, 1790–1820." In *Slavery and Freedom in the Age of the American Revolution*, edited by Ira Berlin and Ronald Hoffman, 143–171. Charlottesville: University Press of Virginia, 1983.

Lanctot, Gustave. *A History of Canada*, vol. 3, *From the Treaty of Utrecht to the Treaty of Paris, 1713–1763.* Translated by Margaret M. Cameron. Toronto and Vancouver: Clarke, Irwin, and Company, Ltd., 1965.

Lemon, James T. *"The Best Poor Man's Country": A Geographical Study of Early Southeastern Pennsylvania.* Baltimore, Md.: Johns Hopkins University Press, 1972.

Levering, Joseph M. *A History of Bethlehem, Pennsylvania, 1741–1892, With Some Account of its Founders and their Early Activity in America.* Bethlehem, Pa.: Times Publishing Co., 1903.

Lockridge, Kenneth A. "Land, Population and the Evolution of New England Society 1630–1790." *Past & Present: A Journal of Historical Studies* 39 (1968), 62–80.

Lodge, Martin E. "The Crisis of the Churches in the Middle Colonies, 1720–1750," *Pennsylvania Magazine of History and Biography* 95 (1971), 195–220.

Main, Jackson T. *Social Structure of Revolutionary America.* Princeton, N.J.: Princeton University Press, 1965.

MacMaster, Richard K. *Land, Piety, Peoplehood: The Establishment of Mennonite Communities in America, 1683–1790.* The Mennonite Experience in America, vol. 1. Scottsdale, Pa., and Kitchener, Ont.: Herald Press, 1985.

McCusker, John J., and Russell R. Menard. *The Economy of British America, 1607–1789.* Chapel Hill: University of North Carolina Press, 1985.

McDonald, Forrest, and Ellen Shapiro McDonald. "The Ethnic Origins of the American People, 1790." *William & Mary Quarterly* 37 (1980), 179–199.

Menard, Russell R. "Migration, Ethnicity, and the Rise of an Atlantic Economy: The Re-Peopling of British America, 1600–1790." In *A Century of European Migrations, 1830–1930*, edited by Rudolph J. Vecoli and Suzanne M. Sinke, 58–77. Urbana and Chicago: University of Illinois Press, 1991.

Merrens, Harry R. *Colonial North Carolina in the Eighteenth Century: A Study in Historical Geography.* Chapel Hill: University of North Carolina Press, 1964.

Meyer, Duane. *The Highland Scots of North Carolina, 1732–1776.* Durham, N.C.: Duke University Press, 1961.

Miller, Kerby A. *Emigrants and Exiles: Ireland and the Irish Exodus to North America.* New York: Oxford University Press, 1985.

Mitchell, Robert D. *Commercialism and Frontier: Perspectives on the Early Shenandoah Valley.* Charlottesville: University Press of Virginia, 1977.

Moltmann, Günther. "Die deutsche Auswanderung in der Kolonialzeit und das Redemptioner-System." *Zeitschrift für Kulturaustausch* 32 (1982), 318–323.

Nash, Gary B. *Red, White, and Black: The Peoples of Early North America,* 3rd ed. Englewood Cliffs, N.J.: Prentice Hall, 1992.

———. *The Urban Crucible: The Northern Seaports and the Origins of the American Revolution.* Cambridge, Mass.: Harvard University Press, 1986.

Neisser, George. *A History of the Beginnings of Moravian Work in America.* Translated and edited by William N. Schwarze and Samuel H. Gapp. Moravian Archives Publications, vol. 1. Bethlehem, Pa.: Archives of the Moravian Church, 1955.

Ornstein, Michael D. and Darroch, A. Gordon. "National Mobility Studies in Past Time: A Sampling Strategy." *Historical Methods* 11 (1978), 152–161.

Parson, William T. "The Bloody Election of 1742." *Pennsylvania History* 36 (1969), 290–306.

Phillips, John A. "Achieving a Critical Mass While Avoiding an Explosion: Letter-Cluster Sampling and Nominal Record Linkage." *Journal of Interdisciplinary History* 9 (1979), 493–508.

Purvis, Thomas L. "The European Ancestry of the United States Population, 1790." *William & Mary Quarterly* 41 (1984), 84–101.

———. "The European Origins of New Jersey's Eighteenth-Century Population." *New Jersey History* 100 (1982), 15–31.

———. "The National Origin of New Yorkers in 1790." *New York History* 67 (1986), 133–153.

———. "Patterns of Ethnic Settlement in Late Eighteenth-Century Pennsylvania." *Western Pennsylvania Historical Magazine* 70 (1987), 107–122.

———. "The Pennsylvania Dutch and the German-American Diaspora in 1790." *Journal of Cultural Geography* 6 (1986), 81–99.

Ramsey, Robert W. *Carolina Cradle: Settlement of the Northwest Carolina Frontier, 1747–1762.* Chapel Hill: University of North Carolina Press, 1964.

Reichel, William C. "Historical Sketch of Nazareth Hall." *Transactions of the Moravian Historical Society* 1 (1876), 1–27.

———. *Historical Sketch of Nazareth Hall, from 1755 to 1869.* Philadelphia: Lippincott & Co., 1869.

———. "Red Rose of the Olden Time and Old Inn, Nazareth." *Transactions of the Moravian Historical Society* 2 (1877–1886), 270–332.

"A Review of the Founding of the Lancaster County Church Settlement Based on the Alms Books and the Ministry." *The Diary* (December 1983), 17–22.

Roeber, A. G. "The Origins and Transfer of German-American Concepts of Property and Inheritance." *Perspectives in American History* n.s. 3 (1986), 115–171.

———. *Palatines, Liberty, and Property: German Lutherans in Colonial America.* Baltimore, Md.: Johns Hopkins University Press, 1993.

Rolland, Susanne M. "From the Rhine to the Catawba: A Study of Eighteenth Century Germanic Migration and Adaptation." Ph.D. diss., Emory University, 1991.

Rothermund, Dietmar. *The Layman's Progress: Religious and Political Experience in Colonial Pennsylvania, 1740–1770.* Philadelphia: University of Pennsylvania Press, 1961.

Rouse, Parke. *The Great Wagon Road from Philadelphia to the South.* New York: McGraw Hill Book Co., 1973.

Sachse, Julius F. *The German Pietists of Provincial Pennsylvania.* Philadelphia: Julius F. Sachse, 1895.

Salinger, Sharon V. *"To Serve Well and Faithfully": Labor and Indentured Servants in Pennsylvania, 1682–1800.* Cambridge: Cambridge University Press, 1987.

Schwartz, Sally. *"A Mixed Multitude": The Struggle for Toleration in Colonial Pennsylvania.* New York: New York University Press, 1987.

Schweinitz, Edmund de. "The Financial History of the Province and its Sustentation Fund." Unpublished typescript in the Moravian Archives. Bethlehem, Pa., 1877.

Schweitzer, Mary M. *Custom and Contract: Household, Government, and the Economy in Colonial Pennsylvania.* New York: Columbia University Press, 1987.

Sellers, Charles C. *Benjamin Franklin in Portraiture.* New Haven, Conn.: Yale University Press, 1962.

Sergeant, Thomas. *View of the Land Laws of Pennsylvania, with Notices of its Early History and Legislation.* Philadelphia and Pittsburgh: James Kay, Jr., and John I. Kay, Co., 1838.

Sheperd, William R. *History of the Proprietary Government in Pennsylvania.* Studies in History, Economics and Public Law, vol. 6. New York: Columbia University, 1896.

Shy, John W. "Migration and Persistence in Revolutionary America." In *Autre Temps, Autre Espace: Etudes sur l'Amérique pré-industrielle,* edited by Elise Marienstras and Barbara Karsky, 215–227. Nancy: Presses universitaires de Nancy, 1986.

Smaby, Beverly P. *The Transformation of Moravian Bethlehem: From Communal Mission to Family Economy.* Philadelphia: University of Pennsylvania Press, 1988.

Smith, C. Henry. *The Mennonite Immigration to Pennsylvania in the Eighteenth Century.* Norristown, Pa.: Pennsylvania German Society, 1929.

Smith, Daniel Scott. "Migration of American Colonial Militiamen: A Comparative Note." *Social Science History* 7 (1983), 475–479.

Stoudt, John J. "Count Zinzendorf and the Pennsylvania Congregation of God in the Spirit: The First American Oecumenical Movement." *Church History* 9 (1940), 366–380.

———. "Pennsylvania and the Oecumenical Ideal." *Bulletin of the Theological Seminary of the Reformed Church in the United States* 12 (1941), 171–197.

Stout, Harry S. "Ethnicity: The Vital Center of Religion in America." *Ethnicity* 2 (1975), 204–224.

Thayer, Theodore. *Pennsylvania Politics and the Growth of Democracy, 1740–1776*. Harrisburg: Pennsylvania Historical Museum Commission, 1953.

Thorp, Daniel B. *The Moravian Community in Colonial North Carolina: Pluralism on the Southern Frontier*. Knoxville: The University of Tennessee Press, 1989.

Tillison, Albert H., Jr. "The Southern Backcountry: A Survey of Current Research." *Virginia Magazine of History and Biography* 98 (1990), 387–422.

Todd, Vincent H. *Christoph von Graffenried's Account of the Founding of New Bern*. Raleigh: Edwards & Broughton Printing Co., 1920.

Trommler, Frank, and Joseph McVeigh, eds. *America and the Germans: An Assessment of a Three-Hundred-Year History*, vol. 2. Philadelphia: University of Pennsylvania Press, 1985.

Tully, Alan. *William Penn's Legacy: Politics and Social Structure in Provincial Pennsylvania, 1726–1755*. The Johns Hopkins University Studies in Historical and Political Science, vol. 2. Baltimore: The Johns Hopkins University Press, 1977.

Turner, Frederick Jackson. *The Frontier in American History*. New York: Henry Holt and Company, 1920.

Villaflor, Georgia C., and Kenneth L. Sokoloff. "Migrations in Colonial America: Evidence from Militia Muster Rolls." *Social Science History* 6 (1982), 539–570.

Vorsey, Louis De, Jr. "The Colonial Georgian Backcountry." In *Colonial Augusta: "Key of the Indian Countrey"*, 3–26. Macon, Ga.: Mercer University Press, 1986.

Wacker, Peter O. *Land and People: A Cultural Geography of Preindustrial New Jersey: Origins and Settlement Patterns*. New Brunswick, N.J.: Rutgers University Press, 1975.

Walsh, Lorena S. "Staying Put or Getting Out: Findings for Charles County, Maryland, 1650–1720." *William & Mary Quarterly* 44 (1987), 89–103.

Weis, Frederick L. *The Colonial Clergy of Virginia, North Carolina and South Carolina*. Baltimore: Genealogical Publishing Co., 1976.

Welker, G. William. "Early German Reformed Settlements in North Carolina." In *The Colonial Records of North Carolina*, edited by William L. Saunders, vol. 8, 727–757. Raleigh, N.C.: P. M. Hale State Printer, 1886–1890.

Wokeck, Marianne. "The Flow and the Composition of German Immigration to Philadelphia, 1683–1776." *Pennsylvania Magazine of History and Biography* 105 (1981), 249–278.

———. "A Tide of Alien Tongues: The Flow and Ebb of German Immigration to Pennsylvania, 1683–1776." Ph.D. diss., Temple University, 1983.

Wolf, Stephanie G. *Urban Village: Population, Community, and Family Structure in Germantown, Pennsylvania, 1683–1800*. Princeton, N.J.: Princeton University Press, 1976.

Wood, Gordon S. *The Radicalism of the American Revolution*. New York: Vintage Books, 1991.

Wood, Jerome H., Jr. *Conestoga Crossroads: Lancaster, Pennsylvania, 1730–1790*. Harrisburg: Pennsylvania Historical and Museum Commission, 1979.

Wood, Peter H. "The Changing Population of the Colonial South: An Overview by Race and Region, 1685–1790." In *Powhatan's Mantle: Indians in the Colonial Southeast*, edited by Peter H. Wood, Gregory A. Waselkov, and M. Thomas Hatley, 35–103. Lincoln: University of Nebraska Press, 1989.

Wust, Klaus. *The Virginia Germans.* Charlottesville: University Press of Virginia, 1969.

Yoder, Don. "Palatine, Hessian, Dutchman: Three Images of the German in America." In *Ebbes fer Alle—Ebbes fer Dich: Something for Everyone—Something for You*, edited by Albert F. Buffington, 107–129. Publications of the Pennsylvania German Society, vol. 14. Breinigsville, Pa.: The Pennsylvania German Society, 1980.

Index of Immigrants and Villagers

General Index

Abzugsfreiheit (freedom of movement), 30
Adelshofen, 43, 48, 56
Advice literature: for new immigrants, 97–99
Africa: contributions to colonial population, 3
African Americans: fertility of, 159; percentage in population, 1–2
African slave imports: estimates of, 176 n.2
African slaves: in America, 153; Moravian mission to, 96, 101; passage mortality of, 209 n.38
Agriculture: disasters causing emigration, 5, 6; methods in southwest Germany and Switzerland, 23–24; practices, changes in, 21
Alexandria (Virginia), 8
Aliens, 138
Allegheny County (Maryland), 8
Allegheny Mountains, 85; as boundary of settlement for Kraichgauers, 74
Allegiance, of German immigrants, 132
Allen (ship), 105
Almanacs (*Calendars*), Pennsylvania German, 97
Alsace, 102, 114
Alsatians, 86
America: low taxes and freedom in, 33; worsening conditions in, 4. *See also* North America
American culture: and Germans, 149, 152–153; Americanization of Germans, 12, 152
American Revolution, Germans in, 152
Amish, 102, 104–105, 106–107, 108, 195 n.15; on the *Charming Nancy*, 75; geographic stability of, 94–95; leaving their community, 201 n.39; use of collective strategy, 125; Amish immigrants, European origins of, 170–171
Amsterdam, 89, 115

Anderson, Virginia DeJohn, 93
Annapolis (Maryland), 8
Anti-Federalist ticket, and Germans in Pennsylvania, 150
Appalachian Mountains, 153
Appomattox River, 208 n.28
Aristocracy: absence of, in American localities, 135 (*see also* Nobility); aristocratic encroachments, in German political rhetoric, 141; aristocratic offensive: in America and France, 215 n.41; in colonial America, 146–147; in Europe, 147; in the Kraichgau, 42–51, 56, 59
Armbrüster, Gotthard, 202 n.42
Assembly elections: and land policy and naturalization, 136; in Pennsylvania (1764), 142. *See also* Elections
Augusta (Georgia), 10
Augustus Lutheran Church (Trappe, Pennsylvania), 88

Backcountry, 117; of Pennsylvania, 140; settlement in, 85. *See also* Greater Pennsylvania; Southern backcountry
Baden, 185 n.21; emigration from, 25–28; inheritance practices in, 25–28; population decline of, 184 n.19; population recovery in, 184 n.20; restrictions on emigration from, 182 n.7
Baden and the Breisgau, 16, 163–164
Baden-Durlach, margravate of, 15, 36, 37, 39; 189 n.37; feudal dues in, 182 n.10; population of, 15–16; 181 n.1; proto-industry in, 183 n.14
Badeners, 72, 86
Baltimore: German immigration society in, 133; as immigration port, 8
Baltimore, Frederic Calvert, Lord, 146
Banat, 187 n.31
Baroque buildings, in the Kraichgau, 46
Basel, 72, 76

This book has been set in Galliard. Galliard was designed for
Mergenthaler in 1978 by Matthew Carter. Galliard retains many of
the features of a sixteenth-century typeface cut by Robert Granjon
but has some modifications that give it a more contemporary look.

Printed on acid-free paper.